GW00456578

Class and Politics in a Northern Industrial Town: Keighley 1880–1914

Class and Politics in a Northern Industrial Town: Keighley 1880–1914

David James

Foreword by Asa Briggs

RYBURN PUBLISHING
KEELE UNIVERSITY PRESS

First published in 1995
by Ryburn Publishing,
an imprint of
Keele University Press
Keele, Staffordshire

Composed by KUP
Printed on acid-free paper
by Hartnolls, Bodmin,
Cornwall, England

ISBN 1 85331 066 2

Contents

Acknowledgements

This book would not have been completed without the help of many individuals and institutions, and it is impossible to name them all. The greatest debts of gratitude are owed to Lord Briggs, who advised me on how to change my original dissertation into a book, and to Professor Keith Laybourn of Huddersfield University, who spent nearly a decade supervising and encouraging me to complete the original Ph.D. The staff of the libraries at Keighley and Bradford have never been anything but helpful, and I must thank Ian Dewhirst, the then Keighley Reference Librarian, whose assistance was unfailing. Elvira Willmott at the Reference Department in Bradford Central Library was kind enough to make the riches of the local history section available to me. The staff of the West Yorkshire Archive Service, especially the Bradford office, should be thanked for their patience when I tried out my ideas and thoughts on them. Other people have also made suggestions or discussed aspects of this work with me. They include Dr Michael Cahill, Dr David Clark, MP, Dr Martin Crick, Professor David Howell, Tony Jowitt, John Palmer, Dr Robert Perks and Dr David Wright. Thanks are owed to them all.

Richard Clark and the staff at Keele University Press have as always been unfailingly encouraging and stoical in the face of delay and I am grateful to them for their patience.

Lastly, and most importantly, I must thank my wife, who patiently spent many uncomplaining nights and days while I wrestled with the complexities of nineteenth-century Keighley.

Foreword

by Asa Briggs

Social historians have devoted far more attention to large cities than they have to small towns. Nevertheless, over recent years there has been a striking increase in the number of detailed local studies of industrial change and of the rise and development of labour movements.

In this careful study, which is based on a wide range of published and unpublished materials, Dr James explores aspects of the economic and political history of Keighley in a formative period of its development. He fully establishes its distinctive identity as a place, an identity which it has subsequently retained despite even greater changes in its social and political structure since 1945. There is a long epilogue to his study which precedes a quite new prelude.

Dr James clearly demonstrates how and why Keighley was at the heart of the labour movement before 1914. He throws new light on Philip Snowden and on the political rank-and-file who supported and, indeed, gained inspiration from Snowden's approach to politics. There was little intimation then that the *dénouement* of the late 1920s and 1930s would follow.

In strictly local terms, this is an absorbing study. In national terms, it has significance when viewed comparatively and when related to major trends in economic and social history.

CHAPTER ONE

Introduction

The reasons for the emergence of a Labour party in the textile region of the West Riding at the end of the nineteenth century can only be understood within the context of the political, social and economic conditions which had evolved in the years after 1850. Before studying the response of the established parties to the rise of labour in Keighley,[1] it is necessary, therefore, to examine how the local élite had succeeded in accommodating the political demands of the working class in the years before 1890.

This élite dominated much of Keighley's public life, and its authority was barely questioned in the mid-Victorian period. Nationally, too, the distinguishing feature of the three decades after 1850 was the relative calm which characterized social relations, which provides a remarkable contrast with the re-emergence of independent and socialist working-class politics and heightened class tensions in the 1880s and 1890s.

A number of explanations have been advanced for the quiescence of the working class during this period. The Webbs suggested that greater prosperity and the willingness of the trade-union leaders to co-operate with the masters produced this peace.[2] This argument lies at the heart of the theory of the labour aristocracy which was expounded by Eric Hobsbawm in a series of essays.[3] He argued that the mid-Victorian peace grew in part from an acceptance of the status quo by a section of the working class – the labour aristocracy. This group, composed of no more than ten to fifteen per cent of the working class, enjoyed high wages and regular employment because of their skills or their ability, through collective action in narrowly defined trade unions, to force employer recognition of their position. In Keighley this group would consist of such people as overlookers in the textile trade and skilled engineers in the machine shops. The difference between them and the unskilled workforce would be emphasized by the fact that many of the latter were, in worsteds at least, women. In addition to their superior economic position, the labour aristocrats could be identified by a characteristic way of life, revolving round the friendly society, the club, the trade union and the notion of respectability. These workers only began to lose their position with the advent of a new round of mechanization in the 1880s and the onset of economic depression. Politically, they supported a slow gradualist approach known as Lib-Labism. It was the threat to their economic and social position at the end of the century that forced this group to abandon its sectional concerns and pursue a more general policy of unionization and political struggle against the manufacturers and the Liberal party which they dominated in the north of England.

Some critics have questioned the value of the concept of the labour aristocracy. Henry Pelling[4] and A. E. Musson[5] detected no great change in the behaviour of trade unions throughout the period and rejected the dichotomy of old and new unionism. Musson argued that the term was either qualified down to nothing or was broadened to include a near-majority of the working class. Pelling noted that, far from being conservative, a number of skilled workers were among the leaders of the fight for greater political rights and swelled the ranks of socialist and labour parties in the 1890s.

Other historians shifted their attention away from the labour aristocracy as an explanation of the political moderation of the working class towards a more complete examination of the forces shaping the life of British workers in general. One group emphasizes the importance of the labour process as a determining factor in the formation of the working class, arguing that an emphasis on the split between adult male workers on the basis of skill ignored important religious and gender distinctions, and that sectional divisions between workers of similar status or wages were equally as important as those between skilled and unskilled in explaining the attitudes of workers. This group sees working life in Victorian Britain as a mixture of argument and agreement, with an inherent tendency towards conflict. Richard Price, one of the leading historians of this school, suggests that the mid-Victorian calm rested on a resolution and containment of industrial conflict that began to come apart in the 1880s.[6]

Another group has focused on the forces that tried to integrate the working class into the mainstream of capitalist society, emphasizing the coercive and paternalistic nature of the process. Richard Storch, for example, in his studies on the police,[7] points to the efforts of the state and voluntary organizations to force their views on the working class, although in his view they failed. H. F. Moorhouse[8] has argued that efforts to control workers generated resistance to the new institutions of repression. Patrick Joyce,[9] on the other hand, believes that social control is not merely an outside force exerted upon workers, but rather a set of internalized values that helps to smooth over the contradictions in British society.

A number of works have examined the ways in which the local manufacturers secured their position in West Yorkshire communities. The starting point is Patrick Joyce, who concentrates on Lancashire but includes references to Yorkshire towns, including Keighley.[10] Jack Reynolds, though disagreeing with Joyce on a number of points, discusses the way that the Bradford bourgeoisie secured their position.[11] Ted Koditschek[12] also discusses Bradford, while a number of authors examine the phenomenon in several West Yorkshire communities, including Halifax and Huddersfield.[13] Keighley, lying on the Lancashire border, with easy communications to the cotton towns on the other side of the Pennines but within ten miles of Bradford and Halifax, is a town where paternalism established a generation of relative industrial and political calm. I will suggest, however, that paternalism was never wholeheartedly accepted by the Keighley working class, and that one reason for this was that the structure of the chief industry of the town, worsteds, made it difficult for a master to be both successful and benevolent.

The examination of obituaries, autobiographies, biographies, business histories, and other sources allows the Keighley élite, together with its attitude to the other social classes of the town, particularly the working classes, to be identified. I will argue that, although socially separate, the manufacturers saw themselves, and were seen by others, as an integral part of local society, with real, if undefined and unspoken, responsibilities. Unlike their Bradford counterparts, who by the end of the nineteenth century were tending to move away from the community and out of a direct role in the worsted industry, many Keighley manufacturers lived in the district and often took part in the day-to-day management of their firms, at least until the end of the First World War. Thus, 'their solid residences dominated the suburbs: the Sugdens at Eastwood House, the Briggs at Guard House, the Greenwoods at the Knowle, the Haggases at Oakworth Hall, the Claphams at Aireworth House'.[14] Their houses and factories were the physical symbols of their power and position in the community, while their wealth enabled them to support a wide range of recreational, educational, religious and other institutions. By studying their financial and other contributions to such organizations as the Mechanics Institute, the Nonconformist chapels, and the temperance movement, it is possible to see how their influence extended to all aspects of the town's life.

However, the ability of the members of the Keighley élite to sustain their position depended ultimately upon their economic prosperity and that of the concerns they owned or managed. The 'great depression', which had a major impact on the West Yorkshire textile trade generally, started in the mid-1870s and eroded the economic base upon which paternalism was founded. The deterioration in the profitability of the worsted trade had a number of consequences, all of which damaged working-class belief in the benevolence of the employers. The fully integrated mill, such as those built by Titus Salt at Saltaire or by the Cloughs at Hainworth in Keighley, became less typical. Workers were put under pressure by management to produce more; the trade became increasingly fragmented and specialized, and working on commission, with its lower overheads, short-term employment and cut-throat competition, was common. To sustain their profits, the manufacturers chose not to invest in new machinery but to seek other ways of cutting the costs of production. They perceived only two areas where this might be done: in the purchase of raw materials and in the price of labour. Although fortunes were made on the Bradford Wool Exchange speculating in wool, the price paid for raw material was largely out of the manufacturers' control; so it was labour which bore the brunt of the cost-cutting exercises. From the 1880s, workers in the West Yorkshire worsted trade were constantly under attack from their employers; more women and half-time workers were taken on; machinery speeds were increased, and employees were expected to be responsible for more machines; piece-rate payments became the norm; and trade unions were discouraged. None of these activities was compatible with the paternalist ideology formally espoused by many of the Keighley élite, among others; as a result, they lost the confidence of their employees and of the working class generally. The outcome was an increase in trade-union activity and growing antagonism between employers and employees. A demand for an independent working-class political voice also developed; and there was something of a move away from Liberalism.[15]

Politically, Keighley, like most West Yorkshire textile towns, was dominated by the Liberal party. This was financed and run by the manufacturers and usually had a majority on the local elected bodies until after the turn of the century. It is necessary to identify the politically active members of the party, and see how they used their powers to maintain their political influence. This is particularly important for the 1890s, when the Independent Labour Party (ILP) was formed. The Liberal manufacturers were quite prepared to intimidate working-class political activists and a number of ILPers lost jobs because of their politics. At the same time, the antagonism between the two political groups should not be exaggerated. The ILPers and the Liberal factory masters could, and did, meet in a number of organizations to work together for common, although often non-political, objectives. Help could also be given at a personal level. For example, B. S. Brigg, a member of an important manufacturing family and a prominent Liberal, provided W. S. Wilkinson, a leading ILPer, with a testimonial when he applied for a teaching post in 1903.[16] These social and semi-official contacts blunted the edge of potential class conflict within the town.

Attention must also be given to the minority of manufacturers who supported the Conservative party, including a number of prominent local families, such as the Haggases, the Butterfields, the Marriners and the Summerscales. The Conservative revival, which began in the late nineteenth century and became a threat to the local Liberals in the early twentieth, needs to be considered. The Borough Council had a Tory majority by 1908, although the constituency returned Liberal MPs from 1885 to the First World War. It is essential to examine the complex relationships between Liberals, Conservatives and Labour. In the 1890s there is evidence that the conflict between Liberals and Conservatives enabled the ILP to obtain political advantages which their numbers did not justify. Thus, in 1896, the Conservative and ILP members of the Borough Council combined to elect Herbert Horner, the first Keighley Labour alderman. At other times, the Conservatives provided the ILP with a platform from which to attack the Liberals. For instance, Tom Mackley, the ILP secretary, wrote a column in the local Conservative newspaper. In the early twentieth century the Liberals and Conservatives combined against Labour candidates in local elections through electoral pacts. Having examined Liberalism and the Conservative revival in Keighley, this study will trace the emergence of the ILP in the town, and the factors which led to its growth. The rise of socialism, and in particular the ILP, was a phenomenon common to much of the West Riding textile belt, but the reasons for its success were varied.

The end of the nineteenth century saw both a revival of interest in socialism nationally and demands for independent working-class organizations, whether in industrial relations with the growth of new unionism, or in politics with the founding of new parties. The Democratic Federation was founded by H. M. Hyndman in 1881, and became the Social Democratic Federation (SDF) in 1884. In the same year, William Morris and a group of followers who disagreed with Hyndman seceded from the SDF to form the Socialist League. In the provinces the SDF and the Socialist League introduced socialism to people who, in the 1890s and early twentieth century, were to provide the working class with much of its leadership. In Bradford, for example, Fred Jowett, Paul Bland, George Minty and James Bartley, all of whom were to play a prominent part in local politics and trade-unionism, were members of the local branch of the Socialist League.[17] Tom Maguire, the Leeds socialist leader, was a member of both the SDF and the Socialist League.[18] The Fabian Society, which provided much of the intellectual stimulus for socialists in the 1890s and beyond, was also founded in 1884. Although often regarded as a London organization, its influence was national, thanks to lecture tours, the sale of its pamphlets, the circulation of book boxes, and the general distribution of practical advice on a variety of subjects. Tom Mackley, the secretary of the Keighley ILP, regularly contacted Edward Pease, the Society's secretary, for help and advice. In addition, a number of provincial Fabian societies existed for a time. John Lister of Halifax[19] and W. H. Drew[20] of Bradford were active members of such organizations, as were many of their West Riding contemporaries.

In West Yorkshire, however, the most important socialist group from the last decade of the nineteenth century until 1914 was the Independent Labour Party. Initially, it was composed of different labour groups which had established themselves independently and which came together to form the ILP in 1893. The inaugural conference was held in Bradford, and the north of England – and particularly the textile belt of West Yorkshire – remained its heartland for many years. At the Bradford conference there were 120 delegates, of whom 48 came from Yorkshire, including 1 from Keighley, and 32 from Lancashire and Cheshire. By 1895 there were 305 branches, of which 102 were in Yorkshire. In 1898 the largest single branch was in Halifax, followed by East Bradford and West Bradford. The town of Keighley, lying equidistant from Halifax and Bradford, was among the twelve largest branches in the country during the 1890s. Many of the party's earliest officials were from West Yorkshire: W. H. Drew, its first secretary, came from Bradford; John Lister of Halifax was the first treasurer; and France Littlewood of Colne Valley succeeded him. Philip Snowden of Keighley was elected to the National Administrative Council of the party in 1898 and was one of its most charismatic and popular figures. For many, the ILP was the chief means of spreading socialism and encouraging labour politics in the north of England.[21]

There have been a number of works which have examined the ILP and the part it played in both national and local politics. The histories of the ILP offered by Henry Pelling[22] and Philip Poirier,[23] although both written over twenty-five years ago, remain indispensable. Later writers, such as Stanley Pierson,[24] have also made notable contributions to our understanding of the party. Important as these works are, however, they have tended to concentrate on the national picture, yet the ILP essentially 'grew from the bottom up' and its 'birthplaces were in those shadowy parts known as the provinces'.[25] The fundamental importance of this is emphasized by David Howell, who argues that 'the analysis of a political organization's growth cannot begin with a study of its formal structure. It must start from an examination of the possible bases of support.'[26] The growing number of books and articles on the ILP in the regions is therefore important. As David Clark points out, 'it is not possible to comprehend fully the nature of the ILP without reference ... to activities at branch level. Yet there has not been a single full length, detailed study of a local Labour Party.'[27] Fortunately, several works have appeared since those words were written, not the least of which is that of Dr Clark himself, with his exposition of Colne Valley.

In addition, Cyril Pearse,[28] Duncan Ross, Jack Reynolds and Keith Laybourn[29] have all contributed to the history of the party in Bradford, while Laybourn and Reynolds have provided an overview of the area as a whole. Robert Perks has examined Huddersfield,[30] and there are also two works on the ILP and the Labour party in Leeds.[31] A biography of John Lister of Halifax has been written;[32] Lister himself wrote a useful, if brief, history of the Halifax branch of the party[33] and there is also a modern study of the same subject.[34] Martin Crick has studied labour politics in Dewsbury and Batley, as well as contributing to the study of Bradford.[35] E. P. Thompson's article 'Homage to Tom Maguire', which surveys the rise of socialism in the West Riding in general and Leeds and Bradford in particular, is an essential starting point.[37] However, apart from sections in the biographies of Philip Snowden by Colin Cross[37] and Keith Laybourn[38] and references in Reynolds and Laybourn,[39] there has been little of relevance written on the Keighley ILP. This book will attempt to fill the gap and contribute to the discussion of how and why the ILP branches developed as they did in West Yorkshire.

The rise of socialism posed a potentially serious threat to the political influence of the Liberal party in West Yorkshire; their reaction to the ILP and their success or otherwise in containing the demands of the working class will be examined. Specifically, it is important to assess the extent of the decline of the Liberals and their replacement by the Labour party as the representatives of the left. Were the Liberals already in irreversible decline, or was the First World War, with the strains it placed on Liberal ideology and the relationships among party leaders, together with the stimulus it provided for a more militant working class, the catalyst for change? The Liberals depended on working-class votes for electoral success; it was important for them to hold on to this base by fighting off the challenge of the labour movement if they were to retain power.

Much recent scholarship has emphasized the success of the Liberal party in responding to this challenge, and a number of explanations have been advanced. First, it has been argued that a New Liberalism emerged in the 1890s which had shed the traditional suspicion of government interference in social policy and, to a lesser degree, in the economy. This enabled Liberal governments between 1906 and 1914 to pass enough social legislation to meet the most critical needs of working-class voters. Second, the agreement between Herbert Gladstone representing the Liberals and Ramsay MacDonald on behalf of the Labour Representation Committee on the allocation of parliamentary seats between the two parties produced a new equilibrium which contained any challenge that Labour may have posed to the Liberals. This agreement, together with the support of the Irish nationalists, enabled the Liberals to win three successive general elections between 1906 and 1910. The stability of this equilibrium, however, depended upon the acquiescence of the rank and file of both parties in the constituencies. The major exponent of this view is P. F. Clarke,[40] who demonstrates the success of the progressive alliance in one of the most important and, at the same time, one of the most individual regions in the country. In Lancashire, working-class conservatism was unusually strong while liberalism was weak, and the Liberals had everything to gain from coming to terms with Labour. It was to their advantage to reach an accommodation, since it was almost always in Conservative-held constituencies that they would back down, leaving Labour to contest the seat.

The West Riding textile belt differed from Lancashire, in that there was a confident, successful and traditional Liberal party which felt no need to compromise its allegiance to free trade, voluntaryism and personal independence in a bid for working-class support. It was not unaware of the New Liberalism and its most notable advocate in the worsted region was W. P. Byles of Bradford, whose stormy career resulted in his being mistrusted by both the ILP and the local Liberal party managers and who was finally obliged to leave the area and follow politics in Salford. As this indicates, New Liberalism was not particularly appealing either to Liberals or to socialists in West Yorkshire. Nevertheless, the Liberals were successful in much of the region for much of the time. In December 1910, in the thirty-eight constituencies of the West Riding, twenty-seven, including Keighley, had Liberal MPs, five had Conservatives and six Labour, and it is clear that the Liberals were attractive to a large section of the electorate.

In examining the question of Liberal support in Wales, Kenneth O. Morgan[41] has suggested that traditional Liberalism was successful in retaining working-class support because of the influence of Nonconformity, temperance, free trade and anti-landlordism. These were also characteristics of much of West Yorkshire Liberalism, in areas such as Keighley, and should be considered in any estimate of Liberal strength in the region. Martin Pugh, however, while recognizing the strength of Morgan's arguments when applied to the West Riding, argues that it was the similarities between Labour and the Liberals which resulted in the failure of the former in parts of the worsted area. He suggests that only the emphasis on having workers represented by working men actually distinguished Labour from Liberal, and that there was not a clear enough difference between the two groups when there was a reforming Liberal government in Westminster, as was the case after 1906.[42] This may be true of Keighley.

In contrast to those works which emphasize the success of Liberalism in the West Riding in the Edwardian years, a number of studies have argued that Labour was in fact replacing the Liberals as the political voice of the working class before 1914. The most wide-ranging of these is by Keith Laybourn and Jack Reynolds,[43] who suggest that the First World War was less significant to Labour's political rise in West Yorkshire than it might have been either nationally or in other parts of the country. By 1910, they argue, the local ILP branches and Labour parties were eroding the political power base of West Yorkshire Liberalism and by 1914 the Liberals were incapable of stopping their growth. Labour's success was partly due to the fact that the political demands of the working class were neglected by the Liberals, resulting in a transfer of support to the ILP. Thus, in Bradford the Liberals 'did nothing to secure the [working-class] vote beyond argue that the Liberal party was the progressive party … Ostensibly they were tending to the interests of the working class. In reality they did very little.'[44] How far this neglect applies to Keighley and whether it was the cause of the growth of the ILP branch is open to question.

There is, therefore, some argument about the success or failure of the Liberals in containing the challenge of the ILP in the West Riding textile belt in the years before the First World War. What cannot be denied is that permanent political organizations were created by the labour movement in the area, and that the most successful was the ILP. A number of reasons have been put forward to explain its appeal.

Keith Laybourn and Jack Reynolds suggest that the key to ILP success is to be found in their alliance with the trade-union movement. They argue that where trade-unionism was firmly established and closely linked with the ILP, powerful and effective labour organizations emerged. But such groups proved to be less resilient in those areas where trade-unionism was weak and where links with the ILP were more tenuous. Discussing the case of Bradford, they show that the key to the ILP's political success did indeed lie with their connection with the trade unions. 'From the outset' they write, 'Bradford trade unionism and the Bradford ILP were seen as two aspects of a single homogeneous labour movement aimed at the emancipation of the working class from poverty and exploitation.'[45] Between 1890 and 1892 the leaders of the Bradford ILP, acting through the trade unions of which they were members, took control of the Bradford Trades Council, removing almost all the previously dominant Lib-Lab group from its executive. The creation of the Workers' Municipal Election Committee in 1901, later to become the Workers' Municipal Federation, a body of trade-union and socialist representatives, gave the ILP much of its organizational strength.

It has been argued that a similar relationship with trade unions was responsible for the success of the ILP in other towns. Patricia Dawson writes that 'the Halifax Labour movement owed much of its existence to the rise of local trade unionism and the "new" unionist ideas of the 1890s'. It was trade-union influence which was 'most important to the Labour movement, which was nurtured within the Trades Council. Afterwards it continued to rely upon and court union allegiances, championing the workers cause during local strikes and defending union interests on the Town Council.'[46] In Dewsbury and Batley 'the emergence of the ILP ... was undoubtedly linked with the resurgence of trade unionism',[47] while in Huddersfield the growth of the Labour party was due to 'the central role played by trade unionism compared to the consistently subordinate influence of Socialism'.[50] Research on towns outside West Yorkshire tends to confirm the importance of trade unions in the creation of a Labour party.[49] In this book, I will examine the importance of trade unions to the success of the ILP in Keighley.

Other writers argue that a connection with trade-unionists, either formal or informal, was not a prerequisite for ILP success. David Clark,[50] in his study of Colne Valley, suggests that the party's growth was not primarily due to trade-union support. He shows how in 1891 only 0.4% of the population belonged to a trade union. In that year, when the Colne Valley Labour Union was founded, there were about 1,000 trade-union members and by 1905 that figure had increased to only 1,024.[51] Trade-unionism, therefore, had little to do with the success of the ILP in this part of Yorkshire, which was largely due, he suggests, to the type of ethical socialism that it preached. This was seen as a doctrine asserting the equality of man, an equality based on the intrinsic value of all human beings. However, it differed from certain other ethical movements in that it believed that its objectives could only be attained if the capitalistic economic system was replaced by a socialist one. Thus, in economic matters its adherents were usually left-wing, calling for the nationalization of the land and of industry. This drastic restructuring of the economic system was justified as being a prerequisite of the new moral order which was desired.[52]

Keighley, which was the town where Philip Snowden made his first impact and which had a popular Labour Church, was very suggestible to the appeal of this semi-religious socialism and this must be taken into account when assessing the growth of the branch.

A further means by which a sustainable socialist organization was created is put forward by Tom Woodhouse when discussing socialism in Leeds. He argues that ideology was the decisive factor, saying that what emerged in Leeds was a Labour party containing not only the strands of parliamentary and municipal reform and popular appeal, but also the influence of a serious and theoretically acute group of socialist leaders whose views were directed by the resurgence of Marxist ideas from the mid-1880s. The Labour party, as it existed in Leeds in 1914, rested on the politics first of populism, second of reform, and third of a combative working-class Marxian socialism. Although by the outbreak of the war the third factor was overlain by the other two, it was still important; indeed, in the early years it was the decisive influence in the continuing success of Labour and the noticeable decline in Liberal fortunes in working-class areas.[53]

There is doubt whether Marxist ideas had a great impact on the members of the Keighley ILP. It is important, nevertheless, to attempt to discover what writers and thinkers influenced them and gave shape to their socialism. There is evidence that Henry George, John Ruskin and Thomas Carlyle all helped to form their beliefs, as did contemporary writers such as the Fabians and Robert Blatchford.[54] The most important influence, however, was probably Philip Snowden, whose beliefs were derived from the works of, among others, H. M. Hyndman and Edward Carpenter, as well as 'old Radical and Socialist books and periodicals and pamphlets dating from the days of Hunt and Owen down to modern times',[55] but who had thought out his political position for himself. The result was a combination of ethical socialism and economic liberalism which was essentially evolutionary and peaceful, and which emphasized parliamentary rather than industrial activity. This ideology, while not particularly profound, was important in shaping the way the branch developed, and many of Snowden's contemporaries, both local and national, found it satisfying, particularly when explained by Snowden himself, with all his passion and rhetoric.

There were also other factors in the development of the ILP in West Yorkshire which need to be considered when discussing the Keighley branch. Perhaps the most important was the creation of social and cultural organizations which were formed initially to complement the political work of the Labour unions. They not only helped to raise money for the branch's political activities, but, more importantly, they helped to create the 'counter culture' which became an integral part of the ILP's appeal. This 'counter culture' was often based on local Labour clubs which brought activists together. Referring to Colne Valley, David Clark writes that:

> This decision [to form Labour Clubs] had wider implications than being merely for administrative convenience or organizational efficiency. For it also meant that the new [Labour] Union was challenging the main political parties each of whom had clubs in most of the larger centres of population. Thus whilst Labour Clubs would provide a place where supporters of independent labour representation could go for social and political intercourse, they also provided venues for formal propaganda meetings. Furthermore they, possibly unwittingly, were to provide the basis of a 'counter culture' which was to become such a strong feature of the Colne Valley labour movement and which was to sustain its very existence in the difficult years ahead.[56]

These remarks apply equally to the ILP clubs in Keighley, Haworth and Wilsden, although it was the Keighley club which dominated the constituency by being both the largest and the best patronized.

Other activities were based on the various Clarion organizations such as cycling clubs, vocal unions and Clarion Scouts. The types of activity organized by these clubs varied from place to place, and need to be explored. In Colne Valley, for example, a vocal union, a socialist brass band and, later, two cycling clubs were adopted.[57] Keighley formed a Clarion Scouts, a vocal union and a cycling club in the 1890s. These Clarion groups, together with the dances, ham teas, concerts, organized walks, 'free and easys' and debates, created a network of interrelated functions which, together with the Labour Church and their directly political activities, gave the Keighley ILPers that 'counter culture' referred to by Dr Clark.

One further development in the Keighley ILP branch should be considered. This was the contribution of certain individuals. Many branches were responsible for the early training of members who were to play an important part in the history of the British labour movement nationally. Fred Jowett in Bradford[58] and Philip Snowden in Keighley[59] are two instances. In addition, there were many people, now almost forgotten, who devoted much of their lives to the movement in their community. In Bradford, Charlie Glyde is an obvious example; Colne Valley had George Garside, who was the first chairman of the Labour Union and, in its early days, its driving force,[60] and in Keighley there were people like the Horner brothers, W. S. Wilkinson, W. F. Hardy and Charles Whitehead, whose talent and hard work gave the branch an importance far outweighing its membership.

The reason why the ILP branches developed as they did in different parts of West Yorkshire are complex. If, in Bradford, the party attracted trade-union support, the appeal of ethical socialism was still strong.[61] At the same time, in Colne Valley the ILP spent a great deal of time trying to increase the number of trade-unionists in the area and convert them to socialism. It must be remembered that the first parliamentary candidate in the constituency was the trade-union leader Tom Mann.[62] In Leeds, the socialist leaders helped to form the local branch of the Gasworkers' and General Labourers' Union and Tom Maguire and John Lincoln Mahon were fully aware of the need for a strong link between politically organized labour and trade unions.[63] In Halifax, the ILP, although dominated by trade-unionists, was influenced by the ideas of a group of local Fabian socialists, particularly John Lister.[64] The cultural side of the party's work, particularly the activities of the various Clarion societies, was also important. Thus the different reasons for the growth of the ILP is a matter of emphasis and Keighley is no exception to this general rule.

It is clear that no one cause can account for the success of the ILP in West Yorkshire. To some extent this is only to be expected, for there is great diversity in an area which ranges from the large urban centre of Leeds, to the overgrown mill town of Bradford, to the thinly populated landscape of the Colne Valley. The other large industrial centres, such as Huddersfield and Halifax, have their own distinct character and history, as have smaller towns such as Pudsey, Hebden Bridge and Morley, to choose three almost at random. Keighley is similar in its individuality. Though smaller than Bradford, it resembles it in that it depended for its prosperity on the worsted trade and, to a lesser extent, on engineering, which was originally established to service the textile industry. However, outside the urban area the parliamentary constituency is more like Colne Valley, dotted as it is with isolated, small industrial towns and villages, such as Haworth, Oxenhope and Cowling. Nevertheless, the town of Keighley dominated the social and political life of the area in a way that none of the villages of the Colne Valley did. Thus the area is different enough from the other worsted textile communities to require its own explanation for the emergence of a local labour movement.

Keighley provides a number of advantages to the historian of the labour movement. Not only did it have one of the larger branches of the ILP, but the sources that have survived are particularly rich. The minute books are complete from 1892, except for the years 1899–1901 and 1911–14. Two letter books covering the period 1897–1907, containing nearly one thousand letters written by the branch secretary, Tom Mackley, have also survived, as has an account book for 1897–1903.[65] In addition, the *Keighley Labour Journal* was for a time the longest-running local ILP newspaper and a nearly complete set is available for the period 1894–1902.[66] There is also a valuable set of pamphlets and newspaper cuttings contained in the

Snowden collection housed at Keighley Library. These records, combined with information on the movement's activities in the local Liberal and Conservative press as well as national labour newspapers such as the *Labour Leader* and the *Clarion*, provide an excellent range of sources for tracing the history of the local branch of the ILP and, later, the LRC. Obviously, there are disappointments; the quality of the minutes varies, those of the later period providing noticeably less information than the early years. It is unfortunate that no membership lists have survived, and although letters written by the secretary are numerous, none received by the branch has been kept. Even so, considering the general paucity of the original ILP branch records for the pre-First World War period in most parts of West Yorkshire, the Keighley material is fine indeed.

Regrettably, the records of local trade-union activity have not survived to anything like the same extent, though relevant material appears in the *Yorkshire Factory Times* and the local press. Some political records of the local Liberal party survive in the form of minutes for the years 1877–1931.[67] In addition, the *Keighley News*[68] was a local paper which reflected the Liberal point of view on most matters, although for much of the time it was owned by the Byles family of Bradford, whose most prominent representative was the New Liberal, William Pollard Byles. Conservative party minutes have also survived[69] and a complete run of the local Tory paper, the *Keighley Herald*,[70] exists. Sources for the political history of the town are therefore good, and in some areas excellent, and provide adequate and illuminating material for this study.

Notes

1. The standard history of Keighley is Ian Dewhirst, *A History of Keighley* (Keighley, 1974), p.45.
2. S. Webb and B. Webb, *The History of British Trade Unionism* (London, 1894, reprinted 1920).
3. E. Hobsbawm, 'The Labour Aristocracy in Nineteenth-Century Britain', in *Labouring Men* (London, 1964), pp.274–316.
4. H. Pelling, 'The Concept of the Labour Aristocracy', in *Popular Politics and Society in Late Victorian Britain* (London, 1968).
5. A. E. Musson, *British Trade Unions* (London, 1972); A. E. Musson, 'Class struggle and the labour aristocracy', *Social History*, vol.1, 3 (1976), pp.335–56.
6. Richard Price, *Masters, Unions and Men* (London, Cambridge University Press, 1980).
7. Robert Storch, 'The Plague of Blue Locusts: Police, Reform and Popular Resistance in Northern England, 1840–1855', *International Review of Social History*, XX, 1 (1975), pp.61–90.
8. H. F. Moorhouse, 'The Marxist Theory of the Labour Aristocracy', *Social History*, vol.3, 1 (1978), pp.61–82; and 'The Significance of the Labour Aristocracy', *Social History*, vol.6, 2 (1981), pp.229–33.

9. P. Joyce, *Work, Society and Politics: the Culture of the Factory in Late Victorian England* (Brighton, 1980).
10. *Ibid.*, pp.22–3, 27, 74, 163–5, 175–6, 219, 322, 325, 335.
11. Jack Reynolds, *The Great Paternalist: Titus Salt and the Growth of Nineteenth-Century Bradford* (London, 1983).
12. T. Koditschek, *Class Formation and Urban-Industrial Society: Bradford 1750–1850* (London, 1990).
13. J. A. Jowitt (ed.), *Model Industrial Communities in Mid-Nineteenth Century Yorkshire* (Bradford, 1986).
14. Dewhirst, *op.cit.*, p.45. For the houses of the Keighley manufacturers, see G. Sheeran, *Brass Castles: West Yorkshire New Rich and their Houses 1800–1914* (Halifax, 1993).
15. E. M. Sigsworth, *Black Dyke Mills* (Liverpool, 1958), pp.72–135; D. James, *Bradford* (Halifax, 1990), pp.49–62.
16. *Keighley News*, 1 January 1938; *Keighley Labour Journal*, February 1901.
17. K. Laybourn and J. Reynolds, *Liberalism and the Rise of Labour* (London, 1984).
18. *Ibid.*, pp.30–2; E. P. Thompson, 'Homage to Tom Maguire', in A. Briggs and J. Saville (eds), *Essays in Labour History* (London, 1960), pp.276–316.
19. H. J. O. Drake, 'John Lister of Shibden Hall: 1847–1933', unpublished Ph.D thesis (University of Bradford, 1973); Laybourn and Reynolds, *op.cit.*, p.35; A. M. McBriar, *Fabian Socialism and English Politics 1880–1914* (London, 1966), ch.10.
20. Laybourn and Reynolds, *op.cit.*
21. K. Laybourn and D. James (eds) *The Rising Sun of Socialism: the Independent Labour Party in the Textile District of the West Riding of Yorkshire between 1890–1914* (Wakefield, 1991); Laybourn and Reynolds, *op.cit.*
22. H. Pelling, *The Origin of the Labour Party 1880–1900* (London, 1954).
23. P. P. Poirier, *The Advent of the Labour Party* (London, 1958).
24. S. Pierson, *British Socialists: the Journey from Fantasy to Politics* (Harvard, 1979).
25. Thompson, *op.cit.*, p.277.
26. D. Howell, *British Workers and the Independent Labour Party 1888–1906* (Manchester, 1983), p.vii.
27. D. Clark, *Colne Valley: Radicalism to Socialism. The portrait of a northern constituency in the formative years of the Labour Party 1890–1910* (London, 1981).
28. C. Pearse, *The Manningham Mills Strike in Bradford, December 1890 – April 1891* (Occasional Papers in Economic and Social History, No.7, Hull, 1975).
29. W. D. Ross, 'Bradford Politics 1880–1906', unpublished Ph.D. thesis (University of Bradford, 1977); K. Laybourn, 'Trade Unions and the ILP; the Manningham Experience', in J. A. Jowitt and R. K. S. Taylor (eds), *Bradford 1890–1914: the Cradle of the Independent Labour Party*, Bradford Centre Occasional Papers, No.2 (Bradford, 1980); J. Reynolds and K. Laybourn, 'The Emergence of the Independent Labour Party in Bradford', *International Review of Social History* (1975).
30. R. B. Perks, 'The Rising Sun of Socialism; Trade Unions and the Independent Labour Party in Huddersfield', in Laybourn and James, *op.cit.*,

pp.158–217; R. B. Perks, 'Liberalism and the Challenge of Labour in West Yorkshire 1885–1914, with special reference to Huddersfield', unpublished Ph.D. thesis (Huddersfield Polytechnic, 1985).

31. T. Woodhouse, 'Trade Unions and Independent Labour Politics in Leeds, 1885–1914', unpublished paper produced in the mid-1970s; T. Woodhouse, 'The Working Class', in D. Fraser (ed.), *A History of Modern Leeds* (Manchester, 1980), pp.353–88.
32. Drake, *op.cit.*
33. J. Lister, 'Early History of the ILP Movement in Halifax', MS copy in West Yorkshire Archive Service, Calderdale.
34. P. Dawson, 'The Halifax Independent Labour Movement: Labour and Liberalism 1890–1914', in Laybourn and James, *op.cit.*, pp.45–75; P. Dawson, 'Halifax Politics 1890–1914', unpublished Ph.D. thesis (Huddersfield Polytechnic, 1987).
35. M. Crick, 'Labour Alliance or Socialist Unity? The Independent Labour Party in the Heavy Woollen Areas of West Yorkshire *c*1893–1902' in Laybourn and James, *op.cit.*, pp.28–45. M. Crick, 'To make Twelve O' Clock at Eleven: the history of the Social-Democratic Federation', unpublished Ph.D. thesis (Huddersfield Polytechnic, 1988), published as M. Crick, *The History of the Social-Democratic Federation* (Keele, 1994); M. Crick, 'A Collection of oddities: the Bradford Branch of the Social Democratic Federation', *The Bradford Antiquary*, Third Series No. 5 (1991).
36. Thompson, *op.cit.*
37. C. Cross, *Philip Snowden* (London, 1966).
38. K. Laybourn, *Philip Snowden: a biography 1864–1937* (London, 1988).
39. Laybourn and Reynolds, *op.cit.*
40. P. F. Clarke, *Lancashire and the New Liberalism* (London, 1971).
41. K. O. Morgan, 'The New Liberalism and the Challenge of Labour: the Welsh Experience', in K. D. Brown (ed.), *Essays in Anti-Labour History* (London, 1974), pp.159–82.
42. M. Pugh, 'Yorkshire and the New Liberalism', *Journal of Modern History*, vol.50, 3 (1978), D1139–55.
43. Laybourn and Reynolds, *op.cit.*
44. K. Laybourn, 'Trade Unions and the ILP', *op.cit.*, p.26.
45. Reynolds and Laybourn, 'The Emergence of the Independent Labour Party in Bradford', *op.cit.*, p.313.
46. Dawson, 'The Halifax Independent Labour Movement' *op.cit.*, p.96.
47. Martin Crick, 'Labour Alliance or Socialist Unity', *op.cit.*, pp.61–94.
48. Perks, 'Rising Sun of Socialism', *op.cit.*, p.160.
49. J. Hill, 'Manchester and Salford Politics and the Early Development of the Independent Labour Party', *International Review of Social History*, 26 (1981), pp.171–201; S. Bryher, *An Account of the Labour and Socialist Movement in Bristol* (Bristol, 1929); R. L. Walton, 'The Labour Movement in Blackburn 1880–1914', unpublished MA thesis (Huddersfield Polytechnic, 1981).
50. Clark, *op.cit.*, pp.145–50, 186–8.
51. *Ibid.*, p.103.
52. *Ibid.*, p.186.
53. Woodhouse, 'Working Class', *op.cit.*, p.358.

54. W. S. Wilkinson of Keighley referred to 'the effect on his mind of reading the *Clarion*, *Merrie England*, and Ruskin's *Unto this Last* and *Sesame and Lilies* ... [and] ... felt it his duty to choose sides ... and take his place under the banner of Labour'; *Keighley Labour Journal*, 14 June 1894.
55. Philip Snowden, *An Autobiography* (London, 1934), p.60.
56. Clark, *op.cit.*, p.32.
57. *Ibid.*, p.125.
58. Fenner Brockway, *Socialism Over Sixty Years: the Life of Jowett of Bradford 1864–1944* (London, 1946), pp.44–64.
59. D. James, 'Philip Snowden and the Keighley Independent Labour Party', in K. Laybourn and D. James (eds), *Philip Snowden: the first Labour Chancellor of the Exchequer* (Bradford, 1987), pp.5–25.
60. Clark, *op.cit.*, p.22.
61. Laybourn, 'Trade Unions and the ILP', *op.cit.*, pp.34–40.
62. Clark, *op.cit.*, pp.39–61.
63. Woodhouse, 'Working Class', *op.cit.*, p.369.
64. Dawson, 'Halifax Independent Labour Movement', *op.cit.*, pp.105–6.
65. Housed in Keighley Reference Library.
66. *Ibid.*
67. *Ibid.*
68. *Ibid.*
69. Housed with West Yorkshire Archive Service, Bradford.
70. Housed in Keighley Reference Library.

CHAPTER TWO

Keighley and the Wool Textile District in the Nineteenth Century

Keighley is part of the West Yorkshire textile district, which is a distinctive area, six hundred square miles in extent, bounded on the north edge by Keighley itself, in the east by Leeds and Wakefield, in the south by the villages of the Holme Valley, and in the west by Hebden Bridge. In the nineteenth century, the main preoccupation of the area was wool, but there were other industries. Coal-mining and ironworks were important in Bradford, as was stone-quarrying. Engineering was widespread, sometimes, as in Halifax, employing more people than the textile trade, and towns often had their own specialisms. Otley, for example, was known for its printing machinery, and Keighley for its washing machines. Engineering and textiles were a useful combination, as they could give a balanced spread of employment. In Keighley, as in similar towns, women and children comprised the majority of the textile workforce, while engineering was the biggest male employer.[1]

Nevertheless, wool was the heart of the region's economy, and in places such as Bradford and Keighley the whole working community ultimately depended upon its prosperity. Recessions produced not only business failures, but short-time working and unemployment, which threw thousands into the arms of the Poor Law Guardians. In 1826 the trade depression led to a financial crisis, known as the Butterfield panic, during which 'the majority of the Keighley tradesmen were ruined', and which fifty years later was still referred to by the people in the town 'with bated breath as if they were talking of one of the world's calamities'.[2] At the height of the 1847–8 depression, the Bradford Poor Law Union was administering outdoor relief to over sixteen thousand people, or about one in ten of the Union's population.

The woollen industry achieved a notable degree of local variation and specialization, but there are two broad categories: woollens and worsteds. Worsteds were not important in Yorkshire before the late seventeenth century, but became increasingly so after 1750. It has been suggested that a number of factors determined whether an area was to be worsted or woollen: where land was unsuitable for arable cultivation; where it was enclosed early; where the influence of the manorial system declined; and where there emerged a large landless class of wage-earning cottagers – in these situations, the transition to a centralized system of production suitable for worsteds was encouraged. On the other hand, the artisanal structure of the woollen side of the industry prevailed in areas where soils were better; where land was held in leasehold or copyhold; where farms were of sufficient size to support a dual economy; and where traditional manorial farms had survived for longer. The manufacture of worsteds differed from woollens in seemingly minor ways. Worsted yarn is made of fibres which, before being spun, are straightened out until they lie parallel with each other. They are combed, while woollen fibres are not. In woollen yarn the fibres cross and intermingle in all possible directions and go through processes called fulling, scribbling and dressing, which worsteds do not. The distinctions between them also contributed to the differences in the development of the two branches of the industry. Worsteds were centred in Bradford, Halifax and Keighley, and by 1851 there were 418 factories, with 746,281 spindles and 30,856 power looms in the region.[3]

From its origin, the structure of the worsted industry was more dependent than woollens on the availability of capital, and the typical worsted entrepreneur was a man of means who organized, but did not necessarily engage in, the actual process of production, or even in some cases have any prior connection with the trade. Known as a stapler, he had to finance the chain of processes which turned the wool, which he usually purchased from Lincolnshire or the East Riding, into the finished cloth which he sold to a merchant, usually, in the case of Keighley, at the Halifax Piece Hall. Having bought his raw material, he would put it out to independent workers who would comb, spin and weave the cloth in their homes. The distribution of this work covered a large area, often as far as Long Preston, Giggleswick, over the Lancashire border, or even Cheshire and Derbyshire.[4] In Keighley, the Cravens started in business as worsted staplers in the eighteenth century and distributed work to Silsden, Sutton, Ickornshaw and Cowling among other places.[5] The stapler not only had to have the money to buy the wool, but also to finance the large number of domestic workers he employed. The Heaton family of Ponden, near Haworth, were typical examples of these early worsted entrepreneurs, and their fortunes have been analysed in several articles.[6] Even before mechanization, therefore, the worsted centres of the West Riding were dominated by wealthy businessmen who organized the trade in their own interests.

However, this 'putting out' system came under increasing pressure as the demand created by the expansion of overseas markets grew in the latter half of the eighteenth century. When it was found that, by adapting machinery used in the nearby cotton industry, it was possible to spin worsted yarn, it was only a matter of time before the trade turned from domestic to factory production.

The mechanization of all stages of worsted production took more than fifty years.[7] The first spinning mills were small and were paralleled by an increase in hand combers and weavers brought about by the general expansion of the trade. The first worsted spinning mill in Yorkshire was opened in 1787 in Addingham, a village seven miles from Keighley in neighbouring Wharfedale. The date of Keighley's earliest worsted spinning mill is not known, but according to John Hodgson[8] three mills were in existence by 1808. Two more were built by 1810, and by 1823 the town had forty-four worsted manufacturers. Among them were families which were to become synonymous with the town's élite; the Marriners, Jonas Sugden, John and William Haggas, Isaac Butterfield. In worsted weaving, the threat of machinery to hand workers became obvious in the 1830s. Progress was slow, however, and early attempts to introduce power weaving were successfully resisted. When James Swarbrick, a manufacturer of Shipley, a town lying about eight miles from Keighley, tried to place a power loom for weaving in his mill as early as 1822, it was destroyed by the hand workers. In 1826 there was a riot in which two people were killed when a mob attacked Horsfalls mill in Bradford, where new weaving machines had been erected. However, in 1834 power weaving looms were installed successfully in Keighley by John Clough, and in the following years they became common.[9] Nevertheless, Clough and other manufacturers continued to employ many hand weavers and it was not until the 1850s that the power loom completely superseded the hand-loom weaver. This was due partly to the crudity of the first machines, which could not match the skill of the hand worker, and partly because the downward pressure on wages made it as cheap to employ hand-loom weavers as to invest in power looms. The problem of a successful combing machine was not solved until the 1840s. The key figure was Samuel Cunliffe Lister, who, with the help of a Leeds engineer, G. E. Donisthorpe, produced a successful combing machine and immediately secured as many patent rights as possible. He managed to obtain a stranglehold on the worsted industry, making his machines for two hundred pounds and selling them for twelve hundred. Even at these prices, manufacturers were forced to buy from him if they wished to stay in business. Thus, Marriners in Keighley installed the new machines as early as 1854.[10] Lister became a very rich man, although his invention meant the demise of the once proud hand combers, who had previously been the best paid of the hand workers.[11]

With the mechanization of these processes, it became possible to employ a workforce entirely in one place, with all the stages of production under one roof. Although a number of these mills were built, most notably by Titus Salt at Saltaire, many manufacturers continued to use several buildings, often on various sites.[12] The Cravens, for example, had three mills in Keighley,[13] while Robert Clough built a large new complex consisting of spinning mills, warehouses and weaving sheds, but still had to lease another site for further spinning.[14]

The industrialization of the worsted industry brought fundamental changes to the physical appearance of the region, and altered the living conditions of the population. The number of people whose lives centred on the trade rose from 292,356 in 1801 to 1,594,904 in 1901. Some of this population growth was due to natural increase, but much of it was a result of immigration. One group, the Irish, was particularly important. By 1851, one person in twenty living in Keighley was Irish or of Irish descent.[15] Largely unskilled, uneducated and unpopular, they were separated from the rest of the population by religion, culture and, on occasion, language, some of them speaking only Gaelic. They were persecuted for their Catholicism: the region was a centre of the Orange Order and anti-Catholic riots were frequent. They lived in the worst of the slums and generally had the least popular, most ill-paid jobs, many of them becoming hand combers in the very years when this job was being replaced by machinery. Faced by widespread prejudice and social ostracism, the Catholics preserved their communal identity through the Church. The priests, curates and nuns were not only spiritual leaders, but also bankers and insurers. They acted as spokespeople for the community, disbursing its charities and generally taking on the role of social leadership. In return, the Catholic Church, unlike other congregations, retained the loyalty of its communicants. It was only with the growth of Irish nationalist groups at the end of the century that any alternative organization developed to represent the Irish community. Politically, too, they were distinct, often voting as a group, usually for the Liberals. In Keighley, at the time that the ILP was being founded and claiming to be the voice of the working class, the Irish were committed to the Liberals, and on occasion were the main reason for that party's electoral success.[16]

This population explosion did not lead, as has been indicated, to a totally urbanized environment, and this factor must be borne in mind when explaining the development of the West Yorkshire ILP. Some communities did grow spectacularly, and by 1900 Leeds, Bradford, Halifax and Huddersfield all had populations exceeding one hundred thousand. Keighley, too, saw a rapid increase, though not on as large a scale. Even so, as late as the early years of the twentieth century, only about half the total population of the Yorkshire textile district lived in the largest towns. Just as typical were the many small and medium centres such as Keighley, Bingley and Silsden, and industrial villages such as Hebden Bridge and Cowling.

Regardless of where workers lived, however, the new industrial system brought them little immediate benefit. Factory owners tended to replace male hand-loom operators with juveniles and females. Wages were low, hours were long, short time was frequent and discipline was harsh. Samuel Rhodes of Keighley, who worked for Mr Mitchell, 'a genuine Christian', told the Sadler Committee in 1832 that discipline was maintained by an overlooker who 'had a strap with nails in it'.[17] However, if conditions in the mill were bad, the position of the hand workers was worse. The 1830s and '40s saw a steady decline in their wages. Weaving wages fell from 9*s.* (45p) to 4*s.* 6*d.* (22.5p) a week between 1833 and 1855, and combers' wages fell from 13*s.*

3*d.* (67.5p) to 7*s.* (35p). The situation was aggravated by the economic pattern of a three-year boom and slump which climaxed in the disastrous years of the 1840s. For the employers, there were certain advantages in having machine and hand production running side by side. In boom periods, hand workers could be taken on to supplement machine output, while in slumps they could be laid off and the capital-intensive power looms be kept running. For the hand workers, there was only constant misery.[18]

Outside work, life was equally difficult. Housing and sanitation were primitive. In Keighley the streets contained standing puddles 'of foul and offensive liquid matter'[19] which seeped through walls and into cellars. Unventilated back-to-back houses reeked with bad air, privies and soil pits; pigsties and heaps of manure stank in yards and snickets. The atmosphere was polluted, and towns like Keighley were covered in a permanent smog created by industrial and domestic processes. There was rarely any fresh water and food was unappealing when it was not adulterated; a hand-loom weaver's diet in the 1840s consisted of 'malt, treacle and bacon'.[20] Inevitably, people's health suffered. Diseases such as smallpox, scarlatina, dysentery and measles killed many, particularly the young. In Haworth in the 1850s the life expectancy was 25.8 years, and forty-one out of every hundred babies never reached the age of six. Rebecca Town, a Keighley woman who died in 1851 aged 44 years, had thirty children who all died in infancy.[21]

Times were also difficult for the manufacturers, and for every successful business there was an equal number or more of failures. Hodgson, writing about the Keighley entrepreneurs in 1879, remarks, 'we well recollect nearly thirty years ago trying to call to mind the names of persons who had been engaged in the worsted trade in this neighbourhood during the previous 25 years, and out of nearly 100 who had been so engaged, less than a score remained in business at that time.'[22] William Wilkinson, a Keighley spinner, was unlucky in the Butterfield banking crash and was reduced to poverty and earning his living as a wool comber, eventually dying in the workhouse.[23] Nevertheless, it was in this period that the chief characteristics of the trade were established. By the middle of the nineteenth century the worsted industry had moved away from its earlier pattern of boom and slump to a more stable and continuously prosperous footing. The 1860s and early 1870s were boom times. The American Civil War created a cotton famine, which favoured worsted goods, and in 1870 the Franco-Prussian war crippled the French industry, providing English manufacturers with even more opportunities. The biographer of Swire Smith, a Keighley spinner, wrote of these years, 'if this were the story of a man who wished to make much money, it would have told how he began to make it in the Franco-Prussian War. The boom in the woollen trades was unsurpassed. Mills were built rapidly throughout the Riding.'[24]

However, as has been indicated, after 1875 the economic climate turned gloomy, with the price of wool, yarn and piece goods falling steadily and continuing to fall for nearly thirty years. There were short-term booms, but wool textiles now entered a period of more or less continual decline until the early years of the twentieth century. This was partly due to increasing competition from abroad. The French quickly recovered from the devastations of the war and found that changing fashion had made their fabrics more popular than those of Yorkshire. At the same time, the doctrine of free trade was challenged by a growing number of countries which erected tariff barriers against British goods. The hardest blow was the introduction of the American McKinley and Dingley tariffs, which irrevocably damaged British wool exports to its largest foreign market. Though the early years of the twentieth century saw a rise in domestic consumption, this obscured a worsening exports situation which constantly undermined the industry's long-term stability. The decline in the worsted industry was a key factor in determining why the ILP developed as it did in West Yorkshire, undermining the Liberal Nonconformist manufacturers who provided the social and political leadership in many of the local communities.[25]

During the period 1850–1914 there were improvements in the environment of the area. Local councils tackled the worst sanitary problems, and by the 1870s the region was sharing in the national decline of typhus and cholera. Many of the smoke nuisances, as contemporaries called the choking mass of poisonous fumes which poured out of factory chimneys, were moderated, although in Keighley the problem was still bad enough to justify the ILP mounting campaigns against offending factory owners throughout the 1890s.[26] Parliamentary Acts and local bye-laws improved the standard of housing, and building societies made property more widely available, although mainly to the middle class and labour aristocrats.[27] It was the ILP who were to agitate for the municipal housing which was to provide proper accommodation for the bulk of the people. Public parks became increasingly available in the latter half of the nineteenth century, providing the working classes for the first time with green space in which to exercise their bodies. Keighley was late in the provision of these facilities, but between 1887 and 1893 no less than three public parks were opened. Similarly, public libraries and museums increasingly gave the public the opportunity to exercise their minds. Keighley, thanks to the friendship between the local manufacturer Swire Smith and Andrew Carnegie, became the first town in England to have a Carnegie Library. Other organizations that were created to help the citizens improve themselves included Mechanics Institutes, debating societies, co-operative societies, friendly societies, burial clubs, temperance groups and coffee taverns.[28] How popular all these institutions were with the workers is debatable, but there was no lack of enthusiasm for providing people with useful ways of spending their time. For many, however, the pub was the most important place of entertainment. The years between 1870 and the First World War saw its heyday and they became ever more elaborate. The temptation for the working man, living in a cramped back-to-back, is obvious, but the middle classes, who rarely actually ventured into pubs, came to regard them with suspicion, seeing them as places where workers were lured into vice and temptation.[29] One strand of the ILP, too, regarded drink with caution, and Philip Snowden remained an advocate of total abstinence all his life.[30]

More important in improving people's standards of living was the general increase in real wages and the decrease in the hours of work. The worsted trade, however, was notorious for its low pay, and Keighley pay rates were regarded as particularly poor.[31] Hours of work, too, remained longer than average in worsteds, although the Nine Hours Movement had considerable success among the engineers and other skilled groups. Textile employers argued that shorter hours would give foreign competition an advantage, that women and children did not work as hard as men and therefore should have longer hours, that piece-rate workers would receive diminished earnings, and that in any case there was no widespread agitation for shorter hours.[32]

Within this general economic and social framework, five factors should be emphasized as being of particular importance in studying the political history of communities like Keighley. These are: the role of the manufacturers in the wider life of the community; the extent of civic pride and local patriotism; the centrality of religion on many people's lives; the importance of politics; and the relative failure of the trade-union movement, particularly in the textile industry.

It is impossible to generalize about the attitudes of mill owners towards their workforce and the communities in which they lived. Whatever their motives, however, a significant number of them had a view of society in which their position conferred power, influence and responsibility. Henry Forbes of Bradford expressed this when he wrote in 1852 that:

> I say not that there are no grasping masters – men ignorant or regardless of their high moral obligations – but I do say that these men are the exception rather than the rule: that we have among us many 'Captains of Industry' between whom and their workmen there is some other connection than mere money payment, who study to promote their welfare and elevation and whose efforts are met by a frank confidence and grateful recognition.[33]

Paternalism such as that advocated by Forbes tended to be most successful in towns where there was a relatively small group of major employers. Local examples include Titus Salt of Bradford and Saltaire,[34] the Crossleys and Ackroyds of Halifax,[35] the Fosters of Queensbury[36] and the Forsters of Burley-in-Wharfedale.[37] In Keighley the Briggs, the Cloughs, Swire Smith and his brother Prince Smith, and a number of others were of the same type. Such people had a hierarchical view of society where each member had his function, his duties, his obligations and his ties of dependency. Ideally, harmony prevailed, but when the structure of the community came under threat, from an industrial dispute, for example, or the work of political activists, then stern measures were taken. Strikers could be dismissed and perhaps turned out of the homes they rented from the master, or socialists blacklisted and forced to find work elsewhere. G. J. Wardle, a leading Keighley ILPer, was placed under considerable pressure to give up his political work. He explained how:

> some of the employers in Keighley … had persecuted him because he dared to have an opinion of his own … he was brought to the headquarters [of the Midland Railway Company] and was made to sign an agreement not to take part in any public meeting belonging to the Independent Labour Party … he signed for the sake of his wife and children.[38]

The co-existence of contradictory characteristics such as power and obligation, cruelty and kindness, oppression and benevolence, exploitation and protection, was at the heart of paternalism, which was essentially a form of authority.[42]

The power of the local employers did not derive solely from their control of job opportunities. A master might also be a town councillor, an alderman, a mayor, a magistrate, a school and hospital governor, a Poor Law Guardian, a church and chapel dignitary and vice-president of various voluntary and charitable bodies. In Keighley, for example, John Brigg was at various times the town's MP, a member of five Liberal associations, an *ex officio* member of the Board of Guardians, a magistrate, a county councillor, as well as being connected with the running of the Mechanics Institute, two schools, two hospitals and the St John's Ambulance, local charities, the Scientific and Literary Society and the football club, not to mention the Chamber of Commerce and the Textile Society. His son Benjamin Septimus was a member of the Local Board and Borough Council for over thirty years.[40] Members of the local élite could thus have several decision-making roles running concurrently, giving them wide-spread influence throughout their communities. This influence was reinforced by the exercise of philanthropy, acts of personal benevolence and voluntary efforts to provide local amenities and foster a sense of civic pride.

Obviously, neither the power nor the influence of the manufacturers was absolute. The growing national legislation relating to public health, education and the franchise was implemented without reference to local opinion, and factory laws, although sometimes ignored, also limited the activities of the employers.

The persistent overlap of economic, social and political leadership is evident in Keighley, and when the ILP started to challenge the employers in the political arena, they found that they were often combating their economic and social influence as well. Working for the local manufacturers was the power of local parochialism. Communities tended to be insular, although this does not mean that they were isolated from national trends. Railways provided reliable communications, and newspapers and journals gave national news and views; businessmen travelled in search of orders, and workers in search of employment. Nevertheless, local loyalties remained strong. In 1876 the Keighley Board of Guardians refused to implement the Vaccination Acts, a piece of legislation much resented locally, and seven of them were arrested and sent to York prison. On their return they received a vote of thanks, endorsing substantial public opinion, 'for the manner in which they have resisted the carrying out of compulsory vaccination in Keighley'.[41] Many northern industrial towns remained essentially clusters of villages, each with its own local loyalties and distinguishable accents. In these communities the millowner might build his mill, establish the Church and Chapel of his choice and provide what amenities he decided. Thus, in Keighley the Sugdens dominated Oakworth, the Ickringills Eastwood, the Cloughs Ingrow and Hainworth,[42] and, to a lesser extent, the Merralls controlled Haworth. Other instances abound: the Fosters at Denholme, the Forsters at Burley-in-Wharfedale and the Fosters at Queensbury. Also in these communities, periods of crisis and prosperity were shared by masters and workers and this created a uniformity of purpose and outlook. Often the outlook adopted was that of the master. The ILP and trade-unionism provided an alternative frame of reference for workers, that of horizontal 'class' loyalties, which was contrary to the vertical framework of allegiance and dependence put forward by the masters. However, local patriotism and the influence of the manufacturer meant that it was frequently difficult for the ILP to get a hearing, and even when they did, they were often listened to with suspicion and mistrust. Thus, when the fledgling Keighley ILPers went to the remote village of Cowling, they were met with abuse, violence and buckets of water.[43] In such remote communities, organizing the ILP branches on any but the most local basis presented problems.

It is significant that some of the most important celebrations of local patriotism took place on essentially religious occasions. Sunday School anniversaries, Whit walks, the opening of a new church or chapel, were enthusiastically adopted as an opportunity to sanctify the achievement of the local community. Although religious leaders, particularly in West Yorkshire's larger towns, found much to depress them in the 1851 religious census and in the occasional censuses taken in individual towns at a later date, the influence of the Church, and more importantly the Chapel, was of central, though declining, importance to all aspects of the region's economic, social and political life throughout the period up to 1914, including the development of the area's own brand of ethical socialism.

The region was a centre of Nonconformity, with only the area around Wakefield being an Anglican stronghold. Keighley was typical of the district.

The Wesleyan circuit had accommodation for 7,175 souls; Devonshire Street Congregational Church contained over 1,000 seats; Albert Street Baptist Chapel had space for 700, and Cavendish Street United Methodist Free Church for 800 people.[44] Many local industrialists saw religious activity as an important part of their social obligations. Thus the Briggs were active Congregationalists,[45] and the Cloughs were Wesleyan Methodists.[46]

After 1850, despite the survival of sects such as the believers in Joanna Southcott, who were still holding meetings in Apple Hall, Bradford in 1881, or the Spiritualists, whose chapel in Keighley held 180 seats in 1886,[47] the older millenarian flavour disappeared from much religious teaching, and a new softer tone emerged. Nonconformist chapels became increasingly ornate and expressive, and part of the local establishment. From the 1890s there was increasing concern among all religious groups at the loss of faith, and about declining congregations and members. Attempts were made by the established churches to counteract this decline, by the introduction of such organizations as the Pleasant Sunday Afternoon movement, but they were not notably successful.[48]

There were several reasons for this failure. Society was growing steadily more secular. Prior to 1850, the bulk of schooling was provided by Sunday Schools; after 1870, the School Boards, and later the local authorities, took increasing responsibility for education. Sport became a popular leisure activity, often at the expense of the church or chapel. Entertainment was increasingly professionalized, so that people went to the music hall, the theatre, the football or cricket match rather than the church hall. The differences between the world of work and the claims of religion were obvious to working men.[49] Employers were closely identified with Nonconformity, and people noticed the contradictions between the manufacturers' behaviour both towards their workers and towards each other, and the teachings of the gospels. In addition, church ministers often sided with the masters in their preaching, thus calling into question the commitment of the Nonconformists to the struggle for equal political rights for the working class. In a period when extension of the franchise was a burning issue, the attitudes of churchmen, both dissenting and established, held little attraction for the working man. In the 1890s increasing numbers directed their enthusiasm into the Labour Churches and the religion of socialism, while others became involved in non-religious activities such as politics and the ILP. Even so, the identification of the Liberal party with Nonconformity and the Conservatives with Anglicanism remained important political factors throughout this period.

Politics always attracted the energies of a portion of the labouring classes. Elections were contested vigorously and party political battles fought continuously. Even without the vote, the workers played an active role in these campaigns. Many electors came from sectors of society which were vulnerable to pressure from the workers, such as shopkeepers or those involved in the drink trade. At a time when there was no secret ballot, the way that people voted was public knowledge, and non-electors could exert considerable influence by boycotting those shopkeepers with whose politics they did not agree and by dealing only with those sympathetic to them. More important, the region stood in the vanguard of virtually every contemporary working-class political movement of size and significance. Agitation from Luddism, Chartism and the creation of a working-class political party in the 1890s had on occasion significant degrees of working-class support throughout the area.[50] It was not unknown for Chartists to draw 10,000 people to a demonstration, for example.[51] That is not to say that all the workers were interested in politics. Probably a majority rarely concerned themselves with radical industrial or political activity. Queensbury, a small industrial hilltop village midway between Halifax and Bradford and ten miles from Keighley, dominated by the paternalism of John Foster and Company, did not experience even the mildest outbreak of Chartist activity. Instead, in 1848 the workforce thanked the master for 'the regular employment their business talents have procured for all employed at Black Dyke of late years and particularly during the panic of 1847'.[52] Over fifty years later the *Keighley Labour Journal* could remark that 'the majority of the electors in Keighley are so deeply sunk in the slough of political party ignorance as to be almost beyond hope, or to be hardly worth troubling to save'.[53] Nevertheless, West Yorkshire was usually prominently represented in the nation's popular political arena.

Between 1850 and 1914 the textile district was a Liberal stronghold. The Liberals offered a view of the world in which unfettered economic activity combined with individual self-help would produce a society where improvements were possible. They supported limited reform and the extension of the franchise, and this allowed them to attract a certain level of support from the working class, while their firm stand on private property and law and order reassured the middle class. The Conservatives enjoyed success only in parts of the Saddleworth district, in the Anglican stronghold of Wakefield, and in Leeds, where the local party had the happy knack of selecting local men of considerable influence, such as George Beecroft, a Leeds ironmaster who succeeded in attracting a considerable number of working men's votes in the 1860s.

Two threats to Liberal supremacy emerged at the end of the nineteenth century: a Tory revival and the foundation of the Independent Labour Party. There had always been a core of Conservative support throughout the region; generally speaking, Anglicans voted Conservative. But after 1875 the party attracted other recruits. Many moderate Liberals were becoming restive; they disliked Gladstone's foreign policy for what they regarded as its weakness; they thought Liberal policy on Ireland was appeasement; and they resented the radicals' support of Charles Bradlaugh. Furthermore, they were hostile to the radical approach to the Local Veto, which would have given localities the right to forbid the licensing of pubs and which brought the Liberals the reputation of being killjoys.[54] A number of them therefore moved into the Tory camp. In Keighley, for example, Richard Longsden Hattersley had been a moderate Liberal throughout the 1880s, but in 1895 he became an active Tory. The Conservatives also appealed to much of the middle-class vote, which had grown towards the end of the nineteenth century with the expansion of jobs in shopkeeping, local government, schoolteaching and clerical work. Many in this group felt threatened by the working class and remained deferential to their social superiors, attracted by the Tory emphasis on firm government, the defence of national institutions, patriotism and the Empire. There was also a group of working-class Conservatives, many of whom were anti-Irish, anti-education, anti-temperance, and fervently nationalistic.

Perhaps most important, however, was the debate over free trade. As the depression and foreign competition threatened the profits of the worsted trade, the unity of local Liberal parties dissolved. For almost fifty years, *laissez faire* had been an article of faith with the worsted manufacturers and the Liberals. Yet the depression brought a revival of protectionist sentiment. The erection of new tariff barriers by Germany, France and the United States convinced some manufacturers that the era of free trade was over and that Britain had to respond in kind. They called for equalized tariffs with other countries and a tax on imported food, in order both to protect home agriculture and to allow Britain to be self-sufficient in food production. They looked to the Empire to replace the markets which were being closed by these new tariff barriers, and wanted the government to encourage and protect trade with the colonies in order to create a market for British goods and an assured supply of raw materials and food at reasonable prices. This debate split the Liberals and drove some of them to the Tories – the party of protection. The most famous local protectionist was Samuel Cunliffe Lister, the Bradford silk manufacturer, but there were many others. In Keighley the Haggas family of spinners split along generations: John Haggas, who died in 1889, had been an active Liberal, while his sons James, Frederick and Herbert, who were politically active from the 1890s, were all Conservatives.[55]

Equally important to the Liberals in the long term was the challenge of Labour, which saw the establishment of a separate political party to represent the working class. Although the growth of the Labour party in West Yorkshire is complex, in general the district showed a preference for the less overtly doctrinaire ILP over organizations such as the Socialist League or the Social Democratic Federation, and it became the area of greatest support for the ILP in Britain. In 1895, two years after the ILP's foundation at the Bradford conference, 79 of its 305 branches were located in the wool textile district. Progress was by no means steady and there were periods, notably in the early twentieth century, when a great deal of the initial momentum was lost. However, by the First World War it was clear that Labour had become an established part of the political landscape. It had 202 representatives on local political bodies. In Bradford it held 20 seats on the Borough Council, in Leeds 16, and in Halifax and Huddersfield 5 and 8 respectively. It had won a number of seats in parliamentary elections, and in certain constituencies could command between a quarter and a third of the vote. In Keighley it had considerable early success and had developed a body of electoral support which made it an influential factor in local politics.[56]

Nevertheless, while the growth of the party was undoubtedly important, it would be wrong to see the ILP either as equally influential in all parts of the district or as the dominant force in political life. Its support was strongest in those areas where the Liberals had either consistently antagonized their working-class supporters or had simply ignored their demands. Middle-class Liberals felt particularly able to ignore calls both for legislation which would serve the interests of the workers and for an increase in the number of working-class candidates in those constituencies where there was no large-scale bloc of working-class votes to be appeased. However, even though the Labour party was gathering increasing support in the years before 1914, and its alliance with the trade unions meant that it was poised for even more growth, yet the region was still a bastion of Liberalism until the outbreak of World War One. However, it was a Liberalism still dominated by the factory master and Nonconformity, which offered self-help and charity rather than intervention and collectivization. It was old-fashioned, and Labour was increasingly eating into its support.

If the region was politically active, trade-unionism was generally regarded as weak. In part this may be due to the structure of the industry. The organization of the worsted trade into a factory system in the 1850s resulted in a marked differentiation of workers based on age, skill and gender. A small group of adult male workers received higher pay and considerable control over the mass of the labour force, largely made up of women or children. The women were generally unmarried, and accepted low wages in the belief that they would not be in the mills for long but would marry and leave. Except for the few boys who stayed on as overlookers or skilled workers in other parts of the trade, most lads left the factory when they were 18 to seek other employment. Such a transient workforce was inevitably difficult to organize, and before the advent of the general unions in the 1880s the worsted industry was characterized by a mass of non-union weaving and spinning workers and a group of small craft unions among the skilled trades. As a self-conscious élite, the unions of skilled men sought to balance conciliation and militancy to achieve their limited aims.[57]

This arrangement suited the manufacturers in many ways. The worsted trade depended for its success upon its ability to produce goods cheaply, and this was achieved largely by cost-cutting. The need to keep prices low exerted pressure on wage rates and led to continual efforts to increase productivity. Manufacturers thus engaged in speed-ups, extensions in the number of looms and spindles minded, cutbacks in employment and unsafe working conditions. The lack of trade-unionism among the unskilled made it easier to achieve these cutbacks. The group which policed these changes was the skilled section of the workforce, such as the overlookers, who also enforced discipline and in practice had the power to employ and sack workers. Thus, the factory workforce was divided and there was very little sense of unity among the skilled and unskilled.[58]

However, while the employers could tolerate the unions of skilled men during the boom years before 1875, the depression raised difficulties. Skilled workers were affected by the downturn in trade, and there were serious problems of unemployment. They therefore tried to use their trade societies to slow the impact of the depression. This brought them into conflict with the masters, and gave them common cause with the unskilled to contest wage cuts and increased workloads. In the 1880s the formation of general unions for the unskilled was often encouraged by members of the skilled unions, and this, linked to the political emergence of the labour movement, brought the skilled and unskilled together in an alliance against the manufacturers and their political party, the Liberals.

Politics was seen as complementing trade-union activity. Some working-class leaders felt that it was futile to expect major improvements to be brought about by unions alone. Change could best be achieved through political action. As the *Keighley Labour Journal* said when discussing the 1896 iron moulders strike:

> But when will working men see how utterly futile strikes are to solve the wages problem? When will they realise the powerful influence of the vote and seek through independent political organization to accomplish the material bettering of their lives which this power gives. Believe me my fellow working men all improvement affected by strike is purchased at too great a sacrifice. If it were the only way, why then nothing could be said against it, but it is not the only way, and if you will only learn the lessons which the present is so plainly teaching you will soon throw over the out of date weapon and take advantage of the political machine ready to hand.[59]

Within this worsted region, Keighley was the most important centre of production, after Bradford and Halifax. It exhibited all the characteristics of the district, yet had its own history and development. In order to understand why it came to the forefront of the area's radical politics, it is important to trace the economic, social and political growth of the town during the nineteenth century.

Notes

1. Dewhirst, *op.cit.*, p.92; D. James, 'Paternalism in Keighley', in Jowitt (ed.), *Model Industrial Communities*, *op.cit.*, p.104. W. Keighley, *Keighley Past and Present* (Keighley, 1879), pp.233–6.
2. Dewhirst, *op.cit.*, p.37.
3. P. Hudson, *The Genesis of Industrial Capital: a study of the West Riding wool textile industry c1750–1850* (London, 1986), pp.25–53; G. Firth, *Bradford and the Industrial Revolution; an economic history 1760–1840* (Halifax, 1990), p.141–69.
4. James, *Bradford*, *op.cit.*, p.20; G. Firth, 'The Genesis of the Industrial Revolution in Bradford 1760–1830', unpublished Ph.D. thesis (University of Bradford, 1974), pp.385–7.
5. J. Hodgson, *Textile Manufacture and Other Industries in Keighley* (Keighley, 1879), p.31.
6. Firth, *Bradford and the Industrial Revolution*, *op.cit.*, pp.147–52; E. M. Sigsworth, 'William Greenwood and Robert Heaton', *Bradford Textile Society Journal* (1951–2), pp.61–72.
7. Sigsworth, *op.cit.*, pp.1–72. G. Firth, 'The Bradford Trade in the Nineteenth Century', in D. G. Wright and J. A. Jowitt (eds), *Victorian Bradford* (Bradford, 1982), pp.7–37.
8. Hodgson, *op.cit.*, p.19.
9. *Ibid.*, p.69. M. Smith, 'Robert Clough Ltd., Grove Mill, Keighley. A Study in Technological Redundancy 1835–1865', MA thesis (University of Leeds, 1982).
10. Hodgson, *op.cit.*, p.55.
11. Sigsworth, *Black Dyke Mills*, *op.cit.*, p.29.
12. Reynolds, *op.cit.*, pp.256–325.
13. Hodgson, *op.cit.*, p.31.
14. *Ibid.*, p.70.
15. C. W. Garnett, 'Irish immigration and the Roman Catholic Church in Bradford, 1835–1870', MA thesis (University of Sheffield, 1983); C. Richardson, 'Irish settlement in mid-nineteenth century Bradford', *Yorkshire Bulletin of Economic and Social Research*, 20 (1968), pp.40–57; Dewhirst, *op.cit.*, p.49.
16. See pp.69–70.
17. Dewhirst, *op.cit.*, p.19.
18. James, *Bradford*, *op.cit.*, p.37.
19. Dewhirst, *op.cit.*, p.52.
20. W. Cudworth, *Condition of the Industrial Classes of Bradford and District* (Bradford, 1887; reprinted Queensbury, 1974), p.46.
21. Dewhirst, *op.cit.*, pp.49–61.
22. Hodgson, *op.cit.*, p.175.
23. *Ibid.*, p.101.
24. K. Snowden, *The Master Spinner: a Life of Sir Swire Smith LL D, MP* (London, 1921), p.73.
25. Sigsworth, *Black Dyke Mills*, *op.cit.*, pp.82–111.
26. Keighley ILP election manifestos 1895–8, in *Keighley Labour Journal.*

27. L. Caffyn, *Workers' Housing in West Yorkshire 1750–1920* (London, 1982), pp.76–81.
28. Dewhirst, *op.cit.*, pp.92–5, 100–4.
29. P. Jennings, *Inns and Pubs of Old Bradford* (Bradford, 1985).
30. Laybourn, *Philip Snowden*, *op.cit.*, p.2.
31. 'Keighley was notorious, not famous, for low wages', *Keighley News*, 7 September 1889.
32. Cudworth, *op.cit.*, pp.31–45.
33. H. Forbes, *The Rise, Progress and Present State of the Worsted, Alpaca and Mohair Manufactures* (Bradford, 1852). Copy in the Federer collection, Reference Department, Bradford Central Library.
34. Reynolds, *op.cit.*
35. J. A. Jowitt, 'Copley, Akroyden and West Hill Park: Moral Reform and Social Improvement in Halifax', in Jowitt (ed.) *Model Industrial Communities*, *op.cit.*, pp.73–89.
36. Sigsworth, *Black Dyke Mills*, *op.cit.*
37. M. Warwick, 'W. E. Forster's Work in Burley-in-Wharfedale, 1850–1886', *Yorkshire Archaeological Journal*, vol.43 (1971), pp.166–74.
38. *Keighley Labour Journal*, 26 March 1898.
39. Joyce, *op.cit.*, pp.135–58.
40. Extracted from *Keighley Year Books*, 1885–1910.
41. Dewhirst, *op.cit.*, pp.78–9.
42. Joyce, *op.cit.*, pp.175–6; Laybourn and Reynolds, *op.cit.*, p.7.
43. Cross, *op.cit.*, p.23.
44. *Keighley Year Book*, 1886.
45. Hodgson, *op.cit.*, p.136.
46. *Ibid.*, p.71.
47. J. A. Jowitt, 'The Pattern of Religion in Victorian Bradford', in Wright and Jowitt, *op.cit.*, p.48; *Keighley Year Book*, 1886.
48. K. S. Inglis, *Churches and the Working Classes in Victorian England* (London, 1963), pp.79–85; L. Smith, *Religion and the Rise of Labour* (Keele, 1994).
49. D. Russell, 'The Pursuit of Leisure', in Wright and Jowitt, *op.cit.*, pp.199–223.
50. F. Peel, *The Risings of the Luddites, Chartists and Plug Drawers* (Heckmondwike, 1881; reprinted 1968); D. G. Wright, *The Chartist Risings in Bradford* (Bradford, 1987).
51. Wright, *Chartist Risings*, *op.cit.*, p.48.
52. Quoted in Sigsworth, *Black Dyke Mills*, p.xii.
53. *Keighley Labour Journal*, 28 November 1902.
54. Ross, *op.cit.*, pp.220–95.
55. Information extracted from the *Keighley Year Books*, 1881–1910.
56. Laybourn and Reynolds, *op.cit.*, p.149.
57. *Ibid.*, pp.40–75.
58. J. A. Jowitt, 'Textiles and Society in Bradford and Lawrence, USA 1880–1920', *Bradford Antiquary* (1991).
59. *Keighley Labour Journal*, 2 May 1896.

CHAPTER THREE

Work, Society and Politics in Nineteenth-Century Keighley

Introduction

During the years between 1820 and 1850, the West Yorkshire textile belt underwent three decades of industrialization and urbanization. This was accompanied by major social and political dislocations which made the region a centre of all the significant mass movements of the period: the factory reform movement, the anti-Poor Law agitation, trade-unionism, machine-breaking and physical-force Chartism. Keighley played its part in all these activities. At a number of points in this period, but particularly in the 1840s, it seemed as if the existing social and political fabric might almost be swept aside. In 1842 the great weaving shed of the Ackroyds at Haley Hill in Halifax was besieged by thousands of Chartists; in the same year at Keighley a company of yeomen galloped to Lees Moor, where a large camp had been reported – it was a congregation of Primitive Methodists;[1] in 1848 Bradford stood on the brink of insurrection and peace was only restored by the arrival of the army from Leeds.[2]

The events of the 1840s had a profound effect on many of the manufacturers, who realized the need to incorporate the industrial working class into the new urban society. Following the demise of Chartism, a range of paternalist initiatives were started by leading millowners. Prominent among them were such things as works brass bands, factory and community sports teams, works trips, works dinners, and social welfare facilities, both within the mill and in the surrounding communities. The object was to heal class divisions and indoctrinate working men and women with the middle-class values of respectability, earnestness and self-help. The master stressed the harmony of interest between worker and manufacturer, the necessity for collaboration and sympathetic understanding between the classes. The image often cited was that of the family, with the employer as a father figure and the workers, their dependents and relatives as his children.[3]

Paternalism was particularly attractive to Yorkshire textile employers in the third quarter of the nineteenth century. The economic situation was much safer than in the 1830s and 1840s, and many of the entrepreneurs' political demands had been met. By 1850 they had the vote, they dominated the local political system, and they had ushered in an era of free trade. The ideology of paternalism buttressed their position of power; they could ape the landed aristocrats by bestowing their munificence on their employees. In addition, the paternalistic ethic chimed in with some of the key notions of Nonconformity and evangelical Anglicanism which predominated in the textile region: in particular, it accorded with the concepts of duty, accountability and work.

On the surface, paternalism successfully imposed an employer hegemony on the West Yorkshire worsted region. Trade-unionism was negligible; class politics remained in abeyance until the rise of the labour movement at the end of the century; strikes and disputes occurred, but were small-scale and relatively rare; politically, the employer provided many of the local councillors and Members of Parliament; individually, the masters were often held in high esteem. In 1891 the *Keighley Argus* held a competition to see who were the most popular people in the town; among the first six were Ira Ickringill, Swire Smith, Benjamin Septimus Brigg, Henry Butterfield and Richard Longsden Hattersley. The only person who was not a major employer was William Weatherhead, an auctioneer. In Haworth the most popular people were Isaac Holden, John Clough and George Merrall, and in Cross Hills, James Lund, John Brigg and John C. Horsfall. All were major employers; most were both Nonconformists and Liberals.[4]

However, the paternalistic ethic was never totally accepted by the working class, who maintained their own culture and their own organizations, such as co-operative societies and, to some extent, trade unions. They also had their own political demands, which were resurrected in the 1890s with the formation of the Independent Labour Party. They may have accepted the reality of the employers' control of the economic, social and political life of the communities in which they lived, but they never entirely believed in the masters' ideology.

It is important, therefore, to examine how paternalism worked in Keighley, to look at factory life, as well as the wider life of the town and local politics and the emergence of the local Labour Union which became a branch of the ILP.

Factory Life

Keighley lies in the corner of the Aire Gap, one of the three great gaps in the Pennine chain. It was here that canal, road and rail linked together the new industrial towns of Lancashire and Yorkshire. The first major improvement in communications was the opening of the Keighley portion of the Leeds and Liverpool Canal in 1773.[5] Despite the nearest wharves being at Stockbridge, a mile from the town, which meant that goods had to be transported on the last leg of their journey by wagon or packhorse, the canal remained important to the town's economic life for much of the nineteenth century. Roads were also developed, and by 1800 a number of turnpike trusts had provided the basis for a comprehensive highway system. Communications were further improved when the Leeds–Bradford railway reached the town in 1847; and in 1849, when a link was made with East Lancashire, through Colne, to Manchester and Liverpool. There were to be further railway connections, and by 1870 Keighley station was passing fourteen trains a day to Bradford and Leeds.[6] This improved transport made Keighley more accessible to the outside world and contributed to the expansion of the town's cotton and, later, its worsted and engineering industries. To service this development, there was a rapid population expansion. There were 5,745 inhabitants in 1801, 18,258 in 1851 and by 1891 there were 36,176. The problems of Keighley in the nineteenth century, therefore, were those of a growing industrialized, urban centre, with all that that implied in terms of environmental squalor:

> Before the introduction of manufacturers, the parish of Keighley did not want its retired glens and well wooded hills; but the clear mountain torrent is now defiled; its scaly inhabitants now suffocated by filth, its murmurs lost in the din of machinery; and the native music in its overhanging groves exchanged for oaths and curses.[7]

However much the author of the above quotation may regret it, industry, and particularly worsteds, was the key to the development of the town. As has been described, a large-scale domestic worsted industry was organized in the area from the middle of the eighteenth century. The capital accumulated from this worsted manufacture was used by a number of Yorkshire masters, including some in Keighley, to build cotton mills, at a time when the worsted trade was badly affected by the American War of Independence and later the French wars. However, as skilled labour for cotton-producing techniques was unusual in West Yorkshire, and as mechanized worsted spinning became feasible, the Keighley cotton trade died out. By 1822 worsteds had become the dominant textile, although for a time some manufacturers ran the two trades together.[8]

The fortunes of many Keighley manufacturers were thus founded on cotton and consolidated with the rise of the worsted factory system. In addition, some individuals, notably the Hattersleys and the Prince Smith family, started engineering firms, initially supplying machinery to the worsted trade and eventually branching out and becoming major local employers themselves. Industrial growth was rapid, and by 1879 it was estimated that the town had 'one-tenth of the mills, nearly one-eighth of the spindles, and nearly one-twelfth of the looms in the worsted trade throughout the United Kingdom'. It also 'nearly monopolised the trade of making worsted machinery; and is also largely employed in making looms'. Other engineering specializations included the manufacture of steam engines, washing machines and sewing machines.[9]

Directing these industries was a small group of businessmen who, having survived the industrial vicissitudes of the early nineteenth century, came to dominate the political and social as well as the economic life of the town. These families had also integrated themselves into the wider West Yorkshire industrial élite, with particularly close connections with Bradford. Asa Briggs notes how Keighley 'fell under the influence of Bradford and most of the movements in Bradford were reflected in Keighley politics'.[10] Isaac Holden, who made his fortune in Bradford and France, became Keighley's first MP in 1885, and built Oakworth House in the town. He married the daughter of Keighley manufacturer Jonas Sugden. Many Keighley manufacturers were members of the Bradford Wool Exchange and the Chamber of Commerce, and a number, such as Ira Ickringill, had mills in both towns. Others had interests in Bradford companies. Benjamin Septimus Brigg, for example, was a director of the Bradford Old Bank. However, notwithstanding these region-wide concerns, the leading Keighley businessmen's interests lay largely with the town in which they had their mills. By the 1880s they had come to see themselves as the natural rulers of Keighley, and this perhaps helps to explain the feelings of perplexity, anger and betrayal with which they faced the rise of the working-class political movement in the 1890s.

Many of the families who made up this Keighley élite were long established and had been in business since before 1800. The Brigg family had been manufacturers since 1780, the Sugdens since 1790 and the Cravens since 1776.[11] In the 1890s John Clough could no longer regard himself as self-made, 'rather after six generations, "self inherited"'.[12] Families such as these established their businesses at the start of the industrial revolution and interrelated with each other through partnerships, marriage and social contact. Thus in 1776 John Craven married the widow of Thomas Brigg and in 1783 he went into partnership with his stepson, also named Thomas Brigg, and Abraham Shackleton 'to carry on the business of spinning cotton'.[13] The very fact that they had survived so long and so successfully gave them the self-confidence to assume that they had the right to organize the town that they commanded economically. They recognized, however, that the wealth which they had derived from the area conferred responsibilities as well as privileges, and some families spent much of their time in public life. In 1925, when William Anderton Brigg was made a freeman of the town, it was remarked that:

> The Brigg family had been connected with the administration of Keighley for a period of over 100 years ... Mr Brigg's grandfather and great grandfather were both trustees of the Bowcock charity, and the town today was receiving the advantage of the careful manipulation of these

> funds in those far off days … two great uncles John Brigg and William Brigg were appointed Commissioners in the Keighley Improvement Act of 1824 … Mr Brigg's father, the late Sir John Brigg, was elected a member of the Local Board in 1867 … he was made Mayor *pro tem* in the interval between the granting of a Charter of Incorporation and the election of the First Town Council, and presented mace.[14]

And, on the same occasion, Philip Snowden remarked about Benjamin Septimus Brigg, another member of the family, that he was 'a man of very rare capacity and ability. If he had not given to Keighley what was intended for a higher sphere of activity he would, I am sure, have attained a high position – one of the highest positions in the councils of the nation – and would have achieved national fame.'[15] Although it seems likely that Snowden was exaggerating Brigg's claim to fame, his speech does show that it was not unusual for the Keighley élite to devote their talents to local life.

Ultimately, however, the manufacturers' dominant position was based on their economic power. It was in the workplace that the relationship between the Keighley bourgeoisie and the working class was defined. This relationship was uneasy from the start of the industrial revolution. As early as November 1812, thirty manufacturers met at the Devonshire Arms to consider the threat posed by a union of wool combers, and resolved 'not to employ or suffer to be employed, any workman who is now or shall continue to be, or who hereafter may be connected with any Society or Societies of a similar nature'.[16] By the 1820s the Keighley workers were organized into combers' clubs and there seems to have been a connection between the local trade societies and national organizations. This link was reinforced in 1825 during the twenty-three-week Bradford wool combers' and weavers' strike, when Keighley contributed £850 to the strike fund and the deputy secretary of the union was James Walworth, a Keighley man.[17] The Keighley masters, for their part, determined 'to turn off all who can be ascertained to support the Combers' and Weavers' Union in any manner'.[18] In the 1830s the town was a centre of the Ten Hours Movement and a short-time committee was established by Joseph Firth, David Weatherhead, and Abraham Wildman, a Sunday School teacher and poet.[19] The workers also strenuously opposed the introduction of the new Poor Law. Tensions between masters and men became so bad during the Plug Plot riots in 1842 that the bookkeeper at Claversyke Mill recorded a three-and-a-half-day stoppage with the laconic comment 'rioting'. In 1843, the wool combers were well enough organized to ask for an all-round increase, for 'through the frequent reductions in our wages and alterations in the wool; an excellent comber has only been able to earn on average about eight or nine shillings a week in full employment'. By 1846 a Protective Society of the Power Weavers of Keighley was established which exercised its influence as far away as Grassington. Almost inevitably there was a strike, which was particularly bitter and centred on Clough's mill. 'I really dare not come into Keighley with my cart until the excitement is over', wrote one manufacturer. Fifteen hundred wool combers were thrown out of work. In 1849 there was another clash, with the wool combers meeting at the Commercial Inn and the masters at the Devonshire Arms.[20]

The 1850s saw widespread economic changes in the worsted industry, and with them came improvements in industrial relations. As in other parts of West Yorkshire, the wool combers who had provided much of the Keighley working class with their radical leadership were in decline. By 1860 the Clough mill employed no hand combers at all.[21] Male combers were replaced by female operatives and there was a decline in the total male textile workforce. Fortunately, the engineering industry expanded, albeit slowly, and by 1901 only sixteen per cent of the town's male workers were employed in textiles, while thirty per cent worked in engineering. Sixty-five per cent of female workers were in textiles.[22]

These technological changes introduced a different relationship between masters and men. The workers no longer questioned the industrial capitalist society which was being created. Instead they saw their economic future as part of the new industrial processes and their political future in working with, not against, their employers. An industrial and social consensus was established which was based on an alliance between the largely Liberal, mostly Nonconformist, factory owners and a section of the working class. This delicate relationship was essentially hierarchical, with the master demanding a deference from the worker which was rarely given wholeheartedly, while the employers wanted concessions from the masters which they were reluctant to make: an extension of the franchise, shorter working hours and better working conditions. It is important, therefore, to examine both the masters' and the labourers' views on paternalism.

Many masters saw the connection between themselves and their workers as being more than financial. Jonas Sugden is a not untypical example of a master whose concern for his employees extended far beyond the economic field. A deeply religious Methodist, he used his power as an employer to establish an elaborate moral code among the people who worked for him. This code pervaded the whole of the life of his workforce and was enforced by the threat of dismissal:

> Notice – Jonas Sugden and Bros. wish and expect, – 1st That every person in their employ attends some place of Divine Worship every Lord's Day.
>
> 2nd That every youth dependent on those whom they employ, attends some Sunday and Day School from the age of six years and upwards.
>
> 3rd That those who are of proper age, and the parents and Guardians of the young, make choice of their own school and place of worship.[23]

In addition, the firm employed no one 'who was known to gamble or to frequent the public house', and 'when young people had fallen into sin, they were required to marry or leave his service'.

Obviously this kind of detailed supervision was not undertaken by every master, though it is worth noting that as late as the beginning of the twentieth century James Ickringill was overseeing a very similar kind of moral discipline among the children of his workforce.[24] James was one of the founders of Ira Ickringill and Co., and in 1911 he started Ira Ickringill's Good Lad's Brigade Brotherhood Class. Their rules included attendance at Sunday School and the Methodist Church, saying grace at every meal, attending Friday Evening Class and being a non-smoker. Not surprisingly, many of the younger workers at his mills were members of the Brigade, and 'to know that they were faithfully performing their duties in the realm of commerce gave him [James] satisfaction and hope'.[25] Clearly, a number of masters over a long period of time felt that they should take a direct interest in the moral welfare of their employees and their families.

Probably more common than this kind of detailed supervision of workers' behaviour was the growth of unspoken understanding which developed over the years between a master and his workforce. Such considerations had much to do with the fact that many of the manufacturers lived among their employees for much of their lives and were seen as an integral part of the local community. They were frequently educated in the town and their houses were often built within the town's boundaries. In many cases they trained at the mill, and grew up to know many of their workmen personally. John Clough, for example, worked as a mill apprentice before going to Cambridge and returned immediately afterwards to take up his responsibilities in the mill. When he became master of his works, he disliked being called 'Sir', having been called 'John' when he worked on the shop floor. He was delighted, therefore, when the old hands continued to address him in that way when he grew up, with the other operatives using the more formal, but still familiar 'Mr John', as they did 'Mr Henry' and so on for the other brothers.[26] James Ickringill also remained close to his workmen even though he employed nearly two thousand of them. In 1908 he told a gathering of his workforce that 'he was pleased he lived within a stone's throw of the place where he served his apprenticeship as an overlooker'.[27] In return, workmen would often stay with the same master for many years. S. B. Clapham had many who 'had been in his employ for the long period of half a century'; James Lund employed a thousand people, 'some of whom had been in the service of the firm all their working lives'.[28]

Swire Smith's biographer describes how this understanding between master and workforce worked in the factory. He wrote that:

> Many workers worked with him for thirty years. Then, although he believed that free competition must determine wages he could help

> rising talent free itself and so the firm paid half the fees of any workers who cared to attend evening classes. Next he knew his hands personally and thought to stand by the worthy ones in any special misfortune. They all saw him twice a day, coming his rounds and he addressed them by their Christian names. Those who lunched at the mill knew he took the same lunch. … His very oversight of work, which was incessant, resembled a personal interest in the spinners; for if the yarn was faulty, he would ask advice about it and talk intimately. … The women and girls in the various rooms took turns in visiting Currer Wood on fine Sunday afternoons and there in those later years, he would join them in their picnic. He was delighted one day to hear a small boy in the street say to another 'See yo; that man works at our mill'. The older hands were pensioned.[29]

Obviously, the point of view of the writer is sympathetic to the manufacturer. Nevertheless, it seems clear that Swire Smith did feel certain responsibilities towards his workforce which he endeavoured to carry out.

It became very easy for the workforce to identify with the factory, especially if the master was generally recognized as a good employer. The mill, inevitably, was one of the chief places around which people's lives revolved, and it could be a social centre as well as a place of work. Employers might encourage the creation of a series of leisure and educational activities. Marriners, for example, had a well-known brass band, and many firms organized works outings, teas and trips. Swire Smith paid half the school fees for his talented workers.[30] Most employees would at least recognize the masters, who would talk to them in a language and accent that was familiar. It was thus natural that people regarded the mill as a familiar place and the manufacturer as a part of everyday life.

However, the relationship between men and master was a complex matter, with each side giving and taking and yet each being aware of its limitations. Jonas Sugden summed up the necessary balance between the aloof and the familiar which it was essential that each employer should maintain. It was said of him that:

> there was no appearance of pride or haughtiness in his bearing, he was not unapproachable, as if his dependents were an inferior race of beings, he conversed with the lowest of them kindly with affability, and yet no one could take advantage of his freedom as he still exercised the dignity required for the exercise of his authority as a master.[31]

The fundamental fact that could never be disguised, or forgotten, was that the manufacturers' economic power over the men was almost total.

Thus, there were difficulties with paternalism as it was practised in the workplace which prevented it ever being completely accepted by the workforce. The prosperity of the worsted trade depended upon its ability to compete within a world market. Manufacturers had to respond to the demands of that market, and for most this meant reducing the costs of production as much as possible. The price of goods was kept low chiefly by pressure on the workpeople, on their wage rates and by continual efforts to raise productivity. There was thus a constant tension between the employer's obligations as a benevolent paternalist and the imperatives of the market. If he took this paternalistic approach seriously, his competitors might reduce their costs enough to price him out of the market; if he was to remain successful, it was at the price of squeezing his workers. This difficulty became more pronounced after the onset of the economic depression in the 1870s, but it was present even during the boom years of the 1850s and 1860s.

All firms faced these problems, but it is likely that the small companies in the industry were affected more than the large, well-established ones, which had more resources with which to endure the bad times. The commission combing shops, the tiny weaving and spinning firms that rented space and power looms, were an important part of the industry. The problems of Ira Ickringill and J. and J. Craven, with two thousand workers each, or Timothy Bairstow, with seven hundred, or the long-established John Clough, with three hundred hands in his Steeton mill, or Richard Fletcher, with two hundred in isolated Silsden,[32] were different from those of establishments with just a few frames, operating on the margin of profit. In good times, such firms would run their machinery as much as possible; in bad times, workers would be laid off and stock laid up in the hope of better prices in the future. In these circumstances, companies relied on credit to stay in business until conditions improved, or, of course, they could always go bankrupt. There were few incentives or resources among such firms to practice the benevolence found in larger mills.

Employers and workers constantly struggled over the hours of work. The Factory Acts were the chief determinant of the maximum hours, but they were generally disliked by the employers, and Keighley manufacturers had a reputation for making their hands work long hours, not only more than other local trades, but also than neighbouring towns. An undated petition, perhaps written in the 1870s, sent to Cloughs by fifty-four male workers makes the point:

> Gentlemen – in October last yr we appealed to you through our committee for a decrease in our working hours viz. to cease work at 12 oc on Saturdays. We then pointed out to you that while Engineers, Millwrights, masons, joiners, plasterers etc were working from 48 to 58 hours per week, we were working 60 hours in an atmosphere as unhealthy as any of the above trades. In addition to the above we now wish to call your attention to what the employers of Bradford and Halifax have done and are doing.[33]

By the late 1880s, Clough employees had achieved the Saturday half day and worked a fifty-six-and-a-half-day week, or, if they worked more, overtime was paid. However, Cloughs, and presumably other local firms, were strict in demanding that employees worked all the hours they wished them to and it was forbidden to leave the mill during working hours. In addition, employers were accused of such mean practices as reducing the dinner-hour or running the machines early in the morning and late in the evening.[34]

Allied to the question of hours of work was the provision of holidays. These took two forms: the statutory holidays allowed at traditional times such as Christmas and Easter, and the treats and excursions given paternally by the masters on special occasions. At the beginning of the nineteenth century, holidays were given at Christmas and Easter, but by the 1840s these seem to have increased, although the number of days varied each year. From 1837 to 1843, between seven and eleven days' holiday a year were given. These might include the old Christmas Day (January 6), Shrove Tuesday, Good Friday and Easter Monday, although some of these would be half, not full, days. In addition, the May and November Keighley Fairs usually warranted two days each; Keighley Parish Feast in July a whole day; and Bingley Feast sometimes a half day. Christmas Day was always a holiday. By the 1890s, holidays were grouped around Easter, Whitsun, the Parish Feast and Christmas, but the amount of time given was not much more than in the 1830s. In 1890 workers received about eight days in four periods, and in 1911 eleven-and-a-half days in the same four periods. In addition, occasional informal holidays were given on special occasions, such as the visit of a circus, or a royal funeral.[35]

Another relief from work was the treat provided by the employer. These might take the form of money, such as in 1862, when Clough gave their workers 1*s.* 6*d.* (7.5p) each to celebrate the coming of age of the Prince of Wales. Fêtes and excursions were more common, however. By 1900, mill suppers and teas were commonplace and trips to Morecambe and Blackpool were usual. The growth of the railway network made the trip to the seaside as easy to arrange as the local fête, and not much more expensive. Some firms, such as Cloughs, had an almost formal set of rules regarding treats; the marriage of a son of the family warranted a trip to Morecambe, the birth of a male child meant the flying of a flag over the mill.[36]

It is clear, then, that masters were reluctant to reduce the hours of work in the mill until they were forced to either by law or custom, nor were they enthusiastic about increasing the number of holidays, for both would add to manufacturing costs. Treats, however, were seen as part of the ritual of paternalism and accepted, at least by the larger firms, as part of factory life.

Apart from regulating the time spent in the mill, there were other attempts to increase productivity without raising costs, and this also exacerbated relations between workers and masters. Thus, although earnings did increase throughout the nineteenth century, there was always a threat of wage reductions, and increases rarely compensated for the extra machines that employees were expected to look after or the extra work they had to do. At Bairstows, for example, a weaver was responsible on average for 1.41 machines in 1866, but by 1891 this had increased to 2.00.[37] The *Yorkshire Factory Times* carries a number of complaints from twisters, weavers, comb and box minders and machine spinners that they were being expected to look after extra pieces of machinery. Employers also tried to reduce piece rates, or make workers take on more work, or run the machines at increased speeds.[38]

These increased workloads could only be imposed by disciplinary measures, and discipline was itself another cause of dissatisfaction among the workers. Factory fines were a particular source of discontent, for they were sometimes exacted for petty reasons, although the most frequent cause seems to have been damage to cloth. For example, at Marriners, in the late 1830s and 1840s, workers were fined for wearing iron-soled clogs in the mill, the money going into a sickness benefit scheme run by the firm.[39] It could be argued that this was all part of the system of paternalism, as was the custom at Jonas Sugden's mill, where if a comber's wages included a farthing, it was put in the missionary box, with the firm adding another farthing.[40] However, at a time when small sums were important to individuals, such authoritarianism could be the cause of discontent. Later in the century, there were complaints about what were considered to be unjust fines, particularly those levied for bad time-keeping. This was especially resented because a worker only had to be a minute late to be fined, but overtime had to be worked for a quarter of an hour before it was paid.[41]

Discipline was maintained in the mill in other ways, most notably by the threat of dismissal. People were sacked most commonly for being ill or otherwise absent from work, for problems with wages, or for poor workmanship. However, workpeople could also be sacked for breaking the management's unspoken rules: for 'cheek', which might include looking up from their work when a manager or director passed by, or even for coming to work in a collar and tie, for it was then evident that a worker was 'thinking too big for his job'.[42] Workers, and the members of their families who worked in the mill, could also, on occasion, be victimized. The *Yorkshire Factory Times* recorded seven examples between 1892 and 1906 of family members being sacked by Keighley firms when one member complained or left the factory, and in the early twentieth century family influence was used to break up a strike by boys. The millowners impressed upon the adult workers that they were losing earnings when the boys stopped working, and so the fathers of those on strike gave them 'a belt over the ear' and sent them back to work again.[43]

The group which kept discipline within the factory was the relatively small number of skilled workmen, who were separated from the mass of workers in various ways. Most obviously, they were men, while in the worsted trade most of the people they supervised were women and children. They were better paid, their earnings were more regular and they often received more fringe benefits than the ordinary worker. The Clough wage books, for example, have several references to skilled workers receiving their basic pay even during short illnesses. It was rare for them to be fined for a misdemeanour and they often enjoyed longer holidays than the average worker. They frequently had to work overtime, but they were sure of receiving extra pay for it. Within the mill, especially the larger establishments, they enjoyed great power and prestige, and often had power to hire and fire. Theoretically, this authority was limited by the oversight of managers and owners, but in practice much of the routine management of the mills remained in the hands of the overlookers. They ruled through a combination of coercion and co-operation. As former factory workers themselves, they understood the nature of the work and the mentality of their workers, but they also had widespread disciplinary powers. Nevertheless, they were subject to the authority of the employer. In times of poor trade, jobs were offered to newly trained skilled workers on low rates of pay, in preference to experienced hands. At Cloughs, an assistant overlooker who had finished his training had to continue on an assistant's wage until there was a vacancy for him to fill; a situation that could continue for some time.[44]

Harsh and sometimes unfair discipline in the mill was not the only element that undermined the ideology of paternalism. Working conditions were rarely satisfactory. By law, mills were supposed to do a certain amount of whitewashing every year, but this did not mean that they were clean and sanitary. There were numerous complaints about sanitation, rats, heating and ventilation. In early 1900 it was alleged that employers did not heat their mills in winter because they believed their employees would work harder in the cold; and, of course, there was a saving on fuel.[45]

As well as being unhygienic, mills could also be dangerous. Many of the Factory Acts were designed to reduce accidents, particularly by forbidding the cleaning of moving machinery and by making the use of machine guards compulsory. However, accidents still happened. Between 1891 and 1913 the *Yorkshire Factory Times* recorded seventy-nine serious accidents in the Keighley worsted mills, the most important single cause being the hoist, which at that time did not have an automatic door, and which led directly to eighteen accidents.[46]

The attitude of the master to the consequences of these accidents as well as to sick pay and leave of absence during sickness or pregnancy was important to the workers. Sick clubs were sometimes organized by the employers. Marriners ran one between 1832 and 1848 and possibly another between 1882 and 1902, and Sugdens also had one. They were financed partly by the employers and partly by the workers. The attitude of the employer to sickness generally, however, was not sympathetic. The *Yorkshire Factory Times* records five cases between 1889 and 1905 of Keighley manufacturers dismissing workers because of sickness, but only three cases of compensation being paid or alternative jobs being provided, and these occurred only after strong pressure or when the accident was the fault of the firm.[47]

Outside the mill, the master could still have direct power over a worker and his family. The house they lived in might have been owned by the firm, and the conditions of tenantry might bind the worker to the mill. Thus Cloughs owned houses and was regarded as a fair landlord as well as a fair employer. However, the houses were for the use of Clough workers only, and if they left their job at the firm, they had to leave the house. This may be accepted as reasonable, and such conditions obtained elsewhere, but more questionable was the tradition that the children of Clough employees who lived in mill houses must work in the mill for perhaps two years before they went to their chosen job, which, of course, may not have been in textiles. In this way, Cloughs ensured itself of a constant supply of young labour. If the tradition was defied, the family was likely to be evicted.[48]

It is clear from the above that there were areas of conflict between workers and masters within the factory which the doctrine of paternalism did little to eliminate. Hours of work remained long, wages were increased only reluctantly, and the threat of dismissal was ever present. Although the masters believed in their own benevolence and felt genuine concern for their workers, the power in the factory lay with them and their employees had little chance of asserting any independence. The most obvious power that the worker had was to withdraw his or her labour, either by striking or changing their job. However, until the advent of the general unions in the 1880s, the worsted industry was characterized by a mass of non-union weaving and spinning workers and a group of small craft unions among the skilled trades.

Manufacturers could call upon more than paternalism to suppress trade-unionism, whose quasi-legal nature, together with the hostility of the legal system in practice to unions, greatly inhibited their organization. The practice of blacklisting appears to have been widespread, and pressure was put on workers to declare that they would not join in industrial action. At Marriners in 1842, for example, forty-nine employees signed a pledge that they 'would not join any riotous assembly but would steadily mind their work and eject any intruders'.[49] The inspectors of the Worsted Committee were also used to control unions and strikes. It was, in any case, difficult to organize the unskilled workers, who lacked permanency in their jobs and did not have the life-long commitment to a single task that informed the view of adult male trade-unionists. In the 1890s, the Weavers' Association, which mainly recruited females, had few members in Keighley. Most unskilled workers retired early and moved on to a new trade or into the home.[50]

Keighley was well known for the weakness of its trade-unionism. Before 1850 the hand workers were involved in major disputes in 1826, 1846, and 1849.[51] After 1850, strikes were primarily the weapon of the skilled male adult, and were chiefly concerned with wage increases or preventing wage reductions, or new systems of payments. Strikes did take place. In the 1870s there were four major outbreaks: of engineers, of spinners at Cravens, of masons, and of weavers at Platts.[52] The most serious dispute, however, was that of the engineers in 1889. It was this event that, more than any other, re-awakened the class consciousness of the Keighley labourers. As at Manningham Mills in Bradford two years later, political and social consensus between the Liberal manufacturers and the workpeople was weakened, though not destroyed, by the strike. This event and its consequences – the forming of a Trades Council and later a Labour Union – will be discussed at length.

Generally speaking, the employed acquiesced in the system and some may even have accepted as legitimate the Keighley élite's claim to leadership and to have endorsed the view of their own subordinate position in the social structure as morally right. A letter written to Robert Clough by a factory girl expresses this view, declaring that 'the rich are appointed by God to defend and protect the poor and how can they better do it than by employing them with labour and giving them a reasonable wage for that labour'.[53] How genuine such an expression is, is not known, and the writer may merely have been saying what she thought the employers wanted to hear. Certainly, it seems likely that the majority of workers accepted, however reluctantly, their own position as inevitable.

Society

One of the reasons why the masters' paternalist ideology was accepted, albeit passively, by the majority of Keighley workpeople was because of its pervasiveness. The manufacturers dominated not only the economic life of the town, but also its public activities.

Before examining this, however, it is worth making two points about the Keighley élite. First, although they were socially distinct from the rest of the town, they belonged to a specific stratum of society and were nowhere equal to the great landed aristocrats. Their connection with trade, and in many cases their Nonconformity, prevented any possibility of this. Even Isaac Holden, reputedly the richest commoner in Parliament, remained separated from the aristocracy. When the Duke of Devonshire opened the Keighley Mechanics Institute in 1870, his guests were Lord Houghton, Lord Frederick Cavendish and Edward Baines. Swire Smith noted that 'the swells went to Ben's [B. S. Brigg, whose family had official connections with the Devonshires] and filled his house out to the door, the second grades such as the Holdens and the Illingworths came to our house'.[54]

Second, and more important, for all their professional rivalries and political differences, the Keighley bourgeoisie was a relatively small group, all of whom knew each other through marriage, business and friendship. Swire Smith's biography shows how tightly knit Keighley society was. Swire was apprenticed to John Brigg, where he met the four Brigg children, Tom, John, William, and Ben. His diary records their social life. He visits their houses, goes to 'Guard House with Ben [Brigg] and to Miss Sugden's', where a 'grand party took place'. He meets 'Emma and Annie ... at our house, having come to dress for a party at Low Mill. We went about seven o' clock and joined thirty more. Had a good dance and "stir".' They all go out together; 'in the afternoon Will., Ben., Ted., Prince [Smith, his cousin], Sam [Clough], Tom Shackleton and I took train to Settle and had tea at Mrs Hartley's, the Golden Lion, after which we set off Christmas singing .... and earned 10*s.* [50p].'[55] John Brigg's wife writes of her son going to Germany 'with two Cravens from Steeton and William Clough'. The men had their own club, the Cavendish, 'for the most influential gentlemen of the town'.[56]

These social ties were often confirmed by marriage. The Brigg and Craven families cemented their business partnership with marriage on three different occasions,[57] and the Briggs also married into the Marriner, the Clapham, the Anderton and the Haggas families. In their turn, the Andertons were connected by marriage with the Haggases, the Marriners and the Greenwoods.[58] Religious and political differences do not seem to have affected these unions; the Briggs were Congregationalists, the Claphams Baptists and the Marriners and Haggases were Anglicans. The Briggs, Claphams, Andertons, and Greenwoods were Liberals and the Marriners were Conservatives, while the Haggases started as Liberals and later became Conservatives.[59]

In the life of the town itself, the masters' influence was considerable. Their economic power did not stop with the people they directly employed, as they generated work in a variety of ways. Mills like Cloughs Grove Mill 'had dynamic business lives that offered major outlets to local suppliers and business'. Extensions and alterations offered work to builders, masons, labourers, quarrymen and carters. Enormous quantities of glass, paint, wood, slate and stone were required for the sort of projects undertaken at Grove Mill in the 1830s and again in the 1860s.[60] Nor was it only the mills that created work. The lifestyle of the successful millowner could result in the employment of a whole range of services. For example, when Isaac Holden built Oakworth Hall, he was careful to employ local men as much as possible. The glazing for the winter garden of the house was done by a Haworth plumber and the plants supplied by a Keighley nursery.[61]

In addition, much of the life and many of the attitudes of the small communities around Keighley were dominated by local millowners. Thus Oakworth was controlled by the Haggases and the Cloughs, splitting into

Church and Chapel, Tory and Liberal, depending on where people lived and who they worked for.[62] In a similar manner, Steeton was commanded by the Dixons and another branch of the Clough family. Cross Roads and Lees were dominated by William Haggas and George Merrall, who together 'have made Cross Roads and Lees one of the most flourishing and prosperous neighbourhoods in this part of Yorkshire', which prosperity was 'doubtless greatly stimulated by the moral and religious character of the people'.[63]

This hold over local communities was reinforced by the isolation of many of the surrounding villages, which led to loyalty being given primarily to a location and resulted in a vertical community structure, with allegiance to the village, the mill and the master, rather than to a larger grouping such as a trade union or a class. The masters encouraged this by identifying themselves with their communities in a variety of ways, particularly through religion and charitable works, but also by supporting educational and social organizations.

Asa Briggs has pointed out how a complete history of nineteenth-century Keighley would need to examine 'in particular the very close relationship between religion and politics',[64] and it has been noted how religion and the various cultural activities associated with religion in Keighley provided an extension of the relationship between masters and men which was formed in the mill:

> In Keighley the employers were Sunday School teachers and superintendent and choir masters. (Having a voice could be a passport to a job). It was in the chapel that the employer was 'got close to', but yet also in which the physical distance appropriate to station was maintained. In Keighley the employers built and supported the churches and expected their workers to attend them.[65]

Religious activities were a way of bringing masters and men together to work for the common good of the community, while at the same time reinforcing the deferential relationship which the élite saw as the natural order of things. By 1900 there were twenty-two Anglican churches within the district; twenty-seven Methodist chapels of various denominations; five Congregational; two Baptist, Catholic, Quaker, Swedenborgian, Salvation Army and Spiritualist places of worship.[66] Most of them were built during the nineteenth century, and nearly all the major employers helped towards their building. John Brigg contributed to the new chapel and minister's house which the Congregationalists built in Devonshire Street. His children continued the tradition and 'it is to a considerable extent through their influence that the beautiful Congregational Chapel at Utley has been built'.[67] They also helped to repair the old chapel in Keighley High Street which became a Mission Chapel and Sunday School. The Marriners, although Anglicans, did not only support the Church of England. When a

Methodist Sunday School was to be built near their works, the oldest partner attended the anniversaries in its early years and kept it functioning with generous donations.[68] The Clough family was 'the principal means of building the beautiful Methodist Chapel and schools at Paper Mill Bridge, and more recently in promoting the extension fund for building several additional Methodist Chapels in the Keighley Circuit'.[69]

The link between religion and business continued well into the twentieth century. In the years after 1900, James Ickringill built, at his own expense, the Oakworth Road Mission Hall, which cost £14,000, and he continued to defray all its expenses for sixteen years. He had no doubt of the close connection between the life of the mill and the life of the chapel. When considering the lessons of his life, he first put down the importance of early piety, but he considered it equally important that 'religion and business may be blended into one harmonious whole'. For 'business and religion are not two antagonistic forces, or two separate streams running in opposite directions, but to all those whose lives are ordered on the Divine Plan, they both mingle together forming one stream of service to God and man'.[70]

Supporting the Church and Chapel meant more than just contributing to the building and upkeep of places of worship. Many prominent members of the Keighley élite were active in the administration and took part in the services at their places of worship. Joseph Summerscales, a washing-machine manufacturer, JP, and member of the School Board; Albert Rishworth, a wealthy miller, corn merchant and leading local Conservative; C. H. Foulds, a leather merchant, alderman and mayor; and John Mitchell of Hattersleys, also a JP and member of the Town Council – all were Anglicans and held posts in the parish church.[71] John Smith Naylor, a brass founder and Poor Law Guardian; Craven Laycock, a leather merchant and member of the School Board; and Jonathan Gill, an iron merchant and member of the Town Council, were important Congregationalists;[72] James Groves and T. S. Clapham of the engineering firm were Baptists, and also took part in the day-to-day running of the church.[73]

Churches were also the centre of a whole range of social, educational and cultural activities. Thus, James Ickringill, having built Oakworth Road Mission School, not only made sure of having the best preachers by securing the services of the leading ministers of the Primitive Methodist Church, but he also established a Sunday School, a choir, a mothers' meeting, which was 'an oasis in the desert to many a toil worn mother', and a holiday club. This last seems to have been very popular with the congregation, for 'the frequent trips into the country or the seaside mean to them recreation and health, so it may truly be said that Oakworth Road Mission Hall is fruitful in blessing to all who are associated with it, and it is to Mr James a source of intense satisfaction and hope'.[74] Jonas Sugden also threw himself vigorously into this aspect of the church's work, being 'the means along with the Reverend W. Exley, of the erection of a school at Lees'. In addition, he encouraged the young men of Oakworth to form an Improvement Society, found them a room, supplied them with books, and attended lectures there.[75]

Obviously, such support for places of worship gave the manufacturers' opinions great weight within the congregations, and the churches found it difficult to oppose their views. The reason why the Keighley élite placed such emphasis on the church was that the moral and social values of the Protestant faith were the touchstones of mid-Victorian middle-class life and the élite sought to spread those values among the workers. Moral education was to be spread through the teachings of the churches and related bodies.

Generally, however, the working class proved indifferent to the blandishments of the Church or Chapel. This is not to say that the image of the chapel-going, respectable working family, teetotal and Liberal, did not have a basis in fact. As will be seen, many of the leading local ILPers were grounded in just this kind of culture, although they rejected the ideas of deference, inequality and acceptance of society as it was which were put forward by the churches. However, it was a minority experience for the working class. Even when they went to church, workers often sought out their own congregations, such as the Primitive Methodists or the Spiritualists,[76] and thus remained somewhat removed from the paternalist messages of the middle-class churches. Furthermore, in an age when appearances counted for much, the mere fact of church attendance helped to satisfy public demands for 'respectability' without necessarily inferring acceptance of the intent and message of the churches. Certainly, the chapel-going ILPers were unconvinced by the social attitudes put forward in the churches they attended, and although they used religious ideas and imagery in their speeches and journalism, the message they delivered was the opposite of the beliefs which the bourgeoisie wanted them to accept.

Despite the encouragement of their employers, therefore, most working people did not go to church. Although there was a tradition of secularism in the area, with wool combers in particular being reputed as free-thinkers, their influence was probably small. For example, Joseph Firth,[77] a Keighley Chartist, was an active secularist, but his chief impact on the town's life was his work with the National Reform League, the campaign against taxes on newspapers, and his membership of the local School Board. More important was the fact that most people had more urgent or more interesting things to do on a Sunday than to attend a place of worship. In a society where the working week could be anything up to sixty hours, Sunday was the one time when most working people could rest, attend to the household chores or play with the children.

The extent to which the churches were under the control of the manufacturers became clear in the 1890s, at the time when religious bodies were usually reluctant to support the awakening social and political demands of the working class. Fred Jowett's well-known remark to the Bradford Congregational ministers, 'If you persist in opposing the Labour movement there will soon be more reason than ever to complain of the absence of working men in your chapels', was as applicable to Keighley as to its neighbour.[78] Indeed, the antagonism of the local churches to the labour movement was noted at the inaugural meeting of the Keighley Labour Union, where James Holmes remarked on 'the pains which the churches are taking to show their dislike of the Labour movement'.[79] This is not to say that all ministers rejected working-class aspirations, and, as will be shown, a number of Keighley ministers were sympathetic to the ILP and trade-unionism.

As it became apparent that the churches were not reaching the workers, a number of attempts were made to make organized religion more attractive. The Pleasant Sunday Afternoon movement, both nationally and in Keighley, was one such attempt. Its object was 'to provide a service which shall be a sort of intermedium between an ordinary religious service and a Sunday concert … not too formal on the one hand to keep away those who do not habitually attend places of worship and on the other hand not too secular to alienate the sympathies of the puritanical'.[80] Unfortunately for the organizers, the majority of the workers remained indifferent to the movement. The *Keighley News* reported that the first service 'had a good congregation, which, however, included not more than a sprinkling of the class for whose benefit the movement had been specially inaugurated',[81] and 'the attendance of persons unconnected with any religious body is not as numerous as the promoters of the movement would desire it to be'.[82] One of the reasons why the movement failed to attract more support may be because it was ideologically committed to the continuation of the social and economic ideas of the Keighley élite, as one of the earliest lectures, on 'Socialism', shows. The lecturer agreed that the 'principle of socialism … [is] … that the good of the individual shall be subordinate to the good of the many which is really borrowed from Christianity', but concluded 'that the welfare of society will not be promoted by the most thorough reconstruction so much as by the improving of the character of the people'.[83] Thus, a better future was to be achieved through the acceptance of the old-fashioned doctrines of self-help and moral improvement. At a time when economic depression had resulted in increasing pressure on the workers and growing political and industrial unrest, such a conclusion was unlikely to have wide appeal.

In addition to their religious activity, the Keighley élite concerned themselves with charitable and other philanthropic work. John Craven, for example, used to:

> drive about the town in his phaeton, and on Monday mornings when he saw any of the butchers with a considerable quantity of beef left over

> from the Saturday market, he would frequently buy the whole stock and then he would give the butcher a list of a number of poor families, ordering him to carry it out in portions varying from seven to four pounds for each family, and this he was in the habit of doing from week to week.[84]

At least part of this charitable work was done face to face with the deprived and this benefited the personal standing of many of the élite with the community. John Hodgson recalls meeting an invalid who was 'almost overcome with joy in consequence of his having been visited by Mr Brigg in his affliction; this old man exclaimed "what a thing it is that a magistrate should visit such a poor old body as me, and talk with me about my soul and pray with me"'.[85] The Cloughs, too, felt that charity should be personal. John Clough, 'notwithstanding his wealth', was as 'humble as a child, and in any case of real necessity being brought before him he was sure to meet with a humble response'.[86]

The masters made other contributions to the good of Keighley. Many were active in the temperance movement. The Band of Hope had 3,000 members in 1893, with William Clough as president and J. J. Brigg and Swire Smith as vice-presidents.[87] The Keighley Coffee House, opened by John Brigg in 1878, provided 'a pleasant retreat where working men may spend an hour or two in social intercourse with one another, free from the besetments of the public house'.[88] They also helped to build and support various welfare institutions, notably the cottage hospital and the workhouse.[89] The former was built in 1876 and was supported by the efforts of the élite; an extension was opened in 1897 for which John (later Sir John) Brigg donated a thousand guineas. Thomas Clough and William Clapham took a special interest in the children in the workhouse and the infirmary, donating large sums to them, while Thomas Clough visited the workhouse every Saturday, where he was 'regarded with great affection by its inmates'.[90] Many of the manufacturers contributed time as well as money to these institutions, acting as chairmen of committees, treasurers and secretaries, and organized and supported fund-raising efforts. They also helped to provide the town with leisure facilities, notably public parks. Between 1887 and 1893 the Corporation was given three large parks. In 1887 the Duke of Devonshire presented the town with Devonshire Park; in 1891 Lund Park, the gift of James Lund, was opened; and in 1893, Isaac Holden, Richard Hattersley, and the Brigg family all gave generously to the purchase of Eastwood House and the surrounding land, which was opened as Victoria Park. The biggest subscription to the latter, however, came from Henry Butterfield, who gave £5,250, but not until an agreement had been made to close a right of way which crossed his land at Cliffe Castle.[91] In smaller communities, the masters' recreational provision could be equally generous. The Cloughs of Steeton provided the village with a memorial park, a children's playground, a public bowling green, and land for a cemetery, as well as Steeton Institute and Public Baths.

Other recreational activities received support from the manufacturers. The Marriners supported two brass bands for many years, and James Ickringill maintained one in the early years of the twentieth century, though his aim was openly didactic, for 'with his usual shrewd insight into the many ways whereby the moral and physical well being of the lads could best be built up he provided the means of forming the band'.[92] Benjamin Septimus Brigg was on the committees of the skating club, the musical union and the Holy Trinity Football Club; John Brigg and John Clough were on the committees of the swimming and football clubs; William Clough was involved with several temperance societies as well as the debating and chess clubs and the Ingrow Football Club. The Marriners were benefactors of football, debating, ornithological, skating and musical societies. Joseph Summerscales seems to have been the most involved of all the manufacturers, sitting on the committees of the football club, the Hornets Football Club, the Parish Church Football Club, the Charity Football Cup, the cricket club, the Albion Cricket Club, the Parish Church Athletic Club, the skating club, and the musical union.[93]

The élite were also concerned with education, though they favoured voluntary provision, as two examples show. Keighley Public Library was built in 1899 and was the first Carnegie Library in England, the result of a close friendship between Andrew Carnegie and Swire Smith. Swire saw it as 'the continuation school through life',[94] and it seems to have been popular. Accurate statistics are difficult to locate, but between November 1904 and October 1905, 93,000 books were loaned to 1,959 people, averaging an impressive 47½ books per person per year, or nearly 1 book per person per week. Borrowers, therefore, made good use of the library, but 1,286 of them lived in the mainly middle-class North West Ward, 418 in South Ward and only 255 in working-class East Ward, the first to return an ILP councillor. Of the 818 borrowers whose occupations have been identified, 397, or nearly half, were clerical or professional people, 216, or nearly a third, were skilled workers, twelve per cent were semi-skilled, and seven per cent were self-employed. Thus the majority of borrowers were middle-class or labour aristocrats, few were unskilled, and the conclusion must therefore be that the benefits of the library went largely to the respectable classes.[95]

A similar situation prevailed in the Mechanics Institute. Founded in 1825 by a group of Keighley labourers as a self-help organization, it was influenced by the Keighley industrialists from the start. It never appealed to the working class as a whole, its members coming chiefly from the shopkeeper and artisan class. Nevertheless, membership grew throughout the nineteenth century until by 1851 over two per cent of the total population or five per cent of the eligible population were on the books. In 1848 there were four hundred members. In the 1850s the Institute ran a Female Improvement Class and a Penny Bank, providing further encouragement for self-help among the respectable classes. However, with the passing of the Education Act in 1870, the Institute lost its role as a primarily educational institution and became more a centre of social and cultural activities. Nevertheless, by the 1870s new premises were urgently needed, and the raising of funds for the new building shows the middle class firmly in control. The committee included Isaac Holden, John Clough, Edward David, Arthur Marriner, William Darling and Thomas Clapham, all leading industrialists. The building was designed by the well-known Bradford firm of Lockwood and Mawson and opened by the Duke of Devonshire, with the foundation stone being laid by Isaac Holden.[96]

The 1870 Education Act itself was disliked by the élite, particularly the Nonconformist members, who resented its support of Anglican schools. They also disliked state intervention generally, and the parochialism of the area manifested itself, among other ways, as a deep suspicion of the London government and its interference in local affairs. Keighley was therefore reluctant to implement the Act, and did not establish its School Board until 1875, when it was dominated by the Liberal Nonconformists, who opened six schools by 1880 but were subject to some criticism. The 'Liberal domination of the School Board ... was one long series of meddling and incessant contention ... owing to the mistakes made by the Board arising from sheer ignorance and incapacity', wrote one commentator.[97] It is clear, therefore, that the Keighley bourgeoisie's influence on the public life of the town was almost as important as their economic power. Just as they had an ideal of the kind of paternal, deferential, hierarchic relationship they wanted with their workforce in the mill, so they had an ideal of the kind of social relations they wanted in the town as a whole. Jonas Sugden's biographer expressed it when he wrote that:

> The vision before him was not that of mansion and equipage and rank, but of prospering brothers, and happy sisters, and thriving relatives; and of a whole neighbourhood, throughout everyone of its classes and constituents, moral in its character, comfortable in its homes, and hallowed in its religious privileges.[98]

However, this ideal rarely became a reality, for if the Keighley middle class had difficulty reconciling the ideology of paternalism in their mills with the facts of international trade, they also had difficulty convincing the working classes of the relevance of their benevolence in the town generally. The working class had their own organizations, which, while accepting the élite's influence, maintained their independence and had their own justifications.

Before discussing these organizations, it is worth examining the social life of the workers in general terms. For just as the Keighley middle class had their society, so did the working class, and the two were quite separate, even though they might overlap, for instance, in the church or on the sports field.

For most working people, there was little time available for leisure. By the 1870s the working week was around fifty-four to fifty-six hours,[99] but when time spent travelling to and from work and eating meals is taken into account, it is clear that the average person spent about seventy hours a week at work. Add to this between thirty-five to fifty hours, at the minimum, for sleep, and there is a total of forty to fifty hours a week left, at most, for all domestic duties and leisure. A worker's free time was increasingly concentrated on the weekend, during Saturday afternoon and Sunday. Saturday afternoon seems to have been the main shopping day for the working class and shops were often open until late, although there was pressure for earlier closing on Saturday nights. Saturday nights were also one of the favourite nights for drinking.

Of all the social pleasures, drink was the most popular. In 1853 there were 46 beershops and inns in the town, one for every 410 inhabitants; by 1884 this had increased to 64, though the rise in population meant that there was now only one for every 535 people.[100] The diary of James Leach, a Keighley constable, gives a graphic picture of the effects of easily available alcohol. People taken to the lock-up were described on a rising scale of drunkenness, as 'rather refreshed', 'part drunk', 'drunk', 'drunk and disorderly', 'fast asleep'. Fights, described as 'Irish rows', frequently took place in or just outside the pub and prostitution was often centred on the inn or beerhouse.[101] Pubs were unknown and regarded suspiciously by the middle classes, who rarely visited them except in a professional capacity. However, they remained an important social centre for the working class, not least because they were a convenient meeting place for societies of all kinds, although other leisure-time activities also became available as the century drew to its close.

Sports in general were popular. By 1900[102] there were seventeen different sports clubs in the town, including cricket, football, rugby, tennis, athletics, swimming, angling, skating, bowls and hockey clubs, most of which were amateur. At the same time, other entertainment was becoming increasingly professionalized. Keighley's first theatre opened in 1880, and the first regular cinema in 1909 at Oakworth.[103] In addition, there were visits by fairs and circuses and regular galas, Sunday School outings, and Band of Hope meetings, factory trips and the outings of clubs and societies.

As well as these activities, there was a range of more formal working-class organizations. Institutions such as the friendly and co-operative societies combined many of the aspects of working-class leisure with the practical goal of self-help. Behind them lurked what was, for the poor, an ever-present concern: the fear of unemployment and poverty which could ultimately mean recourse to the hated Poor Law or an inadequate private charity.

Working men combined together to aid themselves in times of sickness or death. It was this that gave many working-class organizations their special pragmatic and defensive character.

The earliest local benefit society was the Royal Union, which started in 1811. It described itself as 'a society of workmen and other persons', but it was limited to the better-paid worker, since its subscription was 10*s.* 6*d.* (52.5p) per quarter. Benefits were 6*s.* (30p) a week during illness, £2. 2*s.* (£2.10) on the death of a member or his wife and 9*d.* (3.75p) a week for dependents after death. In the 1820s there were two hand combers' clubs operating in a similar way, and they also acted as centres for unemployed combers on the tramp looking for work.[104]

Probably the first permanent friendly society in the town was the Oddfellows, whose lodge was formed in 1823 by working men, 'particularly hand combers, who were advanced politicians (chartists and the like) whose souls revolted against an unprotected and precarious existence'. They believed in 'equal opportunities for all, a fair field to all and a special care for the sick and needy', and elected their own officers, who paid out benefit for sickness, unemployment and death.[105] Membership and the number of lodges increased throughout the nineteenth century, until by 1900 there were 1,151 members in ten lodges throughout the district. Four met in Temperance Halls, four in pubs, and two in other halls. Other friendly societies included the Ancient Shepherds, the Foresters and the Rechabites, all of which were similarly organized and numbered their members in hundreds. Nevertheless, they failed to encompass the mass of the workers, in large part because their monthly subscriptions of two or three shillings were beyond the means of most operatives, and they remained the preserve of the upper working class.[106]

The Keighley Co-operative Society catered for a larger section of the population, although it too appealed particularly to the skilled workers. It also was a self-help organization, believing that 'the working man must not depend for help on the classes above them in the state but must rely on themselves for an improvement in the condition of life'.[107] It was founded, after a number of false starts, in 1860 and, after difficult early years, achieved a steady growth. By 1890 its turnover was £1.5 million, with annual profits of £150,000. It had 4,500 members and in 1896 it was estimated that about eighty per cent of the town's inhabitants were supplied by the Society with at least some of their necessities, and that they were reputed to save about 5*s.* (25p) a week in foodstuffs when they were members.[108] It also supported a wide range of social and cultural activities, such as a newspaper, the *Keighley Co-Operative Bee*, a library of 3,000 volumes, an active lecture programme and a Women's Guild. It dabbled in building and selling houses 'on the building society principle'[109] and established a Penny Bank 'for the encouragement of thrift among the young people'.[110]

The wider responsibilities of the Society were taken seriously and it responded to various appeals, such as the Keighley engineers' lock-out in 1897. It was, however, reluctant to become directly involved in any political action. It contested five seats when the borough was incorporated in 1882, but only one of its candidates was elected. After that, it eschewed politics, so much so that Emanuel Grindrod, 'one of the men who have been brought to the front of the Co-operative movement through his association with the Keighley Society', pronounced when he was on the Parliamentary Committee of the Co-operative Union and the CWS that he:

> had the honour of being in a minority against the proposals to join forces with the Labour party's Parliamentary Committee. In doing so he was acting in harmony with his conviction that if once the Co-operative leaders allowed either politics or theology to come in it would mean the beginning of disintegration.[111]

The Co-operative Society's antipathy to party politics is illustrated by its difficult relationship with the local ILP in the 1890s. A number of ILPers were active in the Keighley Society: G. J. Wardle was on the General Committee, Robert Mackley, an ILP activist and brother of the branch secretary, Tom Mackley, was editor of the *Keighley Co-Operative Bee*, and Philip Snowden was a member and attended a number of meetings. The involvement of leading labour activists in the Co-operative Society is indicative of the kind of people who started the Keighley ILP. However, the two bodies quarrelled on a number of occasions. In 1896 the Society criticized the *Keighley Labour Journal* for urging its readers to buy goods from the private traders who advertised in its paper; there was a disagreement with Herbert Horner, a leading ILPer, over the proposed establishment of a municipal coal depot; and in 1910 Horner criticized the Society for not paying their staff the rate of wages recommended by the Co-operative Congress.[112]

Clearly, none of these organizations seriously questioned the masters' power, yet neither were they dominated by the local middle class. Their aims were pragmatic, even defensive. They wished to offset the worst effects of poverty by providing insurance during unemployment, a decent burial, and cheap, good food. The structure of such organizations expressed the aspirations of the better-off members of the working class to be an association of equals. At the same time, they were built upon the reality of economic insecurity, which encouraged them to seek shelter in mutual benefits. In this need, the skilled and the unskilled shared a common outlook and mentality, one of caution and thrift. Both realized that they were unlikely to escape their status through individual effort alone. Only through collective action, in the Co-op, the friendly society, or through trade-unionism and later political action, could they hope to improve their conditions.

Politics and the Emergence of the Keighley Labour Union

The Keighley Labour Union, which soon became the Keighley branch of the ILP, was formed in 1892. This was not an isolated event, for the town had been a centre for a number of radical groups throughout the nineteenth century, both political and religious. These included an early Spiritualist church, which attracted certain Chartists after the collapse of the movement in the 1850s, and an active branch of David Urquhart's Foreign Affairs Committees, which introduced the Turkish Baths to Keighley and was where a number of ILPers met unofficially in the 1890s.[113]

In the first three decades of the nineteenth century, men and masters in Keighley were often opposed to each other over political questions, with the working class participating in many of the struggles between capital and labour which convulsed West Yorkshire during these years. As has been noted, as early as 1812 there was industrial unrest brought about by the high price of corn; by the 1820s the woollen workers had organized themselves into combers' clubs; and during the 1825 strike in Bradford, Keighley men contributed £837. 6*s*. (£837.30p) to the strike fund, while the Keighley masters showed their solidarity with the Bradford manufacturers by refusing to employ any Bradford men who came looking for work.[114] The town was a centre of Richard Oastler's working-class Toryism, and the workers strenuously opposed the introduction of the New Poor Law.[115] In 1848 the Keighley Chartists joined their comrades from Bradford and Bingley and Halifax to form a crowd of between five and six thousand, which met on Bingley Moor bearing banners with the colours of the French Revolution and the slogan 'The Charter and No Surrender'. They also paid the legal expenses of a group of Bingley Chartists who were tried at York for drilling and riot.[116]

This working-class agitation declined after 1850, with the establishment of social and industrial peace. For a generation the workers channelled their political ambitions and demands for reform into the Liberal party. For the Liberals, the success of this policy can be seen in the careers of three working-class leaders. In the 1830s David Weatherhead[117] was a noted Chartist and radical leader, who helped to establish the Workingman's Hall in 1839. In 1843 he was arrested for refusing Easter dues to the rector. By the 1850s, however, his interests had turned to other areas. He became a leading local Spiritualist and, with his help, the first English Spiritualist journal, *The Yorkshire Spiritual Telegraph*, was issued in Keighley in 1855. By this time he was a prosperous trader, and he built a Sunday School and a Lyceum for the sect. He was a prominent Oddfellow and a member of the Keighley Foreign Affairs Committee, and later was elected to the Local Board of Health. In 1887 his son was a prominent Liberal and became Mayor of Keighley.

Francis Butterfield[118] was another Chartist who was absorbed into the Liberal party. The son of one Chartist and the nephew of another, in the

1850s he too abandoned his earlier beliefs and turned to more acceptable methods of political reform. He helped found the Keighley Foreign Affairs Committee and was a member of the Keighley Co-operative Society Management Committee. He was elected to the Borough Council and was a member of the Chamber of Commerce, after becoming manager of an engineering firm. The third example was Joseph Firth,[119] who moved from Chartism to working for reform within the dominant political structure. He was a Chartist in the 1840s, but later joined the Keighley branch of the National Reform Union and then became a member of the local Board of Health.

A large number of the politically active working class, therefore, joined the manufacturers in the Liberal party. For many skilled workers, both inside and outside the factory, the decision to ally themselves with the middle-class Liberals did not necessarily come as a result of the failure of the various working-class movements, particularly Chartism, in the 1840s. Many of them had already accepted the new industrial order before the collapse of Chartism, whose supporters were often the hand workers who fought in desperation to preserve themselves and their jobs from what they saw as an unjust system. After the end of Chartism, and when the final triumph of the factory method of production had eliminated the hand workers, there was a political vacuum which left the progressive wing of the working class without a home. Given this situation, it is not surprising that they moved into the most promising political organization, the Liberal party, which offered the best chance for the working class to make its voice heard by arguing for the extension of the franchise. By the late 1850s, a new strand of working-class political activity emerged, with the struggle for a new Reform Bill.

However, this struggle brought out the differences in aspiration between the Liberal élite and their working-class supporters. The National Reform Union, primarily a middle-class organization, wished to limit the extension of the franchise to household or rental-based suffrage. The National Reform League, a working-class group, wanted manhood suffrage and the secret ballot. Neither group contemplated universal suffrage. The two groups co-operated in the agitation for a Reform Bill, with the Union supplying the money and the League the manpower. The Union hoped to be able to limit and control the aspirations of the workers, as a letter to potential donors, written in 1866, makes clear:

> Whether or not you agree with the extent of the Suffrage generally sought by the Working classes is not a point to differ about, as it is not likely to be made the basis of a Reform Bill by the leaders of the Liberal Party in Parliament ... They [the workers who do receive the vote] will assist in securing us those measures necessary to peace, retrenchment and religious equality, which have been so long obstructed by the unpopular side of the House of Commons.[120]

It is unlikely that many working-class activists would accept that interpretation of their role in the Liberal party. Working men increasingly demanded a say in politics and, in exchange for their votes, wanted Liberal candidates to support their positions.

There were other tensions between the Liberals' working- and middle-class supporters. Essentially, they wanted different things, and concessions for one group increased concern in the other. As can be seen from the above quotation, many Liberals were wary of extending the franchise too far. For the workers, the existence of legislation such as the Criminal Law Amendment Act, the Masters and Servants Act and the Conspiracy Statute, all of which made effective strike action by unions illegal, were considered threats to their ability to defend their interests. The manufacturers, for their part, considered them a useful means of controlling their employees. Other agitation, such as the Nine Hours Movement and the demand for a paid magistracy, found workers and millowners on different sides.

Despite the differences between employer and employee, the working class failed to create its own political parties until the 1890s, and there were reasons for this. One was political apathy. Furthermore, many working people did not have the vote and, for those who did, the registration procedures tended, in practice, to be more restrictive than for the middle classes. There was also the use of employer pressure, which is impossible to quantify but which seems to have existed. Workers were expected to vote the same way as their master, and it is noticeable that some of the Keighley ILPers found their jobs under threat once their political allegiance was known.[121] Lastly, the working class lacked the financial resources to challenge the wealthy manufacturers who ran the local Liberal associations. This difficulty also faced the local ILP branches, as will be shown, but the alliance with trade unions and prodigious fund-raising efforts, together with the realization that they had to raise their own money if they were to survive, enabled them partially to overcome this handicap.

Perhaps most important in delaying the emergence of a party of labour was the fact that many working-class political activists did believe that their best hope for reform lay with the Liberals. Many skilled workers, who could have led the drive for political independence, actively sought an accommodation with the manufacturers. This is particularly true in the worsted trade, where overlookers and other skilled workers, such as wool sorters, formed a relatively well-paid élite who organized and managed a poorly paid mass of workers. Although these skilled workers might combine with others on factory legislation and political rights, they found they had little in common with them. Most workers viewed the overlooker as the boss's man, and this meant he would have had difficulty leading an independent working-class political movement. It is remarkable how few ILP leaders were skilled worsted workers. In Keighley none of the early leaders was from that stratum of the trade.

For all the tensions, therefore, the working class looked to the Liberals for political leadership in the years after 1850. The Liberals also had other allies. The Irish, who made up almost seven per cent of the Keighley population, were staunchly Liberal. It was said of the 1900 election that 'it was no secret that it was owing to the Irish vote that Mr Brigg was saved from defeat'.[122] Their organizing centre was the Home Rule Club, which in 1876 had 200 members.[123] Their leaders were James Walsh and Michael Howley, both of whom had problems fitting in with the prevalent Nonconformist and temperance strands of the Liberal party. James Walsh was a spirit merchant who was elected both to the Town Council and the Board of Guardians in 1883. He was also a member of the Keighley Burial Board from that year until 1898. Michael Howley was an insurance agent who was elected to the Council in 1895.[124] He was quite willing to side with the ILP on specific issues, with the *Keighley Labour Journal* noting in 1895, for example, that 'they were pleased to see that the efforts of Councillors Howley and Horner are likely to bear fruit in the increase of some of the workmen's wages, and in the heating of Butterfield Hall preparatory to its being put to some useful purpose',[125] but his ultimate loyalty lay with the Liberals.

The Keighley Irish were committed to Home Rule for Ireland, and the Irish National League declared in 1893 that 'Keighley had contributed more money to the Executive for purposes of organization than either of the populous towns of Glasgow or Liverpool'.[126] It was the Liberals' unswerving commitment to the cause of Home Rule that secured Irish loyalty, and in these circumstances it was difficult for any political group to detach them from that party. The ILP were irritated by their fidelity and argued that the Liberals took the Irish for granted, utilizing them 'as the hewers of wood and the drawers of water for the Liberal Party'.[127] In 1896 James Walsh failed to be nominated for mayor, despite his long service on the Council, and in the following year he was not put forward as a magistrate due to pressure by the temperance and Nonconformist sections of the Liberals. The *Keighley Labour Journal* remarked:

> What is the Nonconformist Council and who does it represent? One thing seems pretty certain. It is composed of people whose minds are warped by bigotry, or they would not attempt to frustrate the wishes of the Town Council which is asking for Mr James Walsh (one of its oldest members) to be given a seat on the Magistrates Bench. Mr Walsh is a wine and spirit merchant. He is also an Irishman ... We are sorry to see intolerance carried to such an extent especially by a Council on which so many members of the cloth sit.[128]

The ILP suggested that 'had the Liberal Councillors served the Irish voters one tithe as faithfully as Irishmen served them, the Irishmen of

Keighley would today have been rejoicing that one of their fellow countrymen was occupying the proud position as Mayor elect and First Magistrate of the Borough of Keighley'.[129] Such arguments were of no avail, and it was not until after the First World War that the Irish vote was lost to the Liberals, although there is evidence of it drifting away by 1907, when Francis Hoines, an Irishman, stood as the Labour Representation Committee candidate for the West Ward. He was not elected, but in 1912 Herbert Horner claimed that he had Irish support when he was returned to the Borough Council.[130]

The temperance vote was another important component of support for Liberalism.[131] Temperance was widely supported by the manufacturers and by Nonconformist clergy. William Clough was president of the Keighley and District Band of Hope Union and J. J. Brigg, Swire Smith and J. W. Laycock were among the vice-presidents. All four were members of the Keighley Liberal 300. Swire Smith, his brother Prince, and John Grace of Dean, Smith and Grace, the machine-tool manufacturers, were among those active in the Temperance Society. Again, all were Liberals, active on elected bodies. Robert Holmes, a leading local businessman, was a member of the Local Board and the Town Council for twenty-six continuous years, and for ten years was a member of the committee of the Keighley Coffee House. Many temperance supporters were also active in chapel life. John Simpson, the secretary of the Temperance Society in 1902, was a choirmaster at the Cavendish Street Chapel, and William Wallbank, a prominent temperance worker in the 1890s, held various offices at Temple Street Wesleyan Chapel as well as sitting as a Liberal on the Town Council. The Congregational minister, John Haig, was only one of many clergy who were also involved in the temperance movement.

The alliance of temperance with the Liberals annoyed the ILP. Many ILP supporters, such as Philip Snowden and Herbert and Edward Horner, believed just as sincerely in the virtues of temperance as their Liberal opponents and a few, such as William Moore, were active in the Temperance Society. The debate about whether the ILP club room should sell alcohol roused as much passion as many political questions. However, the ILP argued that drink was not a cause of poverty in itself but was a symptom of greater evils, such as an unhealthy environment. In 1896, when discussing temperance, the *Keighley Labour Journal* remarked:

> We don't want you as teetotallers only. As a matter of fact we've got the cream of the temperance party in the Socialist movement already. But if you are true reformers you ought to know that temperance reform is but one phase of the whole social problem, and that it cannot be dealt with apart from the wider issues involved. If you are teetotallers only, you will stay where you are in the Liberal Party, in the company of the beer house votes, the tied house tenants and the off licence voters.[132]

The Nonconformist churches also tended to support the Liberal party. It has already been shown how many leading Liberals were prominent in local religious life. The Briggs and the Claphams were active Baptists, the Cloughs were Wesleyans, and the list could be extended. As far as can be ascertained, all Liberals elected to the town's public bodies were Nonconformists. The connection between Nonconformity and Liberalism is illustrated by the well-known story about the stranger who visited the town looking for work. He asks:

> What religion be the master here?
> A Liberal
> So be I, and what politics be the master?
> He's a Methody
> So be I. I be a Methody too.[133]

In common with other institutions which depended on voluntary contributions for all or part of their funding, the Nonconformist churches, both in Keighley and nationally, found themselves in the situation noted by Henry Pelling, where 'ministers were often hampered by dependence on the direct support of their congregations, and this frequently meant dependence on support of the most generous laymen'.[134] This point was made frequently by the *Keighley Labour Journal*, where, for example, Herbert Horner wrote in 1898: 'In too many cases a non conformist minister must preach what suits a wealthy manufacturer or those golden pillars of the church will find a means to get someone who will. They are so used to subservient acquiescence in their employees in the shop and factory that they expect the same from their spiritual employees on Sunday.'[135] In 1905, at a local conference held to discuss the hostility shown by the socialists to the churches, one speaker said that 'taking the Church of England as a whole the Socialist found that it was practically a buttress of the Tory party, while the nonconformist clergy were practically a buttress of the Liberal party';[136] and in 1908 Tom Mackley, the secretary of the Keighley ILP, when asking for speakers to counter the local churches' hostility to the labour movement, described the parliamentary division as 'chapel ridden' and wrote that there existed 'much prejudice against the Labour Party by Church and chapel going folk'.[137] Nonconformist ministers who were sympathetic to the labour movement could find themselves in difficulties. S. J. C. Goldsack, a Keighley Nonconformist minister who tried to form a Union of Socialists among his congregation, was forced to resign his pastorate.[138]

The alliance of manufacturers, working-class activists, the Irish, the temperance movement and the Nonconformists was powerful enough to dominate local politics during the second half of the nineteenth century. The Liberals were particularly successful after 1882, when the town became a borough, and 1885, when the Franchise and Redistribution of Seats Act made Keighley the centre of a separate electoral district. The Keighley Conservatives had difficulty finding a candidate for the 1885 election. Isaac Holden, by then 78 years old, had no difficulty in winning the seat for the Liberals by 5,644 votes to 2,818 and went on to sit in Parliament for ten years. He was followed by the Liberals Sir John Brigg (1895), Sir Stanley O. Buckmaster (1911) and Swire Smith (1915). When the first Borough Council elections were held in 1882, two-thirds of the successful candidates were Liberals and they maintained a majority over all other parties combined except for the one year, 1896, when there were eleven Liberals, nine Tories, two ILPers and one Independent. The next year the Liberals were back with an overall majority, and they remained the largest single group on the Borough Council until 1908. In the municipal elections of 1889, they won every seat; between 1891 and 1893, the years when working-class discontent was leading to the creation of the local ILP, the Liberals could nevertheless report that they had not lost a single election, 'while we have secured the election of no less than twenty two Liberal candidates – twelve on the Town Council, four on the Burial Board, four on the Baths Commission and two on the County Council'.[139] A similar situation existed on the School Board, where the Liberals also had a majority the whole time, except for three years between 1887 and 1890 when the Tories prevailed. It was the same on the Board of Guardians and other elective bodies. Thus, in 1892, the Keighley Year Book recorded that 'five members of the Liberal Party were elected to the Burial Board leaving it without Church representatives'.[140] For many years this Liberal dominance was unchallenged and Borough Council elections were often low-key affairs. In 1883 it was noted that 'none of the contests was of a political character'. In 1888 the polling 'passed off very quietly. The contest was almost devoid of interest, the result being a small poll.' In 1891 only one of the six seats was contested, and in 1892 all the retiring councillors were re-elected without a fight. Often vacancies were not contested. Excluding 1882, when the Council was established, and 1895, when the borough boundaries were extended and every seat was contested, there were 102 seats vacant between 1882 and 1900, but of these only 58, or 57 per cent, went to the poll.[141]

It was in the 1890s that the pace of political life quickened and the Liberals were challenged more frequently. Prior to 1895, there were 72 vacancies on the Borough Council. Of these 34, or 47 per cent, were contested. After 1895 the percentage of contested elections increased to around 80 per cent, although the Liberals remained securely in power until after 1900.

Despite their success, there were a number of difficulties which threatened the Liberals. The changed trading climate after the onset of the Great Depression led to an increase in Conservative support among manufacturers, with some being attracted by that party's enthusiasm for imperialism and the replacement of those markets being closed by the new tariff barriers by the colonies. Imperialism also appealed to many working- and middle-class voters, who were attracted to the Tories for other reasons as well. This drift towards the Conservatives is examined below.

The deteriorating economic situation led to increasing demands on the workforce, including the skilled people who made up much of the Liberal party's working-class support. This growing pressure on the workers in the mills and engineering shops tended to bring the different sections of the workforce together. The labour aristocrats, largely skilled men, who had previously underpinned the existing social order through their political attachment to their Liberal masters and had distanced themselves from the rest of the wage-earning class, now found their livelihoods under threat from technological innovations which diminished the value of their skills, and so they drew closer to their less well-qualified comrades. At the same time new categories of semi-skilled workers bridged the gap between the labour aristocrats and the unskilled. Wool sorters, for example, were often ineligible to join the very exclusive Woolsorters' Society, which was composed of highly skilled and highly paid artisans. In 1872 they therefore founded a new Woolsorters' Association for the less qualified, which within twenty years had absorbed the Woolsorters' Society. Thus the working classes started to develop a real consciousness of their common problems. Politically, they had the means of making their views known, through the extended franchise of the 1867 Reform Act and the Municipal Reform Act of 1884, which abolished the property qualification for town councillors. Although there was not universal suffrage, the working-class vote, if it could be organized, could count for much, particularly in urban centres like Keighley.

At the same time, a number of people in the 1880s, both working- and middle-class, had become articulate critics of the economic, social and political order which élites such as the Keighley manufacturers had created and maintained. They did not reject the industrial system, but they did question the basic assumptions of capitalism, that people were merely elements in the process of production and expendable when no longer required.

Finally, the Keighley Liberals remained unwilling to allow their working-class supporters access to, or influence in, the inner councils of the party, or to give them the opportunity to stand as candidates in local elections. Annual reports and balance sheets show how the local party was financed and managed by a small group of wealthy men.[142] In 1898 the Divisional Association reported that John Clough, who had just resigned as treasurer, had paid off all the debts, and it was disclosed that over half the annual income had been contributed by John Brigg. The following year the pattern was repeated, with Clough and Brigg providing half the subscription fees. A similar situation prevailed in the Borough Liberal Association. In

1890 Isaac Holden supplied three-quarters of the funds, and twenty years later John Brigg and John Clough between them provided £300 to pay off the Association's debts. Given that people like John Clough were prepared to support their political beliefs with considerable financial outlay, it is not surprising that they believed that those who contributed most should have the most influence, or that this belief applied not only inside the local political parties, but to society generally. In 1901 Clough attacked Herbert Horner and Philip Snowden on just these grounds, remarking: 'well I don't want to boast at all but my firm pays a fifty-third part of the rates of Keighley and I ought to take some interest. What interest has Philip Snowden? What interest has Horner? I believe he is a burgess, but I think his father's house was transferred in his name in order to make him a burgess.'[143]

In addition, candidates were expected to contribute towards the expense of an election contest.[144] The amount put up by candidates varied. In the East Ward, in the five Council elections contested between 1906 and 1911, the only years for which figures are available, candidates only paid £6. 7*s.* (£6.35p) out of a total of £79. 13*s.* ½*d.* (£79.65p) On the other hand, in the North West Ward they contributed £68. 19*s.* 3*d.* (£68.96p) out of £134. 13*s.* 10½*d.* (£134.69p) and in the Central Ward £34. 19*s.* 1*d.* (£34.95p) out of £60. 5*s* ½*d.* (£60.25p). In these two wards, therefore, more than fifty per cent of the cost was contributed by the candidates. Generally, candidates were expected to provide between a third and a half of the funds needed to fight an election and this was clearly impossible for any working-class activist. Obviously, the local Liberal association could only nominate candidates who were prepared and able to undertake at least part of the expenses of an election campaign, and this effectively excluded working-class representatives from standing as candidates.

Table 3.1 Analysis of cost to Keighley Borough Liberal Association of municipal elections, November 1906–November 1911

Ward	*No. of contests*	*Paid by candidates*	*Paid by Association*	*Cost*
Central	4	£34. 19*s.* 1*d.*	£25. 1*s.* 4½*d.*	£60. 5*s.* 0½*d.*
East	5	£6. 17*s.* 0*d.*	£72. 16*s.* 10½*d.*	£79. 13*s.* 0½*d.*
North-East	7	£33. 9*s.* 8½*d.*	£72. 10*s.* 1*d.*	£105. 19*s.* 9½*d.*
North-West	5	£68. 19*s.* 3*d.*	£65. 16*s.* 7½*d.*	£134. 5*s.* 10½*d.*
South	7	£48. 1*s.* 0*d.*	£92. 2*s.* 9*d.*	£140. 3*s.* 9*d.*
West	7	£47. 2*s.* 10*d.*	£67. 5*s.* 11½*d.*	£114. 8*s.* 9½*d.*
Total	35	£239. 8*s.* 10½*d.*	£395. 12*s.* 10*d.*	£635. 1*s.* 8½*d.*

Average cost of elections

Central	£15. 1*s*. 2½*d*.
East	£15. 18*s*. 7½*d*.
North-East	£15. 2*s*. 10*d*.
North-West	£26. 17*s*. 0*d*.
South	£20. 0*s*. 5*d*.
West	£16. 6*s*. 10*d*.

From the late 1880s, the Liberal alliance was thus under some stress, but the occasion which led to the creation of a separate party of labour was an industrial dispute. The events which took place between the engineers' strike in 1889 and the final formation of the Keighley Labour Union illustrate the way in which resentment of the Liberal manufacturers, the increasing attraction of trade-unionism and an appeal to morality in industrial relations and politics, combined together to make the formation of an independent working-class political party possible. The 1889 Keighley engineers' strike was the climax of a growing dissatisfaction among the workers. Keighley was notorious as a town where engineers' wages were poor, having, it was claimed by the union, the lowest rate in the north of England, at between 15*s*. (75p) and 20*s*. (£1.00) a week.[145] These low wages were accompanied by a general downward pressure on the men's working conditions. In 1872 the Amalgamated Society of Engineers (ASE) had achieved the introduction of a nine-hour day, with overtime rates settled at time-and-a-half, but nine years later the Keighley employers successfully revoked the agreement and forced the workers to accept overtime payments at the same rate as ordinary time. At the same time the *Yorkshire Factory Times* alleged that men who were a quarter of an hour late had an hour docked from their wages.[146]

The strike started in August 1889 in the Midland toolworks of F. and J. Butterfield, where a request to discuss the question of overtime and the 1872 wage rates was dismissed and the workers were told not to waste the management's time.[147] The men at this firm, and at over twenty others, walked out, and George Cooke of the Bradford branch of the ASE was called in to organize them. Although the Keighley branch of the union numbered fewer than 300 members, 3,500 people from 28 firms eventually came out on strike. In the beginning there was considerable ambivalence towards the masters. Although there was massive support for the strike and the wage claim among union and non-union labour, the men were deferential in their statements towards the employers. They indicated that this was the first engineers' strike in the town for seventeen years and that they were eager for a negotiated settlement. The masters, for their part, refused to enter into discussions with the men's representatives. It soon became clear that there was considerable support for the men within the town and almost £700 was quickly collected for the strike fund. The Co-operative Society later contributed a further £100.[148] The masters soon realized that they would either have to give in or accept that the struggle would be a long one, and after a month they made a number of concessions and the men went back to work.

During the strike the masters found it difficult to understand the men's sense of grievance. A representative of F. and J. Butterfield and Co. expressed the belief that most of the workers were content with their conditions. He commented to the *Keighley News* that:

> most of their employees had grown up with the firm, and were really satisfied with the positions they held in the workshop, and all with the exception of the 'riff raff', would willingly return to work were they not afraid of being jeered at and called 'black sheep' by their fellow workmen in the town.[149]

It was hard for the employers to grasp that the strike was threatening the traditional hierarchical relationship between man and master. They suggested that the men were being manipulated by outsiders, by the trade-union organizers who had come into the town to help the strikers. Despite the fact that trade-unionists comprised less than ten per cent of the strike force, they complained that 'the men have allowed themselves to be intimidated by an outside society and [the employers] express their confidence that if the dispute were left to the two parties immediately concerned – employers and employed – it would speedily be settled'.[150]

However, the masters' analysis was wrong. This dispute was not to be settled by appeals to the men's loyalty to their place of employment. The men were convinced they had been unfairly dealt with and were starting to question the system which had governed them for the past forty years. One speaker at a strike meeting made the point that, though Keighley was notable for the excellence of its technical education, it was notorious for its low wages. 'He wanted to put the two together and he wanted to ask them seriously what was the benefit of science and art and technical education unless they put more money in their pockets.'[151] The paternalism exercised by the manufacturers was starting to be seen as irrelevant to the needs of the workers. One striker declared that he:

> believed there were places in Keighley where certain men received high remuneration for their work. The ground on which they were paid seemed to be that they had got the 'gift of the gab' and did a little 'local parsonry' whilst others were blessed with a good voice and were able to sing in a choir.[152]

In addition, the men were increasingly aware that the power of local officialdom lay largely in the hands of the manufacturers, which could be used against them. Their leaders warned them not 'to run themselves into the police court or into the hands of the magistrates, for they would find as a rule that these men were not on the side of labour'.[153] The strikers also saw their action as part of a wider movement of working-class activism. Comparisons were made with the London dock strike, which was taking place at the same time. Samuel Shaftoe, the Bradford trade-union leader, declared that the cases of London and Keighley were almost 'parallel, but the men of Keighley were skilled ... but skilled or unskilled the time had come when the voice of labour would ring above all other cries demanding from the unscrupulous employer and tyrannical capitalist what was their own'.[154]

One immediate result of the success of the strike was an increase in trade-union activity, leading to the formation of a Trades Council in February 1890. A letter to the *Keighley News* reminded the men 'of the necessity of at once joining the various societies which exist for their protection against unscrupulous employers',[155] and a number of new trade-union branches were established, while old ones expanded. These included the iron workers, who formed a branch of the United Machine Workers; the Gasworkers, Brickmakers and General Labourers; the General Railway Workers;[156] and a second branch of the Amalgamated Society of Engineers. A branch of the Teachers' Union was also set up by Herbert Horner, a Liberal activist, who was soon to become the driving force behind the local ILP. Some Liberals welcomed the expansion of trade-unionism, although they were in a minority. The Revd T. Naylor, a prominent local Liberal, argued that 'if three fourths or even one half of the working men in this country were to combine together in a solid labour union, you would find that capital would be their servant, and no longer their master'.[157] The *Keighley News* also approved of the development of trade-unionism, because 'when the men are properly organized and federated there will be less heard of the refusal of masters to treat with duly chosen and responsible representatives of the men'.[158] However, despite this support and the growth of trade-union branches, organized labour remained weak. For example, there is little evidence of the textile workers combining and, as they were the largest group of workers, this naturally weakened the power of trade-unionism generally in the town.

Perhaps as important as the growth of trade-unionism were pointers to the political and ethical approach to social and economic problems which were to become characteristic of the ILP. During the municipal elections of October 1889, James Holmes, a confectioner, stood as a 'representative of labour'. Although he was a Liberal, he 'came forward as a working man's candidate because he believed the time had come when a combination of labour should be put forward in the interests of labour'.[159] His success showed that it was possible for representatives sympathetic to the demands of labour to be elected to public bodies. It also demonstrated that it should have been possible for the Liberals to accommodate working-class demands. However, between 1889 and 1892, as will be shown, it became clear that the Liberals were not prepared to support working-class candidates in local elections.

The phenomenon of ethical socialism will be discussed later, but it is worth noting that the appeal of morality when discussing social problems, which was to be important to the Keighley ILP, also becomes prominent. Even while the engineering strike was in progress, Robert Stansfield, vicar of St Peter's Church in Keighley and, in the 1890s, an ally of the socialists, who eventually married Mary Jane Dixon, an ILP member of the School Board, struck an idealistic note which was to become familiar in countless Keighley ILP articles and speeches. For him, social changes were to be brought about by an appeal to Christianity. In a letter to the *Keighley News* he wrote:

> It is a fiction to say that religion has nothing to do with man's material progress and worldly success. One of its most valuable objects is to inform men that if material goods are increased, that increase should come about rightly and be rightly used. The Christian faith has no want of sympathy with all that even dreamers hope for in a regenerated society, and a better world.[160]

This ethical approach to industrial and political questions was not confined to Robert Stansfield. A letter to the *Keighley News* urged the masters not to forget that 'we are all brothers, and that although they may possess more of the world's goods than others of the family, they are only stewards and not owners'.[161] Again, as had already been noted at a meeting of the Pleasant Sunday Afternoon group, it was accepted that the principle of socialism was that 'the good of the individual shall be subordinate to the good of the many which is really borrowed from Christianity'.[162]

Thus, during the weeks following the engineers' strike, all the factors which shaped the development of the Keighley ILP were already in existence. There was the distrust of the middle-class manufacturers, the growth of trade-unionism, the success of political candidates standing as representatives of the working class, and an increasing emphasis upon ethical approach to solving society's problems. Nevertheless, it was to be a further two years before the ILP became the voice of the politically independent working class. As yet, most workers remained loyal to the Liberal party, but once they had become convinced that the Liberals remained unwilling to take their political interests seriously, the formation of the Labour Union became possible.

It also became clear that, despite the success of the 1889 strike, there were difficulties with using industrial action to achieve the economic objectives of the working class. Trade unions were simply not powerful enough to influence the masters, and the aftermath of the strike saw determined attempts by the manufacturers to isolate trade-unionists from the rest of the workforce. A letter to the *Keighley News* stated that:

> some firms in Keighley intend to weed out all society men and have in fact commenced already operations in that direction. Like the man who cut off his nose to spite his own face they are parting with some of their best and oldest friends, in some cases giving them notice to quit, in others by petty acts of mean despicable tyranny making it impossible for them to remain.[163]

Clearly, a *rapprochement* between masters and men was becoming unlikely, but with the workers vulnerable to victimization in the factory, industrial action was unlikely to be successful. The most effective way to make the voice of labour heard was through political activity; and the question was whether the working class was to function through the Liberal party following the successful election of James Holmes, or was it to form its own alliance.

Given the success of James Holmes, the first alternative offered possibilities. In nearby Shipley in 1891 and 1892 the workers had captured the Liberal party machine and used it to elect W. P. Byles, the most prominent of the Bradford New Liberals, as their MP. Also, some local Liberals had grasped the importance of conceding some of the working-class demands. The *Keighley News* on 20 February 1892 urged the workers to use the Liberals as a vehicle for reform, arguing that they 'have their doors open to the working man' and that, by working with the party, 'they could win with comparative ease far more than by the years of bitterness they are likely to get after disintegrating the Liberal Party'. The paper suggested that:

> through the action of the Liberal Party there were working class representatives before the Independent Labour Party was thought of. What did Independent Labour do, or what did they propose to do that the Liberal Party could not, would not willingly do for them. They wanted something more than to augment labour representation – they wanted payment of members, payment from the rates of returning officers etc [sic]. The Liberal party were quite sound on all these points.[164]

In any case, the paper felt that thinking men 'will not lead to the foolishness of setting up a new political party'.[165]

However, by 1892 mistrust of the Liberals was considerable. One correspondent to the *Keighley News* wrote that 'our political leaders in Keighley are a bad lot' and 'we had some experience of their liberality a little while ago when we asked for a ten per cent advance ... The detective like management makes one feel almost like a slave. They tell us off with our smocks, and roll our shirt sleeves up to our shoulders – so that we can do the extra ten per cent of work, I suppose. These employers, mind you, are the sworn friends of the poor.'[166]

Throughout 1892 there was debate between those who wanted an independent working-class political party and those Liberals who wanted to widen the appeal of their party and keep the loyalty of the workers.[167] Visitors such as Tom Mann, Ben Tillett and John Lister urged that a separate party was the best means of obtaining reform. Others claimed that the 'Liberal Party was the Labour Party' and that they could and would initiate reforms. The difficulty, as far as the working class in Keighley was concerned, was that although the Liberals would pay lip service to the reforms they wanted, it was doubtful whether they could be trusted to keep their word once they had secured the workers' support.

The unwillingness of the Liberal leaders to give working-class political activists a say in local politics became clear in March 1893 at the School Board elections. The Keighley Labour Union had in fact been formed in 1892, but it was still in its infancy and if a compromise had been reached over the School Board, the threat to the Liberals posed by the Labour Union might have been averted. The Trades Council had decided as early as March 1892 to nominate two candidates for the election, Alfred Burrows and George Gill, and in February 1893 negotiations were entered into to see if the Liberals would drop two of their candidates in favour of these two men. In this way a contest could have been avoided. A. B. Smith, the Liberal election agent, admitted to Alfred Burrows, the chairman of the Trades Council, that there was little difference in policy between the two groups,[168] but, nevertheless, the Liberals felt unable to accede to the Trades Council request. John Brigg tried to justify the Liberals' position with a mixture of flattery and technicalities which could not have been overly convincing to the Labour representatives. He said:

> The Liberal Association had every disposition to see Labour represented, and directly represented, on the School Board. He pointed out, however, how delicate were the arrangements for polling and distributing votes, and how easy it was to find one's party in a minority unless these delicate arrangements were faithfully obeyed. It was not with any intention of keeping out the Labour representatives that they could not see their way to withdraw two of their candidates. In fact they looked upon them as another branch of the Liberal party. As far as he could gather the feeling of this Association had been very favourable to Labour representation and it was only this danger of being placed in a minority that caused them to decide that they could not withdraw more than one.[169]

This justification loses its force if the policies of the two groups were similar, as it was agreed that they were, and if the Liberals were sincere in their claims of 'hearty sympathy with the claims of labour – claims which have always been supported and advocated by the Liberal party in Keighley'.[170]

After this rebuff, the Trades Council decided to force a contest and, in the event, both their candidates were successful, so demonstrating that independent political action was an effective way of forwarding working-class demands for reform.

The Keighley Labour Union which was formed on 3 October 1892 at the Albion Hotel was the product of two factors. First, the reluctance of the Liberals to give the working class a voice in their party, and, second, the decision of the local trade-union movement to seek a political vehicle. These two strands were highlighted at the first meeting of the new party. Herbert Horner declared that the object of the Union 'would be to act together with the Trades Council',[171] and the resolution passed by the meeting said that 'Mr Holden [Keighley's Liberal MP] has been rather indifferent of late in his conduct to the labouring portion of his constituents'.[172]

These ideas were repeated on the larger stage of a public meeting in December, when Keir Hardie visited the district. The ubiquitous Herbert Horner made the most of it. He said:

> the rates of wages are too low and the hours of labour are too long and that labour is not properly represented in Parliament, or on local administrative bodies [and we] call on the workers of this district to support their trade unions to the utmost of their power, and to approve the formation of an Independent Labour Party in Parliament.

He added that in 'Keighley much as many of them credited Mr Holden with being an advanced radical, the feeling was growing in the minds of the workers that it was not to the landlords and capitalists but to themselves that they had to look to secure those reforms they so much desired to see realised'.[173] It was this mistrust of existing political parties and the trade-union connection, together with the appeal of ethical socialism, which defined the character of the Keighley ILP and enabled it to survive as an important political group for the twenty-two years from 1892 to 1914.

Notes

1. Dewhirst, *op.cit.*, p.46.
2. Wright, *Chartist Risings*, *op.cit.*, pp.37–62.
3. D. Wright, 'The West Riding Textile Districts in the Mid-Nineteenth Century', in Jowitt (ed.), *Model Industrial Communities*, *op.cit.*, pp.17–43.
4. *Keighley Argus*, October 1891.
5. Dewhirst, *op.cit.*, p.9.

6. *Ibid.*, p.76.
7. T. D. Whitaker, *History and Antiquities of the Deanery of Craven*, quoted in Dewhirst, *op.cit.*, p.10.
8. Hodgson, *op.cit.*, p.19; M. L. Baumber, *From Revival to Regency: a history of Keighley and Haworth 1740–1820* (Keighley, 1983), pp.39–62.
9. Keighley, *op.cit.*, pp.233–6.
10. A. Briggs, 'Industry and Politics in Early Nineteenth Century Keighley', *Bradford Antiquary*, New Series, XXXV (1950), p.312.
11. Hodgson, *op.cit.*, p.36 for Brigg; p.71 for Jonas Sugden; and p.24 for the Cravens.
12. Joyce, *op.cit.*, p.37.
13. Baumber, *Revival to Regency*, *op.cit.*, pp.41, 56–60.
14. *Keighley News*, 21 November 1925.
15. *Ibid.*
16. Quoted in Dewhirst, *op.cit.*, p.14.
17. J. Smith, 'The Strike of 1825', in Wright and Jowitt, *op.cit.*, pp.63–81.
18. Quoted in Dewhirst, *op.cit.*, p.14.
19. Eboracorun Lodge Independent Order of Foresters, *Good Fellowship in Keighley, 1823–1923* (Keighley, 1925), p.54.
20. Dewhirst, *op.cit.*, pp.46–8.
21. This process of technological change is examined in J. Smith, *op.cit.*
22. C. Johnstone, 'The Standard of Living of Worsted Workers in Keighley during the Nineteenth Century', unpublished D.Phil. thesis (University of York, 1976), p.80.
23. R. Spence Hardy, *Memorials of Jonas Sugden* (London, 1858), p.94.
24. A. Almond, *Biography of James Ickringill Esq.* (Keighley, 1919).
25. *Ibid.*, pp.41–2.
26. Joyce, *op.cit.*, p.164.
27. Almond, *op.cit.*, p.21.
28. Hodgson, *op.cit.*, pp.23, 64.
29. Snowden, *op.cit.*, pp.140–1.
30. *Ibid.*, p.140.
31. Spence Hardy, *op.cit.*, p.104.
32. *Men of the Period: Portraits and Pen Pictures of Leading Men* (The Biographical Publishing Company, 1897), pp.321–9.
33. Quoted in Johnstone, *op.cit.*, p.188.
34. *Yorkshire Factory Times*, 26 March 1897, 15 November 1899, 5 September 1902.
35. Johnstone, *op.cit.*, pp.196–7.
36. *Ibid.*, p.197.
37. *Ibid.*, p.189.
38. *Ibid.*, p.190.
39. *Ibid.*
40. Hodgson, *op.cit.*, p.76.
41. Johnstone, *op.cit.*, p.190.
42. *Ibid.*, p.194.
43. *Ibid.*, p.192.
44. *Ibid.*, pp.198–9.

45. *Ibid.*, p.191.
46. *Ibid.*
47. *Ibid.*, p.192.
48. *Ibid.*, p.200.
49. *Ibid.*, p.194.
50. *Ibid.*, p.195.
51. *Ibid.*, p.194.
52. *Keighley Year Books.*
53. Quoted in Briggs, 'Industry and Politics', *op.cit.*, p.316.
54. Snowden, *op.cit.*, p.69.
55. *Ibid.*, p.29.
56. Dewhirst, *op.cit.*, pp.45, 95.
57. Hodgson, *op.cit.*, pp.35–6.
58. Information drawn from the obituaries file in Keighley Reference Library, *Keighley Year Books*, 1885–1910, and Hodgson, *op.cit.*, *passim.*
59. *Keighley Year Books*, 1885–1910.
60. J. Smith, *op.cit.*, p.46.
61. Elizabeth Jennings, 'Sir Isaac Holden 1807–1897: the First Comber in Europe. A Critical appraisal of the career of a Victorian Entrepreneur with special reference to textiles, politics and religion and their interdependence', unpublished Ph.D. thesis (University of Bradford, 1982), pp.312. For the houses of the West Riding manufacturers, including Keighley, see George Sheeran, *Brass Castles: West Yorkshire New Rich and their Houses 1800–1914* (Halifax, 1993).
62. Joyce, *op.cit.*, p.176.
63. Hodgson, *op.cit.*, p.176.
64. Briggs, 'Industry and Politics', *op.cit.*, p.317.
65. Joyce, *op.cit.*, pp.175–6.
66. *Keighley Year Book*, 1901.
67. Hodgson, *op.cit.*, p.43.
68. *Ibid.*, p.55.
69. *Ibid.*, p.67.
70. Almond, *op.cit.*, pp.26, 228–8.
71. Obituary of Albert Rishworth, *Keighley News*, 28 August, 1937; obituary of C. H. Foulds in obituaries file, Keighley Reference Library.
72. Obituary of John Smith Naylor, *Keighley News*, 1 May 1915; obituary of Craven Laycock, *Keighley News*, 27 December 1927; obituary of Jonathan Gill, *Keighley News*, 18 January 1930.
73. Obituary of James Groves, *Keighley News*, 10 June 1916; obituary of T. S. Clapham, *Keighley News*, 20 February 1915.
74. Almond, *op.cit.*, p.27.
75. Spence Hardy, *op.cit.*, pp.158, 161.
76. Keighley was a centre of Spiritualism and the first Spiritualist newspaper, *The Yorkshire Spiritualist Telegraph*, was published in the town. See Logie Barrow, *Independent Spirits: Spiritualism and English Plebians 1850–1910* (London, 1986), pp.4–19; Dewhirst, *op.cit.*, p.68.
77. J. T. Ward, 'Some Industrial Reformers', *Bradford Textile Society Journal* (1962–3), p.132.

78. *Bradford Observer*, 14 June 1892.
79. *Bradford Labour Union Journal*, 28 October 1892.
80. *Keighley News*, 23 November 1889.
81. *Ibid.*, 23 November 1889.
82. *Ibid.*, 14 December 1889.
83. *Ibid.*, 1 February 1890.
84. Hodgson, *op.cit.*, p.130.
85. *Ibid.*, p.43.
86. *Ibid.*, p.70.
87. *Keighley Year Book*, 1894.
88. Keighley, *op.cit.*, p.245.
89. The information in the rest of this paragraph is take from K. M. Feather, 'Nineteenth Century Entrepreneurs in Keighley', unpublished BA dissertation (University of Liverpool, 1983).
90. *Keighley News*, 4 July 1936.
91. Dewhirst, *op.cit.*, p.101.
92. Almond, *op.cit.*, p.62.
93. Information taken from *Keighley Year Books*, 1885–1910.
94. Snowden, *op.cit.*, p.238.
95. Johnstone, *op.cit.*, p.204.
96. Keighley, *op.cit.*, pp.204–14.
97. Spectator (C. W. Craven), *Keighley School Board and its History* (Keighley, 1890), p.10.
98. Spence Hardy, *op.cit.*, p.187.
99. D. Russell, 'The Pursuit of Leisure', in Wright and Jowitt, *op.cit.*, p.202.
100. Johnstone, *op.cit.*, p.203.
101. Diary of James Leach, MS, Keighley Reference Library.
102. *Keighley Year Book*, 1901.
103. *Ibid.*, 1881 and 1910.
104. Dewhirst, *op.cit.*, p.15.
105. *Ibid.*, p.41.
106. Johnstone, *op.cit.*, p.206.
107. Joseph Rhodes, *Half a Century of Co-Operation in Keighley 1860–1910* (Manchester, 1911), p.219.
108. Johnstone, *op.cit.*, p.209.
109. Rhodes, *op.cit.*, p.120.
110. *Ibid.*, p.86.
111. *Ibid.*, pp.140, 143.
112. *Ibid.*, pp.159, 191, 231.
113. A. Briggs, 'David Urquhart and the West Riding Foreign Affairs Committee', *Bradford Antiquary*, New Series, IX (1958), pp.197–207.
114. Dewhirst, *op.cit.*, p.14; J. Smith, *op.cit.*, pp.63–81.
115. Dewhirst, *op.cit.*, p.32.
116. Wright, *Chartist Risings*, pp.59–60.
117. Ward, *op.cit.*, pp.121–35.
118. *Ibid.*; Rhodes, *op.cit.*, p.130.
119. Ward, *op.cit.*, p.132.
120. Quoted in K. Ittmann, 'The Manufactory of Men: Society and Family Life

in Bradford, West Yorkshire 1851–1881', unpublished Ph.D. thesis (University of Princeton, 1989), p.249.

121. See, for example, *Keighley Labour Journal*, 8 March 1896.
122. *Keighley News*, 11 November 1933.
123. Keighley, *op.cit.*, p.242.
124. Obituary of Michael Howley in *Keighley News*, 11 November 1933.
125. *Keighley Labour Journal*, 6 October 1895.
126. *Keighley News*, 22 September 1893.
127. *Keighley Labour Journal*, 24 October 1896.
128. *Ibid.*, 5 June 1897.
129. *Ibid.*, 24 October 1896.
130. *Keighley News*, 2 November 1912.
131. The information in this paragraph is taken from the *Keighley Year Books*, 1885–1910, and the records of the Keighley Borough Liberal Association and the Keighley Divisional Liberal Association.
132. *Keighley Labour Journal*, 21 November 1896.
133. Quoted in Dewhirst, *op.cit.*, p.104.
134. Pelling, *op.cit.*, p.129.
135. *Keighley Labour Journal*, 14 May 1898.
136. *Keighley News*, 17 October 1905.
137. Keighley ILP, Letter Book, 13 May 1908.
138. *Keighley Labour Journal*, 19 September 1895.
139. Keighley Borough Liberal Association, Minutes, 18 February 1893.
140. *Keighley News*, 29 October 1892.
141. Information taken from *Keighley Year Books*, 1884–1910.
142. The information in this paragraph is taken from the Keighley Divisional Liberal Association and the Keighley Borough Liberal Association, Minutes, 1898–1910.
143. *Keighley News*, 14 September 1901.
144. The information in this paragraph is taken from the Keighley Borough Liberal Association, Minutes.
145. J. M. Chambers and T. Holdsworth, 'The Worm Turns: the Amalgamated Society of Engineers in Keighley 1889–1914', unpublished essay deposited in Keighley Library, n.d.
146. *Ibid.*, p.10.
147. The information in this paragraph is taken from *ibid.*, pp.10–11.
148. Rhodes, *op.cit.*, p.126.
149. *Keighley News*, 31 August 1889.
150. *Ibid.*
151. *Ibid.*, 7 September 1889.
152. *Ibid.*, 31 August 1889.
153. *Ibid.*
154. *Ibid.*
155. *Ibid.*, 5 October 1889.
156. *Ibid.*, 28 September and 23 November 1889, 8 February 1890.
157. *Ibid.*, 20 March 1892.
158. *Ibid.*, 8 February 1890.
159. *Ibid.*, 26 October 1889.

160. *Ibid.*, 14 September 1889.
161. *Ibid.*, 5 October 1889.
162. *Ibid.*, 1 February 1890.
163. *Ibid.*, 28 September–February 1889.
164. *Ibid.*, 17 December 1892.
165. *Ibid.*, 20 February 1892.
166. *Ibid.*, 27 February 1892.
167. The information in this paragraph is taken from the *Keighley News*, 1892, *passim*. Tom Mann visited in January, Ben Tillett in February and John Lister in March.
168. Keighley Borough Liberal Association, Minutes, 22 February 1893.
169. *Ibid.*
170. *Ibid.*
171. *Keighley News*, 8 October 1892.
172. Keighley Labour Union, Minutes, 3 October 1892.
173. *Keighley News*, 10 December 1892.

CHAPTER FOUR

Keighley Politics, 1892–1914

The Independent Labour Party

The influence of the ILP and the Labour party on national politics in the years prior to 1914 was small. In West Yorkshire, the Labour party held only three or four parliamentary seats at any one time between 1906 and 1914, while the Liberal party normally gained the other nineteen. There are various reasons for this poor showing. The franchise was limited, and Labour had few full-time agents to represent its supporters at the registration courts; the party was chronically short of money and could not afford to fight as many seats as it wanted; and with national elections only occurring every four or five years, Labour's parliamentary showing lagged behind its true level of success. The real yardstick of Labour and ILP support is to be found in the municipalities and other local representative bodies. By 1900, nationally, the ILP had 63 town, 36 urban, 4 county, 3 rural district and 16 parish councillors; 8 citizens' auditors; 51 members of Boards of Guardians and 66 members of School Boards. By 1906, in West Yorkshire alone, Labour had 89 representatives, 47 on Borough Councils, 36 on County, Urban, Rural District and Parish Councils, and 6 on Boards of Guardians; and by 1913, there were 188, 85 on Borough Councils and the remainder on other elected bodies.[1] A number of ILPers became outstanding local administrators. Fred Jowett of Bradford is perhaps the most notable, but his friend Philip Snowden first showed his skills on the local Borough Council and School Board.[2] This success in local government gave the party valuable administrative experience and political realism. As Fred Brocklehurst said, 'men and women who are daily occupied in administering the Poor Law, educational or civic affairs of the town cannot escape the sobering influence of responsibility'.[3] This 'sobering influence' was a necessary corrective to the ILP's millenarian vision of socialism, which will be discussed later.

Various local studies of the organization and political development of the ILP at branch level have appeared, some of them dealing with West Yorkshire communities.[4] In Keighley, the party was more successful initially than its small numbers might suggest. This was due to a number of factors.

Its policies were cautiously reformist, though it emphasized its separateness from other parties. It established an association with trade unions and articulated their aspirations for better working conditions. It had a number of enthusiastic and able local activists, most famously Philip Snowden, who gave the branch the high quality of leadership that it needed in the face of the animosity of the Liberal manufacturers.

Before examining their political activities in detail, a number of general points should be made. The branch could not compare in size, organization or finance with the local Liberal and Tory parties, both of which had wealthy backers, such as the Briggs and a branch of the Clough family who supported the Liberals, and the Haggases and the Marriners who contributed to the Tories. They had headquarters with extensive facilities, and memberships running into the hundreds; in 1901 the Conservative Club in the centre of Keighley had 500 members, the Eastwood Club had 300 and the Parkwood Club 140. The Liberal clubs were equally well supported.[5] They could employ paid agents and owned newspapers, which were subsidized on occasion. They could mount registration campaigns, canvass the electorate at both local and parliamentary elections and provide other resources, such as transport, for their voters on election days. The Keighley ILP had a membership which rose from 30 in 1892 to about 120 in 1900,[6] a weekly news sheet which expanded into a newspaper, and then declined into a monthly edition, little financial backing and a club room which changed addresses three times in eight years.

Financially, the Keighley ILP was always on the brink of collapse. Unlike other branches, such as those in Bradford, which had the support of Arthur Priestman, or Halifax, with John Lister, or Colne Valley, with France Littlewood, Keighley could depend only on its working-class supporters. One example will illustrate the difference in financial resources between the Keighley ILP and the other parties. In 1895, the ILP campaign to run Philip Snowden as a parliamentary candidate fizzled out because of lack of funds. The party needed £160 to pay its share of the poll costs, without which it could not stand. It obtained £55 and the promise of £35 more, but could not find the other £70. In the same election the successful Liberal candidate, John Brigg, spent £838.[7]

In fact, the branch was never free of debt. Minutes regularly recorded this fact of life:

> That a sub. com. be formed – to consider getting up socials for the wiping out of the debt [1895].
> That the special meeting take into consideration – some means of wiping off the debt [1896].
> That we make a special effort at coming tea to wipe off the debt [1897].[8]

The debt, at least in the early years, seems to have been about £20; not a small sum, but negligible when compared with the resources of the Liberal and Tory parties. Even by 1904 the branch had only 1*s.* (5p) in hand, and its income from members' subscriptions was £28. 0*s.* 3*d.* (£28.02p).[9] In fact, this compares favourably with the subscription income of the other two parties, but in their cases resources were supplemented by donations from wealthy supporters. The branch never did resolve its money problems and this inevitably restricted its development.

To some extent, these financial problems were circumvented by the enthusiasm of the members, who saw themselves as belonging not merely to the smallest political party in Keighley, but rather to a national and international movement. The quarrels between the different branches of socialism were not seen as of major consequence. *Justice* was sold at the Labour Club along with the *Clarion* and the *Labour Leader*, and the branch voted for socialist unity in 1898. It was irrelevant to them that Robert Blatchford and Keir Hardie had quarrelled in the ILP over the Manchester Fourth Clause, which, incidentally, Keighley tended to support.[10] Tom Mackley, the secretary of the branch for many years, when advising the Bingley socialists on setting up their organization, wrote that 'the difference between the SDF and the ILP is practically only a difference in name'.[11] The important point was that people became socialists, and whether they came to that belief through reading Robert Blatchford, William Morris or the Fabians, or through disillusionment with Liberalism, or a sort of religious conversion, was not of vital concern. As Edward Horner said, when talking about G. J. Wardle, 'he [Wardle] had been lead to socialism from its religious standpoint, while he [Edward Horner] had been led to it from its economic standpoint. Thus as all roads led to Rome, so all roads now led to socialism.'[12]

This is not to say that members always acted in harmony. On the contrary, some of them seem to have been difficult to work with. Tom Mackley, for example, was often outspoken, being, as he admitted, 'a curious chap to work with', and on occasion he found it difficult to get people to help him. When looking for an assistant, he wrote: 'I have tried some half doz [sic] who I thought would be most likely and most suitable and have been refused.'[13] One ILPer once described his behaviour when thwarted:

> Mr Mackley resorted to his favourite methods of procedure. With an eloquent burst of his characteristic language he jumped up at the meeting, banged all his books into his desk, and with a threat to resign – left the members of the Executive to suck their thumbs until he chose to allow them to use their own books again.[14]

Herbert Horner also had a reputation for being prickly[15] and Philip Snowden's sharp tongue was well known. Nevertheless, the branch was enthusiastic in the cause of reform, as it had to be, when faced with many difficulties and setbacks.

Overall, the branch was democratic, at least in its early years. The leading ILPer was Herbert Horner, who was the chief instigator in the founding of the branch in 1892 and was a member of the Executive Committee until 1905. His brother Edward remained on the Executive until after 1912, and for most of that time was the branch treasurer. The Liberals liked to identify Herbert as the controller of the local party; for example, after the School Board election of 1896, the *Keighley News* remarked that 'the Liberal party is not the only party in Keighley which has an "I am". After all there is something to be said for a dictator who leads his party to victory. But a dictator who leads his party to defeat is less tolerable.' Commenting on the same elections in 1899, the paper said: 'in other words they [the ILP] wish to have four powers on the Board moving responsive to the will of the one secret player who stands behind the curtains and seeks to control its Councils'. The nomination of Charles Whitehead as an ILP candidate in that election was seen as a master move on the part of Herbert Horner. Whitehead was 'to be kept like a card, tucked up Alderman Horner's sleeve, and to be played or not played as that gentleman pleased'.[16] This assumption that the branch was the creation of one man annoyed the ILPers and led them to minute 'that the first time the newspapers again refer to "Mr Horner and his Party" that an official communique be sent to contradict it'.[17]

In order to assess the extent to which the branch was controlled if not by Herbert Horner, then by a small group of the most active ILPers, figures have been drawn from three sources (Table 4.1, p.124). Where possible, the Executive Committee has been examined to see if the same people were regularly re-elected. The names of those proposing and seconding motions at meetings were examined for the year 1897 to see if the same people were always involved. Finally, those chairing meetings of the Labour Church were examined to see how many were involved in introducing speakers. Obviously, these examinations are not entirely satisfactory. They may indicate a high turnover in membership rather than a high degree of membership participation in the activities of the branch. However, they do seem to indicate that control was not vested in a small cabal. Of the members who sat on the Executive Committee between 1892 and 1900, about seventy-five per cent were elected for two years or less.[18] There is a gap in the Executive Committee minutes between 1900 and 1903, but a similar situation obtains between 1903 and 1910, when 43 out of the 61 people who were on the Executive Committee served for two years or less. The long-established members were Herbert and Edward Horner, W. F. Hardy, W. Robinson, Elizabeth Roe, Tom Mackley, Mary Jane Dixon, and J. W. Waterworth. Philip Snowden, the most charismatic figure in Keighley politics at the time, was not elected to the Executive until 1899. It might be suggested that the long-serving members comprised a group who effectively directed the affairs of the branch, and certainly they were among the most influential ILPers. Nevertheless, a reading of the branch minutes and the local newspapers shows that others, such as William Bland, Philip Snowden, G. J. Wardle, W. S. Wilkinson, were also powerful personalities within the party.

When the people who proposed and seconded motions at the meetings of the Keighley ILP were examined, a similar situation emerges.[19] The 7 people most often elected to the Executive play an important, but not dominating, role. Between January and December 1897, 88 motions were put, each both proposed and seconded. Of these, 18 were by W. H. Hall, 17 by Mrs Roe, 13 by W. Emmott, and 10 by W. F. Hardy, Tom Mackley and G. J. Wardle. Herbert Horner was involved in 9 motions, Edward Horner in 7, W. Robinson in 5 and Mary Jane Dixon in 3. In all, 33 people proposed or seconded motions, which at this time would be about one third of the membership; a relatively high proportion.

An examination of the chairmanship of the Labour Church meetings reveals a similar wide spread of responsibility.[20] Between 1893 and 1899, when meetings are fully reported, 105 Labour Church meetings were held and 44 people shared the chairmanship. The maximum number of services chaired by an individual was 6. Among the long-serving members of the Executive, the Horners and Tom Mackley chaired 6 meetings each, W. Robinson 4, Mary Jane Dixon and Mrs Roe 3 each, and W. F. Hardy 2.

Taken together, these facts indicate that although people like the Horners and Tom Mackley were important in the branch, they did not dominate it. Indeed, on occasion they were made to apologize for their conduct to the branch. After a disagreement at a committee meeting, Tom Mackley wrote: 'my action in leaving the meeting showed a want of respect – There is no doubt I did a wrong action in taking away the books etc. in that I owe an apology to the E.C. and am prepared so to act.'[21] The Keighley ILP appears to have been an open organization, with each member having the opportunity to express his opinions and put forward his ideas. This was in part a reaction against the oligarchic management of the other two party machines; but it was also an expression of what the ILP meant by socialism. Equality meant the opportunity for everyone to have their say in the running of society, for the individual had an important place in their concept of a socialist society.

One last general point should be made. The role of the *Keighley Labour Journal* in informing the local ILPers about what was happening not just locally, but nationally and internationally, should be acknowledged. The paper's first editor was G. J. Wardle, and he was succeeded by Philip Snowden. Under Wardle and Snowden, the paper provided comprehensive accounts of the ILP's activities in the town and commented on borough politics. It helped to direct local political campaigns, telling sympathizers who the ILP candidates were and when and how to vote for them. It noted which speakers visited the area, outlining the main points in their speeches, and describing how they were received by their audiences. Accounts of the various social and cultural activities of the branch were reported, including those of the Clarion Vocal Union, the Clarion Cycling Club, the 'free and easys', the ham teas, the walks, the recruiting expeditions, the Socialist Sunday School and Labour Church meetings. After Wardle left in 1898, Snowden increased the size of the newspaper from quarto size to newspaper size, boosting circulation to five thousand. He was also able to charge a penny (0.4p) a copy, whereas previously it had been free. He wrote much of it himself, under the bylines of 'Robin Redbreast' and 'A Mere Outsider'. Herbert Horner contributed comments on Council activities as 'Scriberius'.

Under Snowden's editorship, the paper was used as a propaganda sheet for the ILP but, more importantly, it acted as a muck-raking journal, exposing what Snowden saw as the corruption of local public affairs. This side of the *Labour Journal*'s activities was summarized by Colin Cross when discussing Snowden's activities as editor: 'One week he was attacking the decision to raise from £300 to £400 the salary of the Borough Surveyor while at the same time the wages of the night soil men were being reduced. Then he turned to the expenses charged by Councillors and officials for trips outside Keighley.'[22] By exposing these and similar activities, the *Keighley Labour Journal* became an important source of information not just for committed socialists, but for every politically aware person living in Keighley.

Unfortunately, Snowden's journalistic ambitions proved too expensive for the local party. His editorship was marked by constant appeals for money to keep the publication going, and, after he had left, the paper changed from a weekly to a monthly and soon appeared only irregularly. It was revived as a weekly in 1905, but collapsed after six months. The printers required 10*s.* 6*d.* (52.5p) a week from the ILP to produce the paper, and the ILP was never able to cover the costs.[23] Nevertheless, while it existed, it was an important means of spreading the party's political message as well as helping to create and sustain the ILP culture and ethical socialism which was an important side of the branch's activities in its early years.

The initial electoral success of the Keighley ILP was dramatic. By January 1899 it had contested sixteen local elections and won seven.[24] Herbert Horner was the first ILPer to stand for the Borough Council in 1893. He was defeated, but was successful a year later. In 1896 Mary Jane Dixon became the first ILP member of the School Board, although Trades Council candidates had previously been elected. In 1898 Herbert Horner became an alderman, with Conservative support. The next year ILP representation on the School Board was increased with the election of Philip Snowden and Charles Whitehead and the re-election of Mary Jane Dixon. By 1900 the Borough Council had four ILP councillors as well as Alderman Horner. James Teal had been elected in 1897, and W. F. Hardy and William Prosser in 1898. Prosser had been 'one of the bitterest opponents we had in Keighley, but like other advanced thinkers he had been forced to abandon his old

Liberal friends'.[25] Philip Snowden became a councillor in 1899, though only by seven votes. In 1901 J. W. Waterworth was voted borough auditor, possibly as a result of Philip Snowden's sustained attack on Liberal extravagance in the *Keighley Labour Journal*. In the same year the party achieved its first success on the Board of Guardians.

These results, combined with Philip Snowden's abortive election campaign in 1895, seem impressive – and in many ways they were. The *Labour Leader* recorded rather exaggeratedly that 'there promises to be a race 'twixt Bradford, Keighley and Halifax as to which shall have the first socialist Mayor in Yorkshire'.[26] However, an examination of the local election results shows that their support was based on insecure foundations. It is true that they had five seats on the Council, but essentially what they captured was a ward. In the years between 1896 and 1900 East Ward returned a Labour candidate four out of five times. The only other Labour success was in 1896 when they returned a candidate for the North-East Ward, but it was not repeated. The North-East Ward voted ILP in 1896, Radical in 1897, Liberal in 1898 and 1899 and Tory in 1900.

After 1900, electoral successes were fewer. Herbert Horner was elected to the West Riding County Council in 1907, remaining a member until 1913. In 1912 he was also re-elected to the Borough Council. In parliamentary elections, Labour put up candidates in 1906, 1911, when there was a by-election brought about by the death of John Brigg, and 1913, when there was another by-election. In the two elections of 1910, it was felt that the position of John Brigg was well-nigh impregnable. In the elections they contested, Labour secured just under a third of the vote. In 1906, W. T. Newlove, a Leeds trade-unionist, stood with the backing of the ILP and the Trades Council, though he was not an agreed candidate under the arrangements made by Gladstone and MacDonald. He secured 3,102 votes, or 26.6 per cent of the turnout. In 1910, W. C. Anderson stood as an official Labour candidate and got 3,452 votes, 28.9 per cent of the poll, and in 1911, William Bland, a local ILPer and trade-unionist, obtained 3,646, or 29.8 per cent of the votes. Labour could thus count on the support of over 3,000 people in a national election, almost as many as the Conservatives, whose poll in the same elections were 3,229 (1906), 3,842 (1911) and 3,852 (1913).

The decline of the local labour movement after 1900 was noted by contemporary Keighley politicians and commentators of all opinions. In 1904 Herbert Horner noted that, where previously there had been four Labour members, now there was one, and in the same year the *Keighley News* wondered why the Keighley ILP had declined so much when nationally it was gaining ground.[27] In 1902, after the defeat of all four of its candidates in the municipal elections, the *Keighley Labour Journal* remarked: 'There is no town in England where the Labour Party has done such good work as Keighley. Every exposure of Corporation extravagance or jobbery, every proposal for municipal reform has come from the Labour party – But their work has been largely thrown away labour.'[28] On the face of it, the Keighley ILP was no worse placed than any other ILP branch. In 1905 it and the Trades Council had formed a local Labour Representation Committee (LRC), and this should have strengthened the movement, particularly as it was dominated by ILPers. The ILP itself nominated six delegates and 'the majority of the delegates from other organizations affiliated are also members of the ILP',[29] and William Bland, prominent in the ILP was the LRC secretary.

Nevertheless, it is clear that Labour did not capitalize on its pre-1900 success and a number of reasons may be put forward to explain this. Herbert Horner considered the problem in 1908. He argued that:

> our success came too soon. We were not really entitled to the representation we won in the early days of the movement – We have to fight our own hands nowadays, whereas in the earlier period, many voted for our candidates simply to spite and defeat the candidates of the opposite orthodox party.[30]

There were other reasons for this failure. A number of Labour activists left the area or dropped out of politics. As early as 1898, G. J. Wardle left to take up a post outside Keighley. After 1900 Philip Snowden was devoting most of his energies to national events. Mary Jane Dixon retired from local politics when the School Boards were dissolved. W. F. Hardy, the ILP councillor, went bankrupt and had to resign his post, and William Prosser, another councillor, developed a drinking habit, which led to his retirement from the Council and the party in 1901. W. S. Wilkinson remained committed to the Clarion Vocal Union, but in 1905, as a result of a decision by the West Riding County Council to raise the status of music teachers, he was obliged to undertake a course of part-time study to achieve the necessary qualifications. Inevitably, such studies limited the time that he could devote to the party.

Then, there were splits among the socialists which diverted their energies. These were exacerbated by personality clashes which became more open after the formation of the LRC. This may, in part, have been the result of tensions between the trade-union side of the party, which tended to become more important as union branches joined the LRC, and the ethical socialists who had hitherto dominated the ILP. However, this is not a complete answer, as many of the early ILPers were active trade-unionists. The Horners were both prominent in the local branch of the Teachers' Union, G. J. Wardle was a member of the ASRS, and Tom Mackley helped to found the local branch of the Carters' Union. Nevertheless, the appeal of socialism as an ethical system was strong in many of the early ILPers. Equally important were difficulties on a personal level. In 1905, John Jervis, who had acted as election agent for Joseph Hargreaves, the ILP candidate in East Ward, in 1904, attacked Herbert Horner and Tom Mackley in the columns of the *Keighley News*, accusing them of making electoral deals with the Tories by agreeing to give them a free run against the Liberals in some wards in exchange for having a straight fight against the Liberals in others, and of not pulling their weight in the election campaigns:

> Both these personages had been loud in their promises of working till midnight every night if necessary, if Mr Hargreaves would only consent to stand. But did they? No. Mr Horner spoke for a few minutes at two meetings, but did not canvass a single door or distribute a single piece of literature during the whole of the election; while the other great man, the real master of the show, Mr T. Mackley, did not put in an appearance, after all his promises from the Sunday prior to the election until the day of the polling.[31]

These splits worsened in the following years. In 1907, Herbert Horner was elected to the County Council. He was successful partly because there were only two candidates, himself and William Weatherhead, who stood as an Independent. Weatherhead had been a founder member of the Keighley Labour Union, but had left after quarrelling with Herbert Horner. Horner also had support from a number of Liberal and Conservative voters and most of the Irish, who voted for him partly because of his opposition in 1902 to the Education Act and his support of denominational schools, and partly because of his sympathies with the working class.[32] The Liberals supported him because he had been persuaded to contest the seat by his union, the Teachers' Association, whose local representative, A. Hirst of Haworth, was a Liberal activist. The ILP, for their part, were divided over the victory. One section 'was not so sure that the victory was an out-and-out triumph for Labour'. Another group insisted that 'it is a Labour victory', and argued that 'it will be better for Keighley when we get rid of that class bitterness and party feeling which we have had in the past'. A third faction argued that whether it was a Labour victory or not was irrelevant, 'we have got a Labour man in and that is everything.'[33]

By 1910 the ILP had divided into the followers of Herbert Horner, who were largely older members, and the supporters of William Bland. By 1913 there was a real possibility that Horner might start a separate ILP in opposition to the branch which he had helped to found over twenty years before. In fact, this never happened, but clearly the party was deeply split along a number of lines. There was a split between the ethical socialists and trade-unionists, who were chiefly interested in improving the lot of the workers. Thus J. Auty, the candidate for South Ward in 1907, 'was a thorough believer in collectivism and municipal enterprise, and also in economy. He did not look upon the municipality as a sponge to be squeezed or a cow to be milked.'[34] There were also those who were prepared to compromise with the other parties if they thought it would help to elect their candidates.

In 1906 one speaker at an election meeting declared that 'his vision was one of compromise, and he hoped that those in the North-West who were of Labour sympathies would return the concession being made to the Labour candidate in the South Ward by giving their vote in favour of the Liberal candidate'.[35] In 1907 the LRC was approached by the Liberals of the North-East Ward to see if an arrangement could be made over the next election in that ward. This led to the Gasworkers' and General Labourers' branch withdrawing from the LRC 'as the strongest protest we can show against the policy they have entered upon, namely of compromising with the local Liberal party, and consider the course they have adopted as being totally opposed to the interests of labour'.[36]

The divisions were worsened by the difficulties over Herbert Horner's candidature as the Labour representative for Keighley. Originally, the local ILP wanted Philip Snowden as their candidate, but after he had agreed to contest Blackburn they had to look elsewhere. In 1906 Newlove stood, but he declined to contest the seat again, so the local LRC chose Herbert Horner as their candidate. He was selected by a large majority, but even so there were those who were unhappy with the decision. The ILP felt it necessary to condemn Joseph Hargreaves for 'making statements at the last LRC meeting charging the ILP with intriguing in the interest of Mr H. Horner (re Parliamentary candidate for this Division) and calls upon him to withdraw the statements at the next meeting of the LRC'.[37] In addition, the national ILP leaders considered Horner a rather weak character, although Philip Snowden spoke up for him, declaring that, 'by his long and effective work on the town and County Councils Mr H. Horner had amply proved his fitness to represent the workers of this constituency in the House of Commons'.[38] From the national ILP viewpoint, the situation was delicate. While John Brigg remained its MP, the town was going to stay Liberal, but it was felt that, when Brigg retired, there was a good possibility of change and Labour might win the seat. However, in the opinion of the Labour party's national agent, Herbert Horner 'would not be a good candidate', but 'if a strong Labour candidate can be secured I am of the opinion, after very careful consideration of the whole position, that we should contest'.[39] In 1911 Brigg died, a by-election was called and the Labour candidate was W. C. Anderson, chairman of the ILP. Herbert Horner was pacified by the promise that he should 'lose nothing through my magnanimity'; but he did, for in the by-election of 1913, William Bland, Horner's local rival, was the Labour candidate. Herbert, therefore, had real reason to feel aggrieved at the way he had been treated. More than anyone else, he had worked for the ILP since the day it was founded, and there seems little doubt that he was shabbily dealt with.[40]

There were other splits among local socialists. In 1908, a branch of the Social Democratic Party was founded. It does not seem to have lasted long, although its first anniversary tea was attended by 120 people and was held in newly opened premises.[41] There is no evidence that it was an important influence on local labour politics, but its very existence and survival indicate that there was discontent with the LRC and ILP branches in the area.

Another reason for the failure of the Keighley ILP after 1900 was its lack of organization. Herbert Horner remarked in 1904 that 'the real reason for this reduction in the number of labour members was that their supporters had been so pleased with the brilliant municipal exposition that had been furnished them by their representatives that they had neglected their organization and it was organization that won'.[42] In part, this was due to shortage of money, but also to every electoral failure reinforcing apathy among the activists, which in turn ensured continued failure. William Pickles, commenting on the County Council elections of 1907, when Herbert Horner was elected, said that:

> their success was due to the fact that they had put more energy and enthusiasm into the contest. For some time past they had been suffering from the depressing influence of a series of defeats, and he felt sure that if they could only stir up the old enthusiasm, the old results would ensue.[43]

The party was well aware of the need for better organization and in 1904 agreed a scheme for appointing captains and lieutenants and ladies to manage each of the wards in the town.[44] However, the scheme seems to have collapsed almost as soon as it was introduced.

A final reason for the failure of the ILP was the strength of Liberalism. Although under pressure from a revived Conservative party and the ILP and LRC, the Liberals nevertheless had no difficulty returning their MPs in every election. Even though it lost control of the Council in 1907, it still seemed a more practical vehicle for reform than the representatives of labour, who were unable to get even one of their members elected for nearly ten years.

But despite the ILP's electoral decline after 1900, the local branch's political impact between 1892 and 1914 was considerable, for which there are a number of reasons. Often, the branch was fortunate in the quality of its candidates. The policies they put forward were tailored to appeal to the working class as a whole and contained little that was overtly ideological, and this enabled them to collect the votes of a number of discontented Liberals.

As an example of the care with which candidates came to be chosen, it is worth examining the ILPers elected to the School Board in 1899. They appealed to a wide section of the electorate, but particularly to the working classes. Mary Jane Dixon was an ethical socialist, a Wesleyan lay preacher, and married to a clergyman who also expressed socialist opinions. By 1899 she was a capable and experienced local politician whose commitment to the workers was always clearly expressed. For example, she commented during the previous School Board election:

> it must not be forgotten that Keighley is a half time district. To compel half timers to take as many extra subjects as day scholars leads to cramming and over pressure. Let those employers who think half timers can do as much work as day scholars, pay their own half timers full time wages.[45]

Philip Snowden, who had previously been elected to the Cowling School Board, was already a national figure and enormously popular in Keighley. He was a leading ethical socialist, a master of debate, and a capable and astute administrator. Even at this early date he was a member of that group of professional politicians who were coming to the top in the national party. Charles Whitehead, by contrast, was a local trade-unionist and secretary of the Trades Council. He represented the trade-union wing of the movement, which, as will be shown in a later chapter, was an essential factor in the development and survival of the branch. The three of them thus appealed to a wide cross-section of the working class:

> While Mrs Stansfield (Mary Jane Dixon) and Mr Snowden from their knowledge and experience of educational work will be able to look after educational policy on the Board, Mr Whitehead from his close acquaintance with labour questions will be most valuable in safeguarding the interests of Labour.[46]

However, it was not always possible to find candidates of such quality; and this was not surprising. A newly formed party with a membership of less than a hundred could not hope to find suitable people to stand in elections immediately. None of the early Keighley ILP candidates had stood for public office before, and their lack of talent for the rough and tumble of local elections clearly comes across on occasion. For instance, in the 1894 municipal elections, the *Keighley Echo* remarked of the ILP candidate that 'nearly every question enumerated in the programme, Mr Roe [the ILP and Trades Council candidate] admitted was too complex for him to explain at a public meeting'.[47] The lack of confidence that this quotation illustrates left the party with little room to manoeuvre. Nevertheless, in this case the *Keighley Labour Journal* somewhat desperately declared that if Mr Roe 'could not explain clearly all the items publicly there is no proof that he did not understand it [the ILP programme] ... Mr Roe would have graced the Council'.[48]

This problem of finding suitable candidates was never completely resolved either by the ILP or the LRC/Labour party. In 1910 the minutes recorded that William Bland, George Town and William Pickles declined to stand as candidates for a municipal by-election, and Herbert Horner reported that a Mr Casson could not stand and nor could S. Rayner. In that particular year, even Herbert Horner showed uncharacteristic reluctance, possibly because of the difficulties he was experiencing with his parliamentary candidature: 'Mr Horner stated that he had no serious objections to having a straight fight either in the West or North West, but he would not say definitely now. He wanted time to consider.'[49] The most objectionable difficulty to finding candidates, however, was the threat of victimization by Liberal factory owners. Active party members were always in some danger of the sack if their political work became too important. The *Keighley Labour Journal* remarked:

> It is not so long since a prominent Liberal candidate told a defeated Labour candidate 'it was a good job for him that he had not won the election as if he had his whole future career would have been blasted'. Nor is it very long since a son of one of our so called Liberal employers told another with respect to a Labour candidate, that 'they would not have such a man about the place' and this ... simply because of his political opinions.[50]

This pressure applied not just to party members, but to anyone considered to have socialist views. The Revd S. J. Goldsack, a Keighley Nonconformist minister and confessed socialist, was forced to resign his pastorate.[51]

In these circumstances, it is not surprising that people were sometimes reluctant to stand for the ILP in elections. The party tended to choose its candidates from the self-employed or from those, like Herbert Horner, who had relatively secure jobs. A number of these self-employed candidates, however, were people who had originally worked in factories but had left, driven out, it would seem, by the opposition of their employers. Thus George Gill had been an engineer but became a newsagent; Alfred Burrows, also an engineer, a trade-unionist and vice-president of the Keighley Labour Union when it was first organized, set up a fish shop; and W. F. Hardy, another engineer, president of the Trades Council and an ILP borough councillor, also became, for a time, a newsagent. Similar candidates were Wilson Roper, who ran a clothes shop, and William Bannister from Haworth, who was a hairdresser.[52] Philip Snowden earned much of his income from lecturing and journalism. Their self-employed status gave them the freedom to pursue their political ambitions, and it also illustrates the depth of their commitment to the party. This is not to suggest that Keighley was unusual. Many early members of the ILP were forced out of their factory jobs. Indeed, it has been suggested that this persecution was one of the reasons for the early bureaucratization of the party. Workmen forced to leave their jobs were found employment within the ILP.

The policies pursued by the Keighley ILP were a mixture of municipal socialism and demands for an improvement in working-class conditions by such means as the implementation of fair contracts clauses; the payment of trade-union rates; and the introduction of the eight-hour day.[53] They also argued that general improvements should be made to enhance the environment, and suggested that ILP policies would be more efficient and cheaper to implement than those of the Liberals. The latter was particularly important in Keighley, where elected members were under considerable pressure to reduce rates. In 1901, an irate ratepayer declared that:

> there was never a time in the history of Keighley when greater need existed for the spending departments of our public bodies to curtail their expenditure within the lowest possible limits. The tradesmen and the working classes had been undergoing a severe financial strain during the last fifteen months, yet our public bodies had spent the public money as though no such severe depression existed.[54]

The ILP's answer was twofold. It blamed the Liberal majority for inefficiency while at the same time it defended the services that the rates provided. Philip Snowden outlined the benefits in a speech in November 1901, talking of parks, police, free education, public health departments, well-lit streets and drains: 'he said this to impress them with the importance of municipal work, to show its benefits and advantages, and to try to divert the interest raised by the high rates into an intelligent investigation of municipal questions'.[55]

The programme of the ILP in the 1895 municipal election is a typical example of the kind of policies they put forward. Among other items, they pledged themselves to the eight-hour day for municipal workers and promised them freedom to join trade unions, for 'there are hundreds of men in Keighley who dare not let it be known that they are trade-unionists ... Employers or workmen should have equal liberty of combination.' They wanted the creation of a municipal coal depot, because 'at least £3,000 a year would be saved'; the building of working-class housing, for 'the Corporation can borrow cheaper and therefore build cheaper than private individuals'; the introduction of a direct works department; and the municipalization of pawn shops and public houses. The ruling Liberal manufacturers were attacked in a pledge to allow the county to pay a part of the salaries of the Medical Officer of Health and the Sanitary Inspector. This, they suggest, had not been done already because:

> Employers ... of whom there are far too many on the Council ... want to keep these officials between their finger and their thumb. With officials backed up by the County Council, the fouling of the becks and of the atmosphere would be more strictly watched and penalties enforced. The gain to the ratepayers would be less rates, less nuisances and better health.[56]

Nine years later, in 1904, the test questions put forward by the ILP were very similar. They included an eight-hour day or forty-eight-hour week for municipal employees, a minimum wage of 24*s*. (£1.20) a week, a 'vigourous' fair wages clause, the establishment of a municipal coal supply, the retention of Corporation land, evening sittings for committees, Sunday opening for the library, the abolition of church rates and the provision of a secular system of national education.[57]

The clearest point about these programmes was that they cannot be described as socialist. The branch argued that the reforms they proposed were steps on the way to socialism, but in themselves they contained nothing that an advanced reformer could not support. Indeed, Michael Howley, the working-class Liberal leader of the Irish community, often did support the ILP on specific measures. The Keighley ILP was not unique in this reformist approach, for the party pursued the same line in most of the places in which it achieved electoral success.

How much the local party achieved in terms of actual reforms is difficult to assess. They were undoubtedly a valuable ginger group, even though their behaviour in the Council Chamber could attract criticism. The *Keighley News* remarked:

> we do not want to see the deterioration which has already set in in our local bodies go any further than it has done already. We are certain that the working men of Keighley have no desire to see the business of the town conducted after the manner of a street row, or to listen to the measureless violence and insulting brutalities in which a certain party carries on its controversies with those who have the misfortune to differ from it.[58]

Nevertheless, it exposed the negligence of the Council on a number of occasions, especially after Snowden became editor of the *Keighley Labour Journal*. His investigative articles showed that the middle-class monopoly of the Council had resulted in some insensitivity and a degree of casualness in local administration. He criticized the expenses charged by the councillors and officials for trips outside Keighley. He discovered that it had cost the ratepayers £119 for silver caskets and illuminated addresses when the Council gave the freedom of the borough to 'four of our distinguished citizens who have chiefly distinguished themselves by growing rich out of the people of Keighley'.[59]

Articles such as these, when combined with attacks in the Council Chamber or on the School Board, introduced a usefully abrasive element into local government. In addition, when, by the end of the century, enough ILPers had been elected to form a significant minority group, their political effectiveness became more noticeable. Herbert Horner was praised for his work on the Sanitary Committee in pursuing landlords of insanitary property. He also claimed responsibility for reforming the milk supply and introducing new regulations concerning cowsheds and ensuring their better ventilation and cleanliness, for organizing a reform of the Town Clerk's Department and suggesting that Keighley should have its own borough magistrates.[60] Philip Snowden, too, claimed that the ILP had been an effective agent of reform. In 1902 he summed up their success. The article is a long one, but worth quoting, for it gives an indication of the extent and limitations of the party's political achievement in its early years.

> I had the satisfaction of knowing that … a very considerable portion of the election programmes … had been carried out, or advanced as far as it is possible to go … Most of the reforms which the Corporation themselves could carry out with their present powers, are today accomplished facts. The Town Clerk's Department has been re-organised at a saving of £700 a year. The Dairies and Cowsheds within the Borough are inspected by a qualified Veterinary Surgeon. The expensive Corporation valuers have been relegated to the less dignified position of private practice. The two guineas a day allowed to Deputationists is now reduced by fifty per cent. The important matter of the re-evaluation of the Union has been definitely embarked upon. The tramways have been municipalised and are already making considerable profits. I along with other members of the Highways Committee, went very carefully into the question of the purchase of the Markets … I induce[d] the Council to offer all surplus lands on lease as an alternative to purchase. My efforts in regard to the public ownership of the Coal Mines and Municipal Fire Insurance had an influence that was felt throughout the Country, and the *Municipal Year Book* has recorded the fact that Keighley has the honour of having first called attention to the importance of the public control of the coal supply; and the question of fire insurance is now receiving the attention of all the largest Councils in the Country.
>
> The other matters such as the taxation of Land Values, reform of Parliamentary Bill procedure, and the control of the Liquor traffic, are matters which can be dealt with only by Parliament and the fact [is] that the Keighley Corporation has municipalised almost everything which can be done in the present state of the law.[61]

Obviously, the implication that there was very little else that could be done is far from the truth. Fred Jowett in Bradford was showing how much more could be achieved on the local level and after 1900 the Keighley ILP's impact in the Council Chamber was minimal. Nor did the Keighley Liberals agree that the local ILP were effective reformers. John Clough dismissed their activities in a speech in 1901. 'They have made a great splutter and noise on the Town Council, but they don't do much work. It is the same on the School Board. Their work on the Committees is small stuff, but when they get before the reporters then they figure as taking a great interest in what is going on.'[62] What is clear, however, is that the Keighley ILP's programme was one of gradual, almost incremental, reform – as, indeed, it had to be, if the necessary support of members of other parties was to be obtained.

By 1900 the Keighley ILP was a permanent part of the political scene. It had significant representation in the Council and on the School Board and Board of Guardians. It had a small but enthusiastic membership and could rely on a body of voters at election times. It boasted of its independence from both political parties, owing its survival to the support of neither of them. Its suspicion of existing parties, particularly the Liberals, is not surprising. Many of the founder members of the Keighley Labour Union were Liberals who were disappointed with that party's refusal to accommodate the political demands of the working class. Yet in the 1890s, particularly in the formative years of the Labour Union, 1892 and 1893, it should have been possible for the Liberals to have minimized the impact of the establishment of the Keighley Labour Union and kept within the Liberal party many people who were to join the ILP.

Liberals and Conservatives

The Keighley Liberals were proud of their reputation as radicals, and the local ILP appropriated many of their policies. At first, there seemed little real difference between the two parties. In 1893, when Alfred Burrows and George Gill stood as Labour candidates for the School Board, the *Keighley News* said that 'the points on which these two gentlemen differ from the members of the existing [Liberal controlled] Board were so few and so trifling that one is at a loss to understand why the first attempts of Labour candidates to enter the public life of Keighley should take this direction'.[63] In 1892, the Revd T. Naylor, a prominent local Liberal, in a speech to the North-East Ward Liberal Association, assured his audience that he was in favour of many of Labour's demands, including the payment of MPs, increased education and land reform.[64] In the same year, a meeting was held between Isaac Holden, the local Liberal MP, and the Keighley Trades Council and labour representatives to discuss the political programme which had been adopted by Labour. The programme contained twelve items divided into four sections. Of these, Holden gave his whole support to nine and conditional support to two. Generally, he appeared to have little quarrel with the Labour manifesto:

> On every item in groups one, two and three Mr Holden gave an answer in the affirmative with the exception of the one relating to the abolition of the Customs and Excise duties ... As to Group IV, he said the railways came within the list of things that he would municipalise or nationalise altogether ... As to the Eight Hours question ... were the miners and railwaymen absolutely to agree on the question he might see his way to vote for a compulsory Bill. He was quite in favour and always had been, of the abolition of all perpetual pensions and sinecure offices.[65]

Similarities between the policies of the two parties continued. In 1895, when Philip Snowden was berating the Liberals in his election speeches, his programme was not seen as particularly distinctive. The *Keighley News*, indeed, attempted to project the ILPers as little more than advanced Liberals, saying: 'we do not say that every Liberal would approve of every item in that programme. But all these items are merely the carrying out of principles accepted and applied already by the party to which Alderman Brigg belongs.'[66]

There were, nevertheless, fundamental differences between the ILP and the Liberals and these will be discussed later. The local Liberals, for their part, had three responses to the emergence of the ILP. One was to ignore the ideological differences and to regard the defectors as advanced radicals who had – understandably perhaps, but wrongly – left the party and should return to it, for it was only the Liberals who had the power to implement the legislation that Labour actually wanted. Thus the *Keighley News* regarded the election of Labour candidates to the School Board in 1893 not as a setback for Liberalism, but as an opportunity for working-class politicians to gain experience in local government. This would prepare them for the work of reform which would be carried out by the Liberal majority. It wrote:

> the responsibility of office is in itself a valuable training … the heedless and ill-guarded utterances of the platform and the public hall find their best corrective in the toilsome and patient details of the Board and Committee Room, where the problems of actual administration have to be faced from week to week and month to month.[67]

This belief that the Liberal party was prepared to accommodate the demands of the workers was put to the test in 1893, when a Labour Electoral Association was formed in the town. This organization, rather than the ILP, was to be the vehicle for achieving the improvements demanded by the organized working class, and its method was 'the permeation and stimulation of the Liberal Party wherever there appears to be undue slackness in the prosecution of the Liberal programme, and in that way … lies the most reasonable hope of practical achievement'.[68] The *Keighley News*, reporting the founding of the Association, urged that 'there is no reason why Labour whatever its special organisation should not continue to work with Liberalism for ends which are in harmony with the tendency of the older body and to a large extent actually parts of its declared programme'.[69]

The difficulty of using the local Liberal party as a vehicle for working-class reform quickly became apparent, however, for the Keighley Labour Electoral Association vanished almost as quickly as it was formed. The Liberal élite who ran the local party was not willing to make any concessions to the workers. The conclusion drawn by the Keighley ILP was that political independence was essential if the workers were to achieve anything. The policy of the ILP was to 'know no party save Labour, to consider no interest paramount to the claims of Labour, to act as intransigents till the battle has been won … This policy may be right or wrong but at least it is clearly defined and different from the one favoured by the LEA.'[70] By contrast, in nearby Bingley, a Labour Electoral Association was successfully established in 1893, while a local ILP branch made no impact, disappeared in less than a year,[71] and was not re-established until 1904.[72] Local circumstances could thus determine the success or failure of attempts to incorporate working-class politicians into the Liberal party. In Keighley, such an attempt failed because the local Liberal leaders were not prepared to pay more than lip service to the aspirations of the workers.

The interpretation of the ILP as representing an advanced form of Liberalism was chiefly favoured by the *Keighley News*. This paper was owned by William Pollard Byles, who was a prominent local Lib-Lab and who almost alone among the Bradford and Keighley business élite wanted to accommodate the aspirations of the working class. He failed to achieve this in Bradford, where he met intransigent opposition from Alfred Illingworth and others, and he failed in Keighley, where there was similar resistance from John Clough and his allies. In Shipley, a small industrial centre situated between the two towns, he proved that it was indeed possible to make the workers an active and relevant component of the Liberal party, but even here his success was short-lived.[73]

A second Liberal response to the ILP was to regard them as impractical idealists. It was an interpretation which was favoured by some local manufacturers. At an election meeting in 1895, Swire Smith used this argument to make his audience laugh with the suggestion that:

> several of the set to whom he had belonged, in the enthusiasm of their youth, had been rather bitten by the socialistic craze. They had, however, recovered to some extent from the severity of the attack, and their hopes for the regeneration of the masses rested chiefly on the cultivation of the intellectual powers and their application to the practical purposes of life.[74]

After the 1895 election, John Clough took an equally patronizing tone towards the ILP, telling his audience that 'a state of Socialism was only possible when there had been a great raising of the moral character of the nation. He [John Clough] had to say that socialism was possible when every man, woman and child was perfect and when that time came socialism would not be required.'[75] This response enabled the Liberals to push the ILP to one side, to that section of the political arena inhabited by cranks and eccentrics, and allowed them to pose as the only practical political party for the working man.

The third Liberal response to the ILP was that they were troublemakers. It was argued that the early ILPers created their own party in order to attack their previous benefactors, the Liberals. For, 'nothing that Liberals do is or can be right with men who hate their old comrades with that malignant bitterness which men who change their colours nearly always show'.[76]

The Liberals concluded, as they did elsewhere, that the activities of the ILP benefited the local Conservative party. Discussing the 1895 election, which resulted in the return of John Brigg as the Liberal MP, the *Keighley News* examined the campaign in some detail, and remarked: 'in claiming the chief honour for the representatives of piety and the pothouse [parsons and publicans] we are not unmindful of the debt of gratitude which they owe to their allies of the Labour party'. The socialists, it suggested, had helped the Conservatives in two ways. First, a number of Labour supporters voted for the Tory candidate, Walter Bairstow, in order to oppose the Liberals: 'in many cases on the principle of cutting one's nose to spite one's face, votes were cast for Mr Bairstow'.[77] Second, a number of Liberals were frightened enough by the ILP to move to the right of Liberalism and vote Conservative. John Brigg commented: 'he knew in this Division that many who had not a bit of Toryism about them had voted against him simply because they were frightened lest Liberalism should lead to Socialism'.[78] This reaction to the ILP as a group of malcontents who objectively helped the Tories was often used by the Liberal party managers to explain poor election results or Tory successes.

By 1900 it had become clear that the ILP was not going to disintegrate into an unimportant group of protesters, it was not going to be reabsorbed into the Liberal party, and it could not be dismissed as a body of naïve idealists. Nevertheless, the Liberals found it hard to accept that the socialists were a permanent fact of local political life. A letter to the *Keighley News* in 1901 shows how sensitive the Liberals had become to the threat of the ILP, while by no means sympathizing with their demands:

> Public life in Keighley has become vulgarised. If I am a candidate I should have to endure questions prompted by the malice of employees whom I have discharged for drunkenness and idleness. There are men who now hold public office in Keighley who make it their business to retail such slanders, and thus prevent the candidature of men of any standing. I may be jaundiced but it seems as if the electors prefer to vote for a man whose reputation has been soiled ... The old spirit of self help and self reliance seems to have died out in Keighley. The popular trick now is to whine about the conditions of life being wrong ... Already I am told Corporation employees help to choose candidates and to pay their election expenses.[79]

The above quotation shows how bitter some Liberals felt towards the Labour party. An analysis of the kind of people who were officers of the

Keighley Liberal party indicates that they were unlikely to be sympathetic towards the aspirations of the ILP. By examining the minute books and extracting the names of the individuals who stood for election to Ward Committees in 1887 and 1890 and who were delegates at the General Meeting in 1893, it is possible to name 442 people who can be considered to be committed Liberals in Keighley when the ILP was formed. Of these 442, the occupations of 275 (62%) have been identified. In Table 4.4 (p.131) these have been divided into 5 occupational categories: (a) managerial/ professional, (b) service and retail, (c) craftsmen, (d) skilled industrial, and (e) clerical. Of these, the managerial and professional group had 101 members, with textiles having 23 representatives, the engineering trade 22, and the professions 15. The service and retail group had 117 members, of which the largest section were shopkeepers, with 11 people actually described this way, a further 26 as grocers and greengrocers, 10 as drapers and 8 as tailors, making 47 shopkeepers in all. The same group also contained 10 coal dealers. The craftsmen had 34 members, including 8 painters and 7 joiners. The skilled industrial workers numbered 16 and included 5 mechanics, 4 overlookers and 3 foremen. The clerical contingent consisted of only 7, with 4 teachers, including the Horner brothers, 2 insurance agents, including Michael Howley, and a clerk. The one person who described himself as a gentleman, and the 9 as private residents, were included in the managerial professional group, as they were largely retired businessmen. No unskilled workers were identified, although they may be included in the 38 per cent whose occupations have not been located. Similarly, few trade-union activists were pin-pointed.[80]

Even with the significant percentage of people whose occupations have not been located, the conclusion can be drawn that the Keighley Liberal party was run largely by people who were employers of labour, whether in a mill, an engineering firm or a retail establishment. As such, most of them were unlikely to be sympathetic to either the political or the economic aspirations of the working class. Among the Liberal activists who were not employers of labour, most who worked in industry were overlookers or foremen with positions of authority, whose views were influenced by their employers. It is not surprising, therefore, that the Liberals paid no more than lip service to trade-union and working-class demands or that their policies would be regarded unsympathetically by the Keighley ILPers. Although Labour and Liberal manifestos often said the same things, the Liberals, typified by someone like John Clough, with his old-fashioned radicalism, were happier demanding traditional reforms such as the disestablishment of the Anglican Church, while the ILP wanted more radical changes.

An example of the way in which the Liberals emphasized issues which were essentially traditional and which the newly emerging Labour party would not regard as central to their concerns can be seen in 1890. A year after the bitter engineering strike, when the Trades Council had just been established and the prospect of an independent party of labour was being seriously considered, the chief concern of the Keighley Liberals was not the industrial and political upheaval taking place in the town, but that the extension of the burial ground should contain both consecrated and unconsecrated portions.[81] Two years later, a Liberal wrote to the *Keighley News*: 'I appeal to the ratepayers to show the spirit of their fathers and defend the position won by struggle and suffering for our predecessors. ... All we ask is an equality ... and ask the friends of Liberty to rally to the old standard tomorrow in the Parish Churchyard.'[82]

It was a topic which raised genuine passions, but it had little to do with the central economic and political topic of the day, which concerned the relations between capital and labour. For the Liberals, however, it was a safe subject which would rally the party against its traditional enemies: the Church of England and the Conservatives. Such religious issues would always unite the Liberals and they returned to them on more than one occasion. In particular, they opposed the 1902 Education Act, which they said 'will do nothing to further the interests of education, but will revive sectarian disputes'.[83] Other traditional issues which concerned the party in the years before 1914 included free trade, which was under attack from Joseph Chamberlain's Fair Trade campaign. The Divisional Liberal Association minuted that 'the tax on corn though a small thing in itself it [the Association] believes it to be the thin edge of the wedge of Protection and enters its protest against a measure that can only lead to dearer bread for the people and increased rents for the landlords'.[84] The interests of temperance were equally important. In 1904 the Keighley Division urged the parliamentary party to make every effort to defeat the Licensing Bill, 'as it creates a vested interest in a yearly licence, and places further obstacles in the way of temperance reform'.[85] During the 1910 House of Lords crisis, the Divisional Association firmly backed the Liberal government, heartily approving:

> the measures which the Government proposes to take in order to limit the veto of the House of Lords on legislation and undertakes to support the King's ministers in their efforts to frustrate the attempts of that Chamber to arrogate to itself exclusive power in the State by depriving the Crown of its exclusive control over the public purse.[86]

The ILP, of course, agreed with the Liberals on many of these measures. Herbert Horner was a passive resister in 1902 and the Keighley ILP resolved that the Education Bill:

> has been formed solely in the interests of the Church and Clergy and that the proposal to disestablish the School Boards of England in favour of a State system of so-called Voluntary Schools is so glaring an injustice

> that if it is not at once withdrawn the only remedy will be to commence an agitation for the immediate disestablishment and disendowment of a church which is no longer a national institution, but the creature of one particular party in the state.[87]

Philip Snowden was a noted advocate of temperance, and the Keighley ILP branch separated itself from the Alice Street ILP Club over the question of drink, with Tom Mackley writing that 'members of the Labour Union severed their connection with them [the Alice Street ILP Club] owing to the fact that they introduced alcoholic drink into their rooms and while keeping the name of the ILP it was nothing more than a social club'.[88] Nor was the House of Lords popular. However, these issues were not central to the Keighley ILP, and on the teetotal question the party argued that 'some temperance speakers are very fond of telling us they "hate the drink" but we go further, and hate the causes that produce drunkenness'.[89] These were, according to the party members, poverty, overwork and the selling of drink for private profit. They saw two difficulties as preventing them from working with the Liberals. The first was ideological: each party had a different set of beliefs. An article in the *Keighley Labour Journal* makes the point:

> There is not a political reform to which the Liberals are pledged, which would not receive the support of Labour members. Payment of Members, one man, one vote, disestablishment, both of the Church and the House of Lords. On these questions the Labour party are as earnest and probably much more so than the Liberals are, only they are not to be bribed by these things by coalition with that party. Why do you ask? Because these are only the mere fringe of what we are desirous of accomplishing. As a party we are not formed to do these things, though we have no objections to help in the doing of them in our own way. Our programme is one which comes into direct conflict with some of the supposed interests of prominent Liberals, and therefore we hold it wise to maintain an independent attitude, and work for the accomplishment of this programme irrespective of the particular wishes or desires of either of the so called great parties. We desire to banish monopoly and competition, to prevent the wholesale robbery of the poor which now takes place, and to banish poverty from the land. Our method of doing this is the municipalisation or nationalisation of the land and the means of production. A proposal founded, as we believe, on the pure right of the worker to the results of his labour.[90]

Second, it was not enough for the ILP simply to reform the existing political and economic system; it had actually to be changed. Clearly, this was a fundamental difference between the two parties and no amount of common ground on individual policies would make it possible for them to work together. In addition, the ILP just did not believe that the Liberals would carry out the parts of their programme which most affected the demands of labour. This distrust is frequently referred to in speeches and articles written by members of the local ILP. For example, in 1895, Philip Snowden, when discussing the payment of MPs, stated that he:

> envied the simple faith of those who believed they were likely to get payment of members from the Liberal Party. They had been in office for three years, pledged to this reform, there had been no obstacle to prevent them giving payment of members, they had simply refused it, and now they came before the people and asked them to return them to power to give payment to members.[91]

Thus, although there could be considerable agreement in their policies, the differences between the two parties made it impossible for them to work together. It is noticeable that in neither the Divisional nor the Borough Liberal Association minutes is there any expression of sympathy towards working-class aspirations and in 1908 the Borough Association gave a tart rebuff to the Keighley Distress Committee. The Committee secretary, J. W. Waterworth, an ILPer who was elected town auditor for a number of years, wrote asking the Liberals to nominate a representative to the Committee, which aimed at 'lessening the severity of the local distress consequent upon unemployment'. The Liberals replied that they could not, as a political organization, appoint representatives on the Distress Committee, which may have been true but which was not seen by the ILP as helpful.[92]

The Liberal programme emphasized the traditional interests of the party – Nonconformity, free trade, temperance and individual freedom – policies which, until 1908, were politically successful even though they did not fulfil the demands of the organized working class, i.e. the eight-hour day, trade-union organization, fair contracts clauses and municipalization. As has been said, the traditional appeal of Liberalism ensured it a majority on the Town Council from 1885 until 1907, and a Liberal MP until 1919. In addition, the threat to Liberalism, when it came, was not only from the left, but also from the Conservative party. Old-fashioned Liberalism retained its appeal amongst much of the electorate, and there was no need for the Keighley Liberals to modify their policies to accommodate the parties to the left of them.

Nevertheless, it was the intransigence of the local Liberal party to the demands of Labour which led to the establishment of the Keighley Labour Union in 1893. Some of the early members of the local ILP had been Liberal activists, although they were far from the real centres of political power. Most prominent among them were the Horner brothers. In 1887 Herbert was elected to the Keighley 300, and in the same year his brother Edward was elected to the North-West Ward Committee. By 1890 Herbert had been elected to the Central Executive Committee of the Borough Liberal Association.[93] Other ILPers who had been active Liberals were Albert Schoon, trade-union leader and organizer of the Merralls strike at Haworth in 1893; in 1887 he was secretary of the South Ward Liberals. In the same year Henry Newton, a founder member of the Labour Union, was nominated by the Liberals as a candidate for the South Ward in the borough elections. In 1887 and 1890 George Gill, who in 1893 was elected as a Labour member of the School Board, was a representative on the North-East Ward Committee of the Liberal party.[94] The best known of these activists who moved from Liberalism to socialism was Philip Snowden, who remained a firm supporter of the Liberal party until the mid-1890s and took part in the activities of the Nelson Liberation Society.

After the founding of the Labour Union, these ex-Liberals often clashed with the Liberal party leaders. Personal antipathy and accusations of betrayal exacerbated political and ideological differences. Many of the early ILPers were stubborn people with intransigent natures, strong personalities and a deep sense of grievance. Philip Snowden was admired, but the violent rhetoric of his speeches and his quick tongue made him many enemies. Herbert Horner had a difficult personality which hindered and eventually blighted his career. As early as his first municipal contest, his obstinacy was noted. The *Keighley News* commented in 1893 that 'Mr Horner is not a pliant candidate, and declined to give pledges which would almost certainly have secured him victory. We do not say this, to his discredit, for pliancy is not the stuff out of which martyrs are made.'[95] He fell out with many politicians, including, eventually, Keir Hardie and, locally, his erstwhile ally Henry Newton. 'Was it Hornerism', a letter writer asked in 1901, 'that drove him [Newton] out of the ILP, or was it Socialism.'[96] By 1901, Horner and John Clough were personal as well as political enemies. Clough reported in a speech that:

> Herbert Horner is only qualified to represent one man, and they call that man Herbert. I have watched that man's career ever since he was known in Keighley, ever since I was a member of the School Board and I know as much about it as most, and I have come to the conclusion that it is simply a question of his own position and of what he can get out of it.[97]

Personal antagonism thus made the possibility of Liberals and ILPers working together more difficult. With John Clough's bluntness and Herbert Horner's suspicion, it was never likely that a working relationship between the two groups would be possible. The arrival of Philip Snowden, with his delight in insult and command of the rhetoric of extremism, made a bad situation worse; it was improbable that John Clough would try to work with a party which described him as a blood-sucking vampire.

Political manoeuvring further widened the differences between the two groups. In particular, in 1898 the ILP made an agreement with the Conservatives to get two Tories and Herbert Horner elected as aldermen. They were successful, but the Liberals never forgot and the ILP was still defensively justifying their piece of political opportunism at the turn of the century. C. H. Brown, on behalf of the ILP, said in 1901:

> I know that the Aldermanic deal of three years ago has been dubbed Hornerism ... I would like to give an explanation of the aldermanic deal as it would appear to the unbiased mind. Since the entry into political circles of the ILP, municipal contests have been round the subject of municipalisation. That being so there is a straight dividing line between the ILP and the other two parties. On this question at any rate they are both as one in supporting private enterprise, so that the point when the ILP members of the Council had to choose between electing three representatives of the private enterprise school who happened to call themselves Liberals, or, on the other hand, voting for two of the same school of thought who called themselves Tories and one ILP man or municipaliser. By choosing the latter course the ILP gained two votes on a division because they got another ILP man on the Council at the bye election. Yet there are some people that have the audacity to blame the ILP for taking the only reasonable course open to them.[98]

To sum up, there was no Lib-Lab agreement in Keighley and it was never likely that the ILP and the Liberals would be able to work together. The Liberals were dominated by a group which had little sympathy for the aspirations of the working class and which regarded the socialists as naïve dreamers or troublemakers. The dependence of the Liberals on the financial backing of this small group meant that the party never made any attempt to win the ILPers back to Liberalism or to create a political alliance with them. Difficulties in personal relations between the socialists and the Liberals aggravated the differences in the policies between the two parties. The Liberal instinct was to continue to emphasize the old-fashioned aspects of Liberalism, and old-fashioned Gladstonian policies still had enough appeal to ensure that the Liberals would remain the strongest political group in the town for much of the period up to 1914.

The Conservative party, on the other hand, achieved its greatest successes in the years after 1900, when it secured control of the Borough Council. However, there had always been a Conservative group in Keighley, dating back to the 1840s and Richard Oastler's Ten Hours Movement. In the 1850s and '60s the party was seen as the political arm of the Church of England and its chief concern was the defence of the Church's position against the disestablishment campaign of the Nonconformist radicals, in which many of Keighley's leading Liberals, such as the Clough and Brigg families, participated. In 1873, a Conservative newspaper, the *Keighley Herald*, was established, lasting until 1911. This paper was seen as an essential adjunct of the local organization, and the local Conservative agent urged everyone to buy it, for it was a 'silent and sure means of influencing and consolidating the principles of Constitutionalism in the minds of the electors', being 'really an official document in which letters of advice, advertisements and news appealing to his party appeared'.[99] In 1903, the owner of the *Herald* decided to shut it down, largely because he wished to retire; after various expedients had been tried, the party decided to take over responsibility for the paper itself.[100] The alternative was to let reports of its activities be published by the Liberal *Keighley News*.

Nationally, a number of moderate Liberals in the 1880s were becoming restive and inclining towards the Tories. As has been noted, many disliked Gladstone's foreign policy for what they regarded as its weakness. They thought government policy in Ireland was appeasement. Locally, this was a sensitive issue with, on the one hand, the large Irish community being committed to Home Rule and thus the Liberal party, and, on the other, anti-Irish feelings always simmering among those who resented the immigrants. They resented the radicals' support of Charles Bradlaugh, who was elected to Parliament but was not allowed to take his seat because he would not take the oath, and they were also hostile to the radical proposal for the Local Veto, which would have given localities the right to forbid the licensing of pubs and which brought the Liberals the reputation of being killjoys. It is, perhaps, not surprising that Timothy Taylor, Keighley's most prominent brewer, was a member of the Conservative party, although he took no active part in town life or in the work of the party. Some Liberals were attracted by the Conservatives' enthusiasm for imperialism, which appealed to many of the middle and working classes and to local businessmen who were looking to the Empire to replace markets which were being closed to them by new tariff barriers. In May 1886, the Keighley Conservative Association resolved 'that this meeting distrusts any measure tending to the dismemberment of the Empire'.[101] Moderate Liberals also found themselves excluded from influence within the local Liberal associations. They therefore started to drift into the Conservative party, a trend which was emphasized after 1886 when Gladstone's Home Rule Bill for Ireland split the Liberals nationally, causing many moderates to turn to the Conservatives or the Liberal Unionists. The latter were opposed to Home Rule in Ireland and soon became an adjunct of the Conservatives. By 1890, in Keighley, the Conservatives were meeting with the Liberal Unionists to find a suitable parliamentary candidate, and the following year the Conservative agent was being offered to the Unionists to help them in their campaigns.[102] However, personal commitment to Sir Isaac Holden, the Division's Liberal MP, and, after his retirement, to John Brigg, who succeeded him, kept many Liberals loyal.

The Conservatives also attracted increased rank-and-file support. They appealed to much of the lower-middle-class vote, which had increased towards the end of the century with the expansion of jobs in shopkeeping, local government, schoolteaching and clerical work. Many of this group felt threatened by the working class and deferential to their social superiors and were attracted to the Conservative emphasis on firm government, the defence of national institutions, patriotism and the Empire. The Keighley District Association routinely sent resolutions to the government praising the Empire. In 1906 it expressed 'its hearty welcome to the colonial premiers on their visit to the Mother Country and earnestly entreats them not to desist from their efforts to promote the cause of Imperial unity'.[103] There were also a number of working-class Conservatives, some of whom could trace the support of their families back to the 1840s and the Factory Reform movement. Some working-class support, however, was anti-Irish, anti-education, anti-temperance, and fervently nationalistic, and the Tories were not averse to accepting such votes.

In 1885, the Third Reform Act created the Keighley Parliamentary Division. In April of that year the Central Conservative Association for the Division was formed.[104] Those who formed the Association included a number of leading textile millowners, such as the Merrall family of Haworth, the Marriners, and their family and business associate William Naylor, Richard Edmundson, and, most notably, Joseph Ellison Haggas. Other businessmen included John Spencer and the Summerscales family, who were engineers, and C. H. Foulds, who was a tanner. However, most of the Conservative activists were in the professions. These included William and R. B. Broster, who were architects; W. L. Brown, a banker; Edwin Chaffers, a doctor; James Clarkson, a solicitor; Hiram France, who managed a newspaper; Robert Lister, a china merchant; and Thomas Lister, an auctioneer. Thus, although the structure of the party was similar in some ways to the Liberals, having a number of textile manufacturers and engineers at the top providing much of the money, many prominent local Conservatives were from a slightly different social group.[105]

The Conservatives had to wait twenty years before they achieved major political success. It was not until 1908 that they got a majority on the Borough Council, but from then on they rarely lost control. By 1911, when a by-election took place, they had reduced the Liberal MP's majority to less than a thousand.

In their struggle for electoral success, the Conservatives had a number of advantages. From the start, they were well organized. They always had a full-time agent, though he never stayed very long, probably because the pay was poor. The first agent was paid £100 a year and by 1914 this had risen to £130. The agents introduced systematic canvassing, paid careful attention to registration, formed Ward Committees and encouraged the creation of Conservative social clubs, which became important centres of Tory activity.

The Division was divided into districts, each with its own committee, and the Borough of Keighley itself was organized by Ward Committees. In addition, a series of Conservative Clubs were formed. These were seen as particularly important for educating people in Conservative principles, although they were also social centres, for 'if the young men join an opposition club for the sake of company or a game of billiards, they imbibe Liberalism from the conversation which goes on around them, and then follows a natural desire to be on the side of the majority'.[106] They were used for talks and debates on political subjects, particularly at election times. In 1892, the Conservative agent outlined the role of the clubs in the Division.

> There has been a quickening of political life throughout the Division. In all the clubs there has been organised a system of periodical political debates. These discussions serve a double purpose, they supply the members with information and they bring young speakers to the front and encourage the diffident to take a fair share in the debate. It is highly desirable they should be energetically pushed forward in every club until an army of local speakers is produced, able to influence public opinion in a Conservative direction. Wilsden is to be congratulated on its excellent course of lectures just completed. Thornton, Denholme Gate and Denholme have had almost as good a series ... Haworth dovetails its lectures into its smoking concerts and so secures a good attendance.[107]

However, the hope of combining political education with social life tended to break down, and the clubs were always likely to become mere drinking places; 'the working men's club at Thwaite's is perfectly useless as a political machine and the committee declined to have a course of lectures in the building, although offered free of expense to them'.[108]

Nevertheless, the clubs remained important to the party. They also spent much time organizing the committees which ran the divisional party. In April 1895 the *Annual Report* remarked that 'special attention has been given to organisation. Branch Associations have been formed at Sutton, Glusburn and Steeton. In other parts of the Division, Ward and Polling District Committees have been formed.'[109] Twelve years later J. E. Haggas, President of both the Borough and Divisional Associations, said:

> He should like to see formed in some of the out districts small associations within the Divisional Association. Spade work was really the best and most effective part of the organisation. Public meetings did not benefit a party to the extent that was done by steady plodding work, week by week, and month by month ... They knew that Haworth did carry on this spade work, and he hoped that good results would come of it, and Wilsden always set a good example to some of the outlying parts of the Division ... he was convinced that this was one of the most

> important parts of their work – spade work – organisation – the education of those that really did not know what benefits they could get from holding Unionist principles.[110]

James Ellison Haggas emphasized the need for an efficient political machine. He was a man of great ability and dynamism and his talents were widely appreciated in the party. Sam Clough of Steeton said in 1905 that 'Mr Haggas had whipped the party into more energetic life and it behoved the members of the party to support him whole-heartedly', a sentiment that was repeated frequently over the years.[111] He realized the importance of the party having its own newspaper and ensured the survival of the *Keighley Herald*, negotiating with the owner when he wished to close it down, then with the *Bradford Argus* to see if they would print it, and finally putting together a local group of Tories to publish the paper themselves. He, more than any other activist, realized the importance of developing an organized party machine, of keeping up the members' enthusiasm and not letting it run down in the periods between elections. As late as 1911, when he was succeeded by C. H. Foulds on the Borough Association, he was urging the Annual General Meeting to 'try and get more enthusiasm into not only their workers, but also into their supporters'.[112] He remained president of the Divisional Association until after 1914, and under his general leadership the Keighley Conservatives secured their first majority on the Council.

The Conservatives achieved their political success not only by the efficiency of their party machine or by utilizing national sentiments, such as enthusiasm for the Empire, but also by exploiting splits in the local Liberal party and attacking their record when they were in power. They condemned the Liberals for being extravagant and put themselves forward as being prudent managers of ratepayers' money. J. E. Haggas declared, in the year that the Conservatives took control of the Council, that:

> they had taught their opponents that they could not spend ratepayers money as they liked without hearing anything about it. The result had been very satisfactory to them as a party, and it ought to be satisfactory to them as ratepayers. They had got control of the Council ... by putting on the Council those they thought would be more careful in the way they spent the ratepayers money.[113]

The Tories also portrayed themselves as exponents of open government, promising in 1908 that 'there should be no hole and corner work in any shape or form. Everything would have to be exposed to the public gaze.'[114] It was, of course, a simple matter to make these claims before they achieved a working majority on the Council. However, it is interesting to note that, once they had achieved a majority, they were perfectly willing to come to an electoral agreement with the Liberals in order to 'retain as far as possible personnel on the Council on account of the important works and undertakings now being carried on'.[115]

Splits among the Liberals helped the Tories in various ways. There were some defections in the 1880s over Ireland, when, for example, the Hattersleys and the Lunds changed their political views, and in 1891 Benjamin Septimus Brigg, a scion of one of the leading Liberal families, was approached to see if he would contest the Division in the Unionist cause.[116] Nothing more was heard of the suggestion, and Brigg continued on the Town Council as a Liberal. The Boer War and the 1902 Education Act also caused some Liberals to reconsider their position. In 1906 the Borough Association's *Annual Report* remarks that Central Ward was won by a Liberal, but one who declared himself a supporter of the Education Bill, and in 1907 West Ward was won by a Liberal 'whose views seem to be considerably elastic', being 'a denominationalist over education and a supporter of Liberal politics on other fronts'.[117] In the same year there are indications that the hitherto strongly Liberal Catholic vote was becoming less tied to that party. The Conservative Borough Association minutes record that the Catholic vote was 'going with the Conservative party'.[118]

Nevertheless, it took the Conservatives many years to gain control of the Council and they did not succeed in electing an MP for the Division until after the First World War. Liberalism remained strong, particularly in the districts outside the borough. In 1907 Haggas said that 'the great weakness of their [the Conservative] party was not in the borough, but in the outside districts'. Two years later he was wishing 'they could have Cowling, Crosshills and Steeton brought up to the same extent as had marked Haworth, Wilsden and Denholme', in which case 'the office of President of the Keighley Conservative Division Association would be even a pleasanter one'.[119]

A major problem with winning the parliamentary seat was the difficulty of finding a suitable candidate. The Liberals always chose local men, either Isaac Holden or John Brigg, who were major employers and well respected locally. This gave them an advantage over the Conservatives, who had to import candidates and accept anyone who was prepared to stand in what was always going to be a difficult seat to win. Standing as a candidate was expensive and although the local party was prepared to contribute some funds, a candidate had to be willing to 'pay all election costs, above the amount promised'.[120] There were, therefore, difficulties involved in securing a representative. For example, in July 1885 H. E. Foster was invited to stand for the Division. In September he declined. In October, R. C. Gill of London was invited, and it was agreed that, if he refused, John Birbeck of Settle would be asked, and if he did not accept, Mr Johnson of London should be approached. None of these potential candidates felt able to accept the invitation, so H. E. Foster was asked again. He refused again and W. H. C. Dunhill was approached. He also refused, and Walter Bairstow was invited. He did agree to contest the Division, but only if Isaac Holden was not the Liberal candidate. This was accepted, but then Bairstow and the Executive Committee of the Conservative Association quarrelled, so R. L. Hattersley was asked, but he declined. By this time it was March 1889, and the question of finding a candidate was dropped. The matter was raised at a meeting in June 1892, but the only agreement that could be reached was that, 'on the understanding that Mr Holden will certainly seek re-election, out of respect for him, and in consideration of his advanced age, the Executive of the Conservative Association on receiving his assurance that he will seek re-election, refrain from opposing him'.[121] Not surprisingly, Holden graciously 'expressed his deep gratification that the Unionist Party at his age had not put him to the physical fatigue of a contest'.[122]

Similar problems were experienced in the years before 1914. Walter Bairstow contested the elections of 1900, but was not prepared to carry on nursing the seat. In April 1902, therefore:

> the name of Mr Frank Hatchard was suggested at the meeting and it was agreed that Mr Wyvill should ask if he would entertain the suggestion if asked by the committee. In the event of Mr Hatchard not consenting to consider the matter it was agreed that Mr Wyvill communicate with Mr Porter, a son of Sir William Porter, sounding him on the matter. If, however, Mr Wyvill came across any other gentlemen, he should see what they thought and report to a further meeting to be held for that purpose.[123]

By January 1903, Myles Stapleton, Amcott Wilson, Whitaker Thompson, Clement Thompson and W. Sheepshanks had also been approached. W. M. Acworth finally agreed to be the candidate, and he also stood, though reluctantly, in the first election of 1910. In November 1910 the Conservatives again had to admit defeat, and resolved that 'in the event of Sir John Brigg being adopted as the Liberal candidate for the Division, he shall not be opposed'.[124] He did stand and he was not opposed. In 1911 Sir John Brigg died and there was a by-election. Acworth stood again and lost. Then Lord Lascelles, son of the Earl of Harewood, agreed to stand, but he too lost in the contest of 1913.

The Conservatives soon realized that the chief difficulty with their candidates was that they were not local men. In 1902 it was 'suggested that it would probably be best if the Committee could persuade a local gentleman to become a candidate'.[125] In the inquest over the defeat of 1910, Sam Clough said: 'perhaps Mr Acworth's weakness ... was that he was not a local man',[126] and this after Acworth had fought the seat three times. Not even Lascelles, who was 'a Yorkshireman who lived within easy distance of the constituency ... [and was] almost a local man',[127] could quite match Isaac Holden or John Brigg. As late as 1913, members of the Executive Committee were 'of the opinion that if Keighley was to be won by the Conservative Party they must have a local businessman as their candidate'.[128]

Nor was it just parliamentary elections that posed difficulties. In local elections, too, the Conservatives found it difficult to get people to stand. In 1892 the minutes of the Annual General Meeting recorded that 'one difficulty is the want of candidates, another is the question of expenses. Moreover the character of some of our public bodies does not seem to hold out sufficient inducement for the most able men to join them.'[129]

The main problem with getting local men to stand for elected positions was, as the above quotation notes, the expense. Sam Clough summed up the dilemma of the local politician in 1910, when he said: 'the demands of parliament were such that a Member must live in London. That meant that a local man had practically to break up his home and sever all his family ties. That was a big sacrifice for a man to make for so uncertain a thing as politics.'[130] Even for J. E. Haggas, who was the obvious local candidate, there were problems, 'because his business held him tight and it was almost impossible for him to stand'.[131] The Holdens and the Briggs might have the leisure and desire as well as the wealth to be able to take up politics as a full-time career, but none of the local Tories had either the commitment or the money.

A further problem for the Conservatives was that the Liberals had been dominant for so long that people assumed that they almost had a right to run local elected bodies. The Liberals had dug themselves into the political infrastructure of the town to such a degree that it took the Conservatives two decades to get them out. The *Keighley Herald* describes the problem in 1905. Quoting Sam Clough, it said the Conservatives:

> wanted young men to take up positions which became vacant. The great strength of the Liberal party in the Keighley Division had come largely in that way. Whenever there had been a good position open it had seemed to be filled by a man who was Liberal in politics. He did not know why it had been so, but he had noticed it for many years past. Said Mr Clough: 'We want to get the positions filled by Unionists and so gradually get hold, socially and politically of the people in the Division.'[132]

Lastly, the Conservatives had the problem of the challenge of the ILP. This was not as great a threat to them as it was to the Liberals, but the ILP was seen as a nuisance and perhaps more, for it took away some working-class votes which would otherwise have gone to the Tories. In 1906, for example, the Tories held the Labour candidate responsible for their defeat. James Haggas said that the ILP had split the Unionist vote. The Liberals:

> thought that they, the Unionists, had been the means of bringing forward a Labour candidate. He believed that some radicals honestly

> thought that the Labour candidates expenses were being subscribed by the leaders of the Unionist party ... [but] ... from the very first he felt that the advent of a Labour candidate would work against their having any satisfactory result ... In the Borough where the great strength of the Unionist party lay the Labour candidate succeeded in winning over a good many of those whom they had every right to look upon as active supporters of Mr Acworth and but for Mr Newlove's advent he had not the slightest hesitation in saying that their votes would be recorded for Unionism.

The same danger was perceived in the run up to the 1910 election, when the Conservatives thought they had a chance of victory, but:

> the danger to their party would lie in the votes which might be taken away by the Labour Party; but if the trade-unionists could only be got to realise that the Conservative Party was the one to support and help them, then the Conservative Party would poll its own votes and Mr Acworth would be returned.[133]

There was thus a three-way struggle for votes in Keighley in the years between 1885 and 1914. The ILP took support from the Liberals and, to a lesser extent, from the Tories. The Tories took votes from the Liberals and tried to limit the appeal of the ILP among their supporters. The Liberals lost votes to both parties, but such was their pre-eminence in local politics that they could afford to see a rise in support for the two other parties without losing their dominance as the most important political group until 1908, when they lost control of the Borough Council, but they retained their ability to elect the local MP until after 1918.

Notes

1. K. Laybourn, *The Rise of Labour: the British Labour Party 1880–1979* (London, 1988), pp.15–16.
2. James, 'Philip Snowden and the Keighley Independent Labour Party', in Laybourn and James, *op.cit.*, *Philip Snowden*.
3. *The Clarion*, 21 April 1900.
4. Reynolds and Laybourn, 'The Emergence of the Independent Labour Party in Bradford', *op.cit.*; Laybourn and James (eds), *The Rising Sun of Socialism*, *op.cit.*; Clark, *op.cit.*; Woodhouse, *op.cit.*; Hill, *op.cit.*; Walton, *op.cit.*
5. *Keighley Year Book*, 1902.
6. 'During the past year 19 old names have been struck off the books, 45 new members have been added leaving the membership at 133 new members.' Report of the secretary for 1903, Keighley ILP, Letter Book, January 1904.
7. Cross, *op.cit.*, p.33.

8. Keighley ILP, Minutes, 12 November 1895, 22 September 1896, 7 February 1897.
9. Report of the secretary for 1903, Keighley ILP, Letter Book, January 1904.
10. Keighley ILP, Minutes, 4 April 1895.
11. Keighley ILP, Letter Book, 27 April 1904.
12. *Keighley Labour Journal*, 1 April 1898.
13. Keighley ILP, Letter Book, 17 June 1904.
14. *Keighley News*, 18 October 1905.
15. 'Mr Horner is not a pliant candidate and declined to give pledges which would almost certainly have secured his victory. We do not say this to his discredit, for pliancy is not the stuff out of which martyrs are made.' *Keighley News*, 4 November 1893.
16. *Ibid.*, 28 March 1896, 18 March 1899.
17. Keighley ILP, Minutes, 8 November 1894.
18. See Table 4.1.
19. This information is taken from the Keighley ILP, Minutes, January–December 1897.
20. See Table 6.1.
21. Keighley ILP, Letter Book, 25 February 1905.
22. Cross, *op.cit.*, p.44.
23. Keighley ILP, Minutes, March–November 1905, *passim*.
24. *Keighley Labour Journal*, 28 January 1899.
25. *Labour Leader*, 10 September 1898.
26. *Ibid.*, 3 December 1898.
27. *Keighley News*, 29 October, 5 November 1904.
28. *Keighley Labour Journal*, 28 November 1902.
29. Letter to *Keighley News*, 28 October 1905.
30. *Yorkshire Factory Times*, 27 March 1908.
31. *Keighley News*, 29 October 1905.
32. *Keighley Herald*, 8 March 1907.
33. *Ibid.*, 8 March 1907.
34. *Ibid.*, 27 September 1907.
35. *Ibid.*, 26 October 1906.
36. *Ibid.*, 19 July 1907.
37. Keighley ILP, Minutes, 7 January 1907.
38. *Keighley Herald*, 28 August 1908.
39. National Labour Party, Agent's report, October 1911.
40. Laybourn and Reynolds, *Liberalism and the Rise of Labour*, *op.cit.*, pp.165–6.
41. *Keighley Herald*, 19 February 1909.
42. *Keighley News*, 29 October 1904.
43. *Keighley Herald*, 8 March 1907.
44. Keighley ILP, Minutes, 18 February 1904.
45. *Keighley Labour Journal*, 22 March 1896.
46. *Ibid.*, 21 March 1899.
47. *Keighley Echo*, 7 November 1894.
48. *Keighley Labour Journal*, 18 November 1894.
49. Keighley ILP, Minutes, 9 November 1910.
50. *Keighley Labour Journal*, 8 March 1896.

51. *Ibid.*, 20 March 1897.
52. This information is derived largely from the *Keighley Labour Journal*, *passim*.
53. See Table 4.3.
54. *Keighley News*, 19 October 1901.
55. *Ibid.*, 2 November 1901.
56. The information in this paragraph comes from *Keighley Labour Journal*, 20 October 1905.
57. *Keighley News*, 29 October 1904.
58. *Ibid.*, 12 October 1901.
59. Cross, *op.cit.*, pp.44–5.
60. *Keighley Labour Journal*, 18 March 1905.
61. *Ibid.*, 26 September 1902.
62. *Keighley News*, 14 September 1901.
63. *Ibid.*, 7 January 1893.
64. *Ibid.*, 26 March 1892.
65. *Ibid.*, 22 October 1892.
66. *Ibid.*, 6 July 1895.
67. *Ibid.*, 1 April 1893.
68. *Ibid.*, 17 June 1893.
69. *Ibid.*
70. *Ibid.*, 24 June 1893.
71. *Ibid.*, 7 October 1893. The 'Independent Labour Party, which started with something like a flourish of trumpets a few months ago has not "caught on" at Bingley.'
72. Keighley ILP, Letter Book, 11 May 1904.
73. Laybourn and Reynolds, *Liberalism and the Rise of Labour*, *op.cit.*, pp.81–9.
74. *Keighley News*, 27 April 1895.
75. *Ibid.*, 27 April 1895.
76. *Ibid.*, 6 July 1895.
77. *Ibid.*, 20 July 1895.
78. *Ibid.*, 27 July 1895.
79. *Ibid.*, 19 October 1901.
80. This information was extracted from the Keighley Borough Liberal Association, Minutes, and the Keighley Divisional Liberal Association, Minutes.
81. Keighley Borough Liberal Association, Annual Report, 1891–3, contained in Keighley Borough Liberal Association, Minutes, 18 February 1893.
82. *Keighley News*, 18 February 1893.
83. Keighley Divisional Liberal Association, Minutes, 3 May 1902.
84. *Ibid.*
85. *Ibid.*, 14 May 1904.
86. *Ibid.*, 11 June 1910.
87. Keighley ILP, Letter Book, May 1902, no day given.
88. *Ibid.*, January 1903, no day given.
89. *Keighley Labour Journal*, 9 December 1894.
90. *Ibid.*, 17 February 1895.
91. *Keighley News*, 13 July 1895.
92. Keighley Borough Liberal Association, Minutes, 1908.
93. *Ibid.*, 4 April 1887, 14 June 1890.

94. *Ibid.*, 1887–90, *passim*.
95. *Keighley News*, 4 November 1893.
96. *Ibid.*, 9 November 1901.
97. *Ibid.*, 14 September 1901.
98. *Ibid.*, 9 November 1901.
99. *Keighley Herald*, 27 May 1891.
100. Keighley Divisional Conservative Association, Minutes, 1903–1905, *passim*.
101. Keighley Central Conservative Association, Minutes, 7 May 1886.
102. *Ibid.*, 13 October 1890, 11 November 1891.
103. Keighley Divisional Conservative Association, Minutes, 8 April 1906.
104. Keighley Central Conservative Association, Minutes, 25 April 1885.
105. *Ibid.*, 25 April, 20 May 1885.
106. *Ibid.*, 27 May 1892.
107. *Ibid.*
108. *Ibid.*
109. *Ibid.*, 27 April 1895.
110. Keighley Divisional Conservative Association, Minutes, 30 April 1907.
111. *Ibid.*, 10 May 1905.
112. *Ibid.*, 8 May 1911.
113. Keighley Borough Conservative Association, Minutes, 30 March 1908.
114. *Ibid.*
115. *Ibid.*
116. Keighley Divisional Conservative and Liberal Unionist Meetings, 13 May 1891.
117. Keighley Borough Conservative Association, Minutes, 21 March 1906, 20 March 1907.
118. *Ibid.*, 9 September 1907.
119. Keighley Divisional Conservative Association, Minutes, 30 April 1907, 17 May 1909.
120. Keighley Central Conservative Association, Minutes, 28 September 1885.
121. *Ibid.*, 9 June 1892.
122. *Ibid.*, 4 August 1892.
123. Keighley Divisional Conservative Association Executive Committee, Minutes, 7 April 1902.
124. Keighley Divisional Conservative Association, Minutes, 14 November 1910.
125. Keighley Divisional Conservative Association Executive Committee, Minutes, 7 April 1902.
126. Keighley Divisional Conservative Association, Minutes, 25 May 1910.
127. *Ibid.*, 28 October 1912.
128. *Ibid.*, 24 November 1913.
129. *Ibid.*, 27 May 1902.
130. *Ibid.*, 25 May 1910.
131. Keighley Borough Conservative Association, Minutes, 30 March 1908.
132. Keighley Divisional Conservative Association, Minutes, 10 May 1905.
133. *Ibid.*, 15 May 1906.

Table 4.1 Keighley ILP officers and Committee members, 1892–1900

October 1892	
Committee:	H. Horner, N. Roper, W. F. Hardy, A. Burrows, Richardson, A. Barnes, B. Spencer, G. J. Wardle, W. H. Thompson, B. Ogden, Bryce, A. E. Schoon
October 1892	
President:	Councillor Henry Newton
Vice-president:	A. Burrows
Treasurer:	B. Ogden
Secretary:	Nelson Roper
Executive Committee:	A. E. Schoon, G. J. Wardle, W. H. Thompson, H. Horner, Richardson, W. F. Hardy, Bateman, W. Robinson, Howells, Harrison, Booth
December 1893	
President:	W. Robinson
Vice-presidents:	John Moor, William Butler
Secretary:	H. Horner
Financial Secretary:	D. Parkinson
Treasurer:	E. Horner
Executive Committee:	W. Clayton, B. Spencer, R. Mackley, Mrs Roe, George Sewell, Bruce Atkinson, Sugden Holmes, M. R. Bignall, T. Dewhirst, F. Scott, Tom Mackley, A. Green, W. H. Thompson, Ed. Carter, George Steel, H. Armstrong
December 1894	
President:	Thomas Mackley
Vice-presidents:	Mrs Roe and John Moor
Financial Secretary:	Sugden Holmes
General Secretary:	H. Horner
Executive Committee:	Arthur Mackeen, Alex Bartle, E. Horner, Smith Wilcock, David Parkinson, W. F. Hardy, Mrs Schofield, W. Brown, Ernest Butterfield, William Butler, Mrs Slater, Ernest Utley, William Bramshaw, Robert Thistlethwaite, Henry Armstrong, Mrs Spencer

December 1895

President:	R. Thistlethwaite
Vice-presidents:	Ellis Foster and Heaton Hollings
Treasurer:	W. Robinson
Financial Secretary:	Sugden Holmes
General Secretary:	H. Horner
Lecture Secretary:	Ernest Butterfield
Assistant Secretary:	John Fergueson
Auditors:	Frank Smithson, Bruce Atkinson
Executive Committee:	N. W. Schofield, Miss Dixon, Mrs Roe, W. Parker, John Fergueson, Ernest Butterfield, William Emsworth, Tyndall Bland, Joseph Dixon, Mitchell Dixon, E. Horner, W. F. Hardy, Ernest Uttley, Smith Wilcock, Bruce Atkinson, Abraham Barnes

November 1896

Number of meetings attended in brackets after names (*=not recorded); 11 meetings held

President:	E. Horner (8)
Vice-presidents:	W. F. Hardy (7) and Sugden Holmes (3)
Treasurer:	W. Robinson (3)
Financial and General Secretary:	T. Mackley (11)
Auditors:	G. J. Wardle (3) and Philip Pickles (*)
Executive Committee:	Mary Jane Dixon (6), G. J. Wardle (3), Mrs Roe (11), William Parker (5), James Teal (2), H. Horner (8), John Fergueson (10), William Emmott (9), R. Hall (11), William Brown (2), Robert Thistlethwaite (4), John Sabey (6), G. R. Heiner (1), William Young (0), Mitchell Dixon (2)

December 1897

President:	E. Horner
Vice-presidents:	David Townson and W. F. Hardy
Treasurer:	G. J. Wardle
Financial and General Secretary:	T. Mackley
Auditors:	William Pickles and J. W. Bell
Executive Committee:	W. L. Wright, William Emmott, Miss Pickles, Mrs Roe, M. J. Dixon, John Fergueson, C. Whitehead, R. Thistlethwaite, W. R. Hall, H. Horner, F. Sabey, W. Parker, E. Uttley, R. Mackley, F. Appleby, John Rose

January 1899

Number of meetings attended in brackets after names; 12 meetings held

President:	W. F. Hardy (7)
Vice-presidents:	J. Teal (1) and Tom Mackley (12)
Treasurer:	E. Horner (8)
General Secretary:	E. Horner (8)
General Secretary:	T. Mackley (12)
Auditors:	W. Ellis, J. R. Green
Executive Committee:	P. Snowden (7), H. Horner (12), Mrs Barnes (9), Mrs Roe (10), Mrs Stell (8), W. R. Wright (11), Mrs Stansfield (5), B. Roff (12), W. Pickles (10), J. Scruton (5), R. Bradley (10), W. R. Hall (12), Miss Pickles (10), S. P. Holmes (4), Mrs Emmott (12), William Prosser (8), W. Richardson (7), R. Mackley (1)

January 1900

Number of meetings attended in brackets after names (*=not recorded); 14 meetings held

President:	J. Hargreaves (14)
Vice-presidents:	B. R. Roff (11) and C. Whitehead (6)
General Secretary:	Tom Mackley (14)
Assistant General Secretary:	J. H. Scruton (*)
Treasurer:	E. Horner (*)
Executive Committee:	H. Horner (11), W. Prosser (4), W. F. Hardy (4), P. Snowden (1), Mrs Stansfield (6), W. Pickles (13), W. Emmott (8), W. R. Hall (11), Mrs Roe (14), Mrs Emmott (8), W. Fisher (12), A. Ridding (10), W. Richardson (7), W. Bannister (6), R. Bradley (7), W. Brown (0)

Table 4.2 Alphabetical list of members of Keighley ILP Executive Committee, 1892–1900

	1892	1893	1894	1895	1896	1897	1898	1899	1900
F. Appleby							◆		
H. Armstrong			◆	◆					
B. Atkinson			◆		◆				
W. Bannister									◆
A. Barnes	◆				◆				
Miss Barnes								◆	
A. Bartle				◆					
Bateman		◆							
J. W. Bell							◆		
M. R. Bignall			◆						
T. Bland				◆					
Booth		◆							
R. Bradley							◆	◆	
W. Bramshaw				◆					
W. Brown				◆					
A. Burrows	◆	◆							
W. Butler			◆	◆					
E. Butterfield				◆	◆				
E. Carter			◆						
W. Clayton			◆						
T. Dewhirst			◆						
J. Dixon					◆				
Mitchell Dixon					◆	◆			
M. J. Dixon					◆	◆	◆	◆	◆
W. Emmott						◆		◆	◆
W. Ensworth					◆				
J. Fergueson					◆	◆	◆		
W. Fisher									◆
Ellis Foster					◆				
A. Green			◆						
R. Hall						◆	◆	◆	◆
W. F. Hardy	◆	◆		◆	◆	◆	◆	◆	
J. Hargreaves									◆
Harrison		◆							
G. R. Heiner					◆				
M. Hollings					◆				
E. Horner	◆	◆	◆	◆	◆	◆	◆	◆	◆
H. Horner		◆	◆	◆	◆	◆	◆	◆	◆
Howells		◆							
A. McKeen				◆					

	1892	1893	1894	1895	1896	1897	1898	1899	1900
R. Mackley			◆					◆	
T. Mackley			◆	◆		◆	◆	◆	◆
H. Newton		◆							
B. Ogden	◆	◆							
W. Parker				◆	◆	◆			
D. Parkinson			◆	◆					
Mrs Pickles							◆	◆	
P. Pickles						◆			
W. Pickles						◆	◆	◆	◆
W. Prosser								◆	◆
Richardson	◆	◆							
W. Robinson		◆	◆	◆	◆	◆			
Mrs Roe			◆	◆		◆	◆	◆	◆
B. Roff								◆	◆
Nelson Roper	◆	◆							
J. Rose							◆		
J. Sabey					◆	◆			
Mrs Schofield				◆	◆				
A. E. Schoon	◆	◆							
F. Scott			◆						
G. Sewell			◆						
Mrs Slater				◆					
F. Smithson					◆				
P. Snowden								◆	◆
B. Spencer	◆	◆							
Mrs Spencer				◆					
G. Steel			◆						
J. Teale						◆		◆	
R. Thistlethwaite			◆	◆	◆	◆			
W. H. Thompson	◆	◆							
D. Townson							◆		
E. Uttley			◆	◆		◆			
G. J. Wardle	◆	◆				◆			
C. Whitehead						◆			◆
S. Wilcock				◆	◆				
W. L. Wright						◆	◆		
W. Young						◆			

Note: ◆ indicates year on the Committee

Table 4.3 ILP election addresses, 1895–1898: summaries of programmes

Municipal Election 1895

1. Oppose increases in big salaries of officials
2. County Council to pay half the salaries of Medical Officer of Health and Sanitary Inspector
3. Eight-hour day for all municipal employees
4. Taxation of ground values
5. Municipal coal depot
6. Enforce Acts relating to smoke control, river pollution, etc
7. Erection of artisans' dwellings by the Corporation
8. Retention of land in possession of Corporation
9. Direct employment of labour by the Corporation
10. Municipal employees to be allowed to join trade unions

School Board Election 1896

1. Supports unsectarian policy
2. Doctor to visit schools and advise on blindness and deafness
3. Schoolchildren not to be pressured into taking up too many subjects
4. The distinction between locally trained and college-trained teachers to be abolished
5. School accommodation to be increased
6. Fair contracts clause

Municipal Election 1897

1. Fair wages clauses in municipal contracts
2. Eight-hour day for municipal employees
3. Taxation of ground values
4. Municipal coal depot
5. Retention of land in possession of the Corporation
6. Establishment of a free library service
7. Drinking fountains to be built in public streets
8. Erection of artisans' dwellings by the Corporation
9. Erection of municipal lodging house by the Corporation
10. Reassessment of property on a rental basis
11. Establishment of the B. Butterfield Hall and Museum
12. Smoke nuisance regulations to be enforced
13. Night soil depot to be built for Low Bridge
14. Licences for public houses to be retained by the Corporation

Board of Guardians Election 1898

1. More adequate outdoor relief for the old
2. Useful work for the unemployed in times of depression
3. Fair wages clause in Guardians' contracts
4. Re-evaluation of the union

Municipal Election 1898

1. Reduction in price of gas
2. Electric lighting to be introduced in streets
3. Taxation of land values
4. Deputation allowance to be reduced
5. Big salaries to be kept down
6. Corporation inn licences to be renewed
7. Borough magistracy
8. Retention of Corporation land by the Council
9. Fair wages clauses in municipal contracts
10. Establishment of a Direct Labour Department by the Corporation
11. Eight-hour day for municipal employees
12. Establishment of a municipal lodging house
13. Prevention of smoke nuisances
14. Removal of slum properties

Municipal Election 1899

1. Taxation of land values
2. Appointment of a full-time Town Clerk
3. Establishment of a municipal tram service
4. The retention of Corporation land
5. The establishment of a municipal slaughter house
6. The removal of insanitary areas
7. The building of municipal dwelling houses
8. Enforcement of sanitary laws
9. The inspection of dairies and cowsheds
10. Purchase of markets
11. Development of Public Baths
12. Establishment of Direct Works Department
13. Council to be a model employer
14. Municipalization of the liquor traffic
15. Reduction of deputation expenses
16. Re-evaluation of the Union
17. Reform of Parliamentary Bill procedure

School Board Election 1899

1. Free education
2. Education to be non-sectarian
3. Medical officer to examine children; school meals to be introduced
4. Maximum class of forty
5. Generous treatment of teachers
6. Fair wages clause in School Board contracts
7. Cost of education to be a national charge

Table 4.4 Keighley Liberal party: analysis of occupations of Ward Committee members, 1887–1890

Occupation	Number
Managerial/Professional	
Textile	
belt manufacturer	1
bobbin maker	2
commission wool comber	1
dyer	1
machine wool comber	1
reed and hield maker	1
spinner and manufacturer	2
stuff finisher	1
stuff manufacturer	2
wool manufacturer	2
worsted spinner	9
Engineering	
engineer	1
hot-water engineer	1
iron founder	4
metal merchant	1
machine maker	3
machine-tool maker	4
shuttle and piece maker	1
spindly-fly maker	1
washing-machine manufacturer	5
wool-combing machine manufacturer	1
Miscellaneous Business	
brass founder	1
mineral-water manufacturer	1
paper manufacturer	2
quarry owner	1
tanner	3
rope maker	1
leather merchant	3
soap manufacturer	1
manager	8
professional accountant	1
architect	3
auctioneer	3
chemist/herbalist	3
dentist	1
newspaper editor	1
solicitor	3
gentlemen	1
private residents	9
Miscellaneous	
bookkeeper	3
agent for canal company	1
farmer	5
shipping agent	1
Service/Retail	
beerhouse keeper	1
bookseller	1
boot/clog dealer	3
butler	1
butcher	4
cattle dealer	1
clothier	1
coachman	1
coal dealer	10
commercial traveller	2
confectioner	4
curator, Liberal club	1
draper	10
dressmaker	1
druggist	1
emigration agent	1
fish/fruit dealer	33
furniture dealer	1
general dealer	1
glass dealer	2
greengrocer/grocer	26
hatter	1
house furnisher	1
ironmonger	1
Liberal agent	1
lodging-house proprietor	1
market gardener	1
milk dealer	1
piano dealer	1
plasterer/builder	1
printer	2
secretary	2
shopkeeper	11
stationer	1
superintendent	1
tailor	8
traveller	4
victualler	1
wholesale merchant	1
yeast dealer	1

Clerical

clerk	1
insurance agent	2
teacher	4

Skilled Industrial

engine driver	1
engineers	1
factory foreman	3
gas-works engineer	1
overlooker	4
tinplate worker	1

Craftsmen

blacksmith	2
bookmaker	2
cabinet maker	4
carpenter	1
cask maker	1
chair manufacturer	1
gardener	1
iron turner	1
joiner	7
mason	1
painter	8
polisher	12
roller coverer	1
wheelwright	2
wood turner	1

CHAPTER FIVE

Trade Unions and the Keighley Independent Labour Party

Most research into the causes of the rise of the ILP in the West Yorkshire textile belt has emphasized the importance of support of organized labour. For Bradford, E. P. Thompson and K. Laybourn and J. Reynolds have argued that the Manningham Mills strike of 1890–1 was the catalyst which turned many trade-unionists away from support for the Liberal party and towards an independent political party which would represent their interests and those of the working class. For Huddersfield, Robert Perks has noted the 'central role played by trade-unionism compared to the consistently subordinate influence of Socialism' in the emergence of the local Labour party. In Halifax, the Labour movement 'owed much of its existence to the rise of local trade-unionism and "new" unionist ideas in the 1890s'. Similar research on Manchester, Bristol, Blackburn and London tends to confirm the importance of trade-unionism to the development of local Labour parties.[1] There are exceptions, notably from David Clark, who argued that in Colne Valley 'trade unionism is not an essential pre-requisite for Socialism',[2] and a study in Wales has emphasized Fabian socialism rather than trade-unionism as the decisive factor in the development of a local political labour organization.[3]

Clearly, therefore, it is important to assess the role of the trade unions in the emergence of the Keighley ILP and later the LRC. However, it should be emphasized that, in Yorkshire, trade-union membership was patchy and that the worsted industry was notoriously unorganized. Within that industry, Keighley was well known for being particularly poorly unionized. An alliance with trade unions was not necessarily an automatic recipe for political success. Indeed, it was the almost endemic weakness of organized labour which convinced local Liberal leaders that there was no need to make any serious accommodation with the labour groups that were formed in the 1890s.

It has been shown that the period after the 1889 strike was a time of increased trade-union activity in Keighley. This growth of trade-union branches and of industrial unrest continued throughout the 1890s and played an important part in awakening the class consciousness of labouring men and women. Many workers in Keighley, as elsewhere, came to the conclusion that if the masters could not be trusted in the economic field, then neither could they be trusted politically. They should therefore be represented by members of their own class on local elected bodies, and ultimately in Parliament. Political and trade-union work thus went hand in hand. It was argued that if an industrial dispute was successful and the masters were defeated, then such action should be followed by activity in the political field. If a strike failed, political success became even more important to counterbalance the industrial defeat. The workers thought that political success could lead to limitations being imposed on the employers through the introduction of such constraints as fair wages clauses in local government contracts. Conversely, the political defeat of the workers would give the masters a greater confidence when imposing unfair working conditions upon the men. Nationally, the Taff Vale decision and the Osborne judgement showed that there were cases where trade-union defeats could only be reversed by political decisions. This belief that political and industrial activity went together was expressed in 1892 by Fred Hammill, when he addressed the Keighley branch of the Vehicular Traffic Workers' Union. He spoke of:

> the need of labour representation upon all the public bodies stating that it was their duty as trade-unionists to permeate these public bodies and even Parliament and by thus concentrating their forces against the buttresses which had been set before them for so long they could knock down the walls of their opponents, and so overturn the constitution in twelve months.[4]

Hammill was a regular visitor to Keighley at this time, and at another meeting a year later he pointed out how political action could be used to save the workers the trouble and expense of industrial conflict, which was inevitably costly both financially and for the strikers' quality of life. He argued that people should join trade unions, but that 'strikes emptied their exchequers and brought in their train starving husbands, starving wives and starving children, and there was a weapon at their disposal which they were going to use preferentially … The weapon was to send men of their own class to the House of Commons.'[5]

The local ILP activists also emphasized that trade-unionism and politics should work together. 'You have already combined inside your workshop', the *Keighley Labour Journal* wrote, urging the labourers to 'now combine politically outside the workshop.'[6] For 'working men have begun to learn the power of combination and when they have fully realised it and combine at the ballot box as they do now in their Trades Unions and Co-Operative Societies the tyranny of Landlords and capitalists will be approaching its end'.[7] There was, therefore, agreement among both trade-unionists and labour politicians that they should work together. However, before this could happen, local trade-union leaders had to be convinced of the necessity of trade unions supporting independent working-class political activity. In Keighley, unlike Bradford, this was comparatively easy. The Trades Council was established as a result of a strike against the Liberal manufacturers and there was a growing mistrust of this local élite from 1889. Throughout the 1890s the Trades Council generally worked closely with the local ILP. The trade-union influence was particularly prominent at the early socialist meetings. For example, during Keir Hardie's visit in 1892, the local people on the platform to greet him included Herbert and Edward Horner, delegates to the Trades Council and members of the Teachers' Union; Alfred Burrows of the Iron Founders' Union; and W. F. Hardy, president of the Trades Council.

Other trade-union officials who were leading members of the Labour Union from its establishment were G. J. Wardle of the ASRS and the first editor of the *Keighley Labour Journal*, who was also a founder member of the party, as was Tom Mackley of the Vehicular Traffic Workers, who for many years was the Keighley ILP branch secretary. Charles Whitehead, William Robinson, Eli Gledhill and Alan Woodman of Haworth were also early trade-union and ILP activists. Close relations between the ILP and trade unions, established in 1892, continued throughout the decade, reaching their apogee in 1899, when Herbert Horner became president of the Trades Council. The ILP's importance on the Council was confirmed before that, however, for by 1897 the president, secretary and treasurer of the Council were all ILPers. Relations between the ILP and the Trades Council nevertheless contained tensions. Trade-unionists could regard the ILP and later the Labour party as its political arm; but the ILP did not believe that its members had to be trade-unionists, desirable though that may have been. In 1907, Tom Mackley wrote to the secretary of the local branch of the Gas Workers' and General Labourers' Union that although ILPers were:

> all anxious that wherever possible the members of the ILP should also be members of their respective 'trade unions' ... they also wish me to say that while expressing the above opinions they do not wish to coerce the ILP members to join such trades unions ... Lastly they desire me to protest most emphatically against that part of your letter describing non trade union members of the ILP as 'no better than any ordinary blacklegs'. We do not ask a man or a woman who wishes to join us whether they are trades unionists or not. If we are satisfied they are socialists they are welcome. It is for the ordinary trades unionist to convert him to the need for industrial combination.[8]

It is obvious that the aims of the ILP and the trade unions were not always identical. The ILP was a more radical organization whose ideology was sometimes different from that of the trade unions. For example, the appeal of ethical socialism was strong among the ILPers and while many trade-unionists may have been attracted to these beliefs, they had little to do with day-to-day trade-union activity. The ILP tended to concentrate on politics rather than on the economic struggle. The chief aim of many trade-union branches was to protect the interests of their members and not to prosecute political objectives. For the trade unions, there was always the temptation to work within the economic system to achieve their aims. The nearby Bingley branch of the ASRS, for example, declared that:

> Their society was not of a defiant character, but for defence, they were banded together for their own protection, knowing from experience they would not be fully doing their duty if they did not do all in their power to minimise accidents and to help the widows and the children of those who met with accidents.[9]

Some masters were happy to accommodate this kind of trade-unionism. J. C. Horsfall, when president of the Keighley Chamber of Commerce, discussing the establishment of a Conciliation Board, considered that capital and unions 'ought to be brothers or at any rate first cousins; their interests were identical; it was impossible to benefit one without benefiting the other, and he trusted that the time might come when both capital and labour might see this'.[10] There was thus always a possibility that the unions might be incorporated into the existing Liberal consensus. How easily this could happen is shown by a comparatively trivial incident in 1893. The Trades Council representatives were invited to a dinner held by the Chamber of Commerce. In his report to the Trades Council, its secretary, John Bateman, a founder member of the Keighley Labour Union, who had clearly enjoyed himself enormously, said: 'it was grand to live at the rate of £10,000 a year for ten minutes' and added that:

> there were men at the soirée whom he truly respected and the kind manner with which they treated the labour delegates made him feel he could truly praise them. He was not so bitter against his masters or the masters of any place, as some people would pretend to make out that he was.[11]

Clearly, if an ILP activist could be so easily attracted by the employers, there was a danger that the local trade unions as a whole could lose their aggression and become partners rather than enemies of the masters.

Another tension was that the ILP was too radical for many trade-unionists and there was a danger that the two groups would split up because of the extremism of the political party. This threatened to occur during the 1896 School Board election. During this contest, the Trades Council nominated Alfred Burrows and George Gill, the two successful candidates of 1893. The ILP nominated its own candidate, Mary Jane Dixon, an ethical socialist. The ILP and Trades Council campaigned separately and it is clear that there was a breach between them. It seems likely that the ILP was considered too advanced by certain elements in the Trades Council, although whether there was a specific cause for the disagreement between them is not clear. The minutes of the ILP merely record that 'Messrs Burrows and Gill be asked if they will pledge themselves to our programme' and that a 'deput[ation] of 3 go to see the Trades Council'.[12] No results are given of this enquiry by the ILP. The two Trades Council candidates were defeated, while Mary Jane Dixon topped the poll. The *Labour Journal*, commenting on the result, implied that Burrows and Gill had been left behind by the politicization of the working class. 'Today the tide has set in another direction ... they [Burrows and Gill] have underestimated its power, or were not prepared to go along with it, and so they have been left stranded.'[13] However, in this particular instance the ILP quickly repaired its fences. It nominated the chairman of the Trades Council as its candidate for a seat on the Borough Council in a by-election that was taking place at the same time as the School Board election.

The last tension was that the ILP did not always appreciate that partnership with the trade unions meant respecting the basic tenets of unionism. Thus in 1896 it was discovered that a number of ILPers were blacklegs in the iron workers' strike of that year. The guilty members were expelled from the party, but the fact that such a thing could happen indicates that not all ILPers were sympathetic to the ideals of trade unions. This incident soured relations between the branch and the local ASE. The ILP attempted to heal the breach by sending copies of the resolution of expulsion to the local branch of the Engineers' Union and asking them 'to urge all their members to vote for none but Socialist candidates for all public bodies and so help to bring about a time when strikers and blacklegs shall be no more'.[14] Even so, such incidents were not helpful in cementing a partnership between the two groups. Nevertheless, relations between them survived these and similar difficulties, and they worked closely together throughout the early years of the party. The ILP candidates in local elections were usually also trade-unionists and were often nominated in conjunction with the Trades Council. Thus in 1894 Herbert Horner and Thomas Roe were nominated jointly by the two bodies. Among the other election candidates put forward at various times were Tom Mackley, who was active in the National Vehicular Traffic Workers' Union; his brother Robert, who was secretary of the local branch of the ASRS; William Robinson, president of the Trades Council in 1896, who was 'in thorough sympathy with labour both from a Trades Union and political standpoint';[15] W. F. Hardy, who was secretary to the Trades Council and a member of the ASRS; William Pickles, secretary to the Alliance Cabinet Makers' Association and vice-president of the Trades Council in 1901; Charles Whitehead, secretary of the Keighley branch of the Mill Sawyers' and Woodcutting

Machinists' Union and secretary of the Trades Council in 1902; Herbert Horner who was in the Teachers' Union; and William Prosser and James Teal, who were also trade-unionists. When such people were nominated, the trade-union connection was emphasized:

> Once more we are appealing to the electors of East ward for their support on behalf of a Labour candidate. We have nominated Mr William Robinson, the President of the Trades and Labour Council, a proved friend of the workers, who is in thorough sympathy with Labour from both a Trades Union and political standpoint.[16]

ILP activists would sometimes emphasize their trade-unionism in preference to their political work. Herbert Horner, for example, was described as a 'member of the Town Council and a well known trades unionist' in 1896.[17] No mention was made of his political affiliation. The party also continually urged the Keighley workmen to join their trade-union branches. Philip Snowden, although he was never closely associated with trade-unionism, or a trade-unionist, wished 'to see every non-unionist in Keighley who was eligible enrolled within the ranks of the unions as soon as possible'.[18] The solid advantages of membership were emphasized by the *Keighley Labour Journal*, for 'wherever trade unionism is strong wages are from 15 to 25 per cent higher than those who paid for similar work where unionism is weak or non existent'.[19] The folly of not belonging to a union was hammered home in both speeches and articles. For example, the *Keighley Labour Journal* argued that:

> for want of trade unionism and organisation amongst the workers, whether men, women or half timers, the whole working community are having to suffer. Non unionists are so frightened that some body is going to make something out of their small union subscriptions that rather than pay a few pence weekly for something that will give them direct benefits, they will present their employer with thrice the amount of trade union subscription by working for so much less wages. Unity is strength in nearly every large town in England, but not in Keighley.[20]

In their election manifestos, too, the ILP expressed solidarity with trade unions. In the municipal elections of 1895, 1897 and 1898, they pledged to fight for an eight-hour day for municipal workers, and in 1899 they wanted to turn the Corporation into a model employer.[21] They also wanted a fair wages clause in contracts granted by the Council so that firms should 'pay the trade union or standard rate of wages and to observe the conditions prevailing in that particular trade'.[22] In addition, they stressed the need for a Direct Works Department and for Council workers to be allowed to join trade unions, for 'employers and workmen should have equal liberty of combination'.[23] In the School Board and Board of Guardians elections, their manifestos included fair wages clauses. Attempts to implement these demands were not successful, although ILP-elected members regularly put them forward. For example, in 1897 Herbert Horner tried to have the *Burgess Lists* printed by a firm recognized by the Typographical Society as a fair house, and Mary Jane Dixon attempted to get a fair wages clause inserted into contracts made by the School Board. Such efforts resulted in the ILP and trade unions working closer together. Thus, after Herbert Horner's failure with the *Burgess Lists*, the Trades Council made a fair contracts clause its test question in the next municipal election.[24]

The connection between the ILP and the trade unions grew closer in 1905, with the establishment of a local Labour Representation Committee whose object was to 'unite the forces of Labour in order to secure the election of Independent Representation on all local and national governing bodies and to keep an oversight on all matters affecting labour'.[25] Discussions started in March of that year, and by May the *Keighley Labour Journal*, which had been revived, reported that 'the trade-unionists, following the example of more advanced towns are slowly but surely getting into harness and a local Labour Representation Committee seems assured in the near future',[26] but it was not until September that the LRC was finally established. Although its members argued that 'it was not the ILP under another name',[27] there seems to be little doubt that ILPers had a major, if not absolute, influence in the new organization. Fourteen of the thirty-three delegates were members of the ILP, six from the party itself and the rest from trade unions, and it was said that non-ILP delegates 'didn't know much about politics' and could therefore be guided by the political activists.[28] The first major effort by the LRC was the 1906 general election, where the Labour candidate, W. T. Newlove, won over three thousand votes. It cemented the ILP/trade-union alliance and ensured that any future labour political developments would take account of the interests of the unions.

Nevertheless, the ILP always emphasized that trade-union action had to be linked to political work; 'for nothing can be long denied well directed labour and given unity in industrial and political affairs, the monopolies from which working men suffer, would soon be undermined and overthrown', and when 'working men combine at the ballot box the tyranny of landlords and Capitalists will be approaching its end'. As these quotations show, the emphasis was often on political rather than industrial action, a perspective which was affirmed by the *Keighley Labour Journal* when it wrote in May 1896: 'But when will working men see how utterly futile strikes are to solve the wages problem? When will they realise the powerful influence of the vote and seek through independent political organisation to accomplish the material bettering of their lives which this power gives?'[29]

The implication of the above extracts is that trade unions within the town were neither well organized nor influential, and this view is largely borne out by an examination of the work of individual branches and the local Trades Council. The Keighley Trades Council, as has been mentioned, was started by the ASE and the iron founders with support from the machine makers, the ASRS and the tailors. By 1891 the Trades Council had 8 branches and 19 delegates; by 1892 there were 11 branches and 26 delegates. This grew to 21 societies and 47 delegates in 1893, but thereafter it declined to somewhat fewer than 20 societies and about 34 delegates. Thus in 1901 there were only 16 unions affiliated, although there were also 12 non-affiliated societies in the town. By 1909 the Council had recovered to its 1893 figures with 22 unions affiliated. There were, however, still 8 non-affiliated societies.[30]

The difficulties of retaining membership are illustrated by the troubled history of the ASE branches and the Trades Council. Although it was one of the founder members of the Council, the Keighley ASE No. 2 Branch withdrew in 1904 only to rejoin two years later. The No. 1 Branch did not affiliate until 1905.[31] In addition to its problems with the Council, the ASE had trouble recruiting members to the union, as the *Keighley Labour Journal* noted: 'When we look at the number of mechanics working in our town and then have to confess that there are only 500 of them members of the ASE it is a sad state of things.' Other engineering unions experienced the same difficulties: 'when we look at the machine makers … to find only about twenty who have the courage and foresight to combine for the common good, it makes one feel ashamed'.[32]

Nevertheless, the trade unions made strenuous recruiting efforts in the area. The initial drive after the 1889 engineers' strike was maintained. In 1892, for example, the Typographical Association, the Vehicular Traffic Workers, the plumbers, the tram drivers, and wood machinists formed branches,[33] and the wool sorters, painters and decorators and five other groups became affiliated to the Trades Council.[34] The following year, the Overlookers' Union, led by A. E. Schoon, an ex-Liberal and founder member of the Labour Union, boasted that it had 'latterly increased its membership very considerably and it has rarely been in such a good position'.[35]

Membership figures are hard to find, but in 1902 the Trades Council could claim to represent only 1,302 members; and union membership was generally recognized as being low and patchy. The textile industry in particular was unorganized. In 1901, the only affiliated textile unions were the Power Loom Overlookers, the Aire and Worth Valley Twisters and Drawers and the West Riding Textile Weavers. This last branch disappeared after 1906. By 1909, the only additional textile union was a branch of the Society of Dyers and Finishers. Textile workers were notoriously difficult to recruit. In the words of Ben Turner, 'the organising work that has been put into Keighley and District has been immense. I have seen us have meetings there of three or four folks after tremendous publicity has been given to them … The workers were in a black leg area and would not come.'[36]

Particular efforts were made to encourage the Keighley women worsted workers to join their local branches, but without effect. There were various reasons for this: if conditions in one mill were poor, women could easily move to another; they were often unmarried and accepted low wages in the belief that they would not be in the mills for long, but would marry and leave; even when they were married, their money was only part of a family wage, the largest part of which was contributed by the man of the house; trade-unionists could be victimized by the management and lose their jobs. All these causes contributed to the difficulty of recruiting women into the unions. In 1893, Isabella Ford attended a meeting in Keighley to give 'an impetus to the local branch of the Weavers' Association and to organise the women workers in general'. She attacked the apathy of the Keighley women workers with vigour:

> she must say that she thought it was a perfect disgrace to this part of Yorkshire that there were not more of them in the Union and that those who were in the Union did not spread their principles more widely and freely. She was eager to see the women leave their life of laziness and easy enjoyment and enter upon the possession of those things which conduced to the real enjoyment and the real happiness of life. Apart from pecuniary gain there was a gain in mental happiness, for what, she asked, increased the happiness of life more than having an interest in the world outside, in having something to think of besides what was going on within the four walls of their homes? She answered, nothing. Women were citizens of the world as well as men, womens' acts were of as much consequence as mens'; and those women by feeling an interest in the social and political questions of the day would be ennobled and made happier. She thought that a woman who took no interest in politics was a tiresome being. She did not put the whole of the blame for this state of things upon women themselves, and she was of the opinion that men were responsible very largely because they did not insist upon their wives and their daughters, if they were in employment, joining the trade union.[37]

In 1896 Katharine Conway, who was particularly popular in the area because of her ethical socialism, gave a series of talks in the Aire Valley on behalf of the Weavers' Union. Haworth weavers were exhorted to 'look out your old friend Katharine St John Conway is coming'.[38] Such appeals, however, were unsuccessful, and the women remained unorganized. Men, too, were hard to convince. An 1894 meeting, under the chairmanship of A. E. Schoon, to form a branch of the Ironworkers' Union, was typical of the apathy of the workers of the period. It had to be abandoned because of the poor response.[39] The minutes of the National Woolsorters' Union Executive testify to the difficulty of organizing in Keighley. Attempts were regularly made by the Bradford branch to unionize the Keighley sorters. In November 1900 it was resolved 'to promote an organising meeting in the Keighley District'. A meeting was held in February 1901 and deemed 'satisfactory'. A follow-up meeting was held in April, but there was obviously a falling away in the next twelve months, because in 1903 another meeting was held. This met with little success, for by May 1905 the secretary had to be 'instructed to make an estimate of our members who are residing in Keighley and district with a view to making a further effort at organising there'. The following year the secretary was again 'instructed to go down to Keighley and make arrangements for holding an organizing meeting at a place which appears to be the most convenient for the largest number'. The union subsequently contacted the ILP and asked to use their room for the meeting. In 1907 the union was again in the town 'enrolling members and if possible establishing a branch there'; a branch was eventually formed, seven years after the first organizing meeting was held in the town.[40]

Trade-unionism in the town, therefore, was generally weak; and the groups that had organized themselves best tended to be those that were not central to the economic well-being of the town – were not, in fact, the textile workers. However, this did not mean that there were no strikes or industrial disputes. In the years after 1889 there were struggles between masters and men which were sometimes fought with great bitterness. As far as the ILP was concerned, these conflicts were valuable in politicizing the working class and breaking down the consensus between masters and men which had been so successful in previous times. Industrial disputes enabled the ILP to emphasize their argument that the masters could not be trusted to look after the interests of their workforce, and that industrial and political action must accompany each other. Only by capturing the elected offices of the state, both local and national, the ILP argued, could the workplace interests of labour be protected and increased.

The impact of industrial disputes in sharpening the differences between masters and men can be demonstrated by examining some local disagreements. In 1892 and 1893 there was a series of disputes between the municipal gas workers who were members of the Birmingham Gas Workers' Union, and the Gas Committee of the Council. In 1892 the introduction of new stoking machines raised difficulties which were exacerbated by the men's fear that certain employees were being discriminated against because they said there was a 'policy for the gradual discharge of all the old hands, an opinion which they [the men] say admits of no doubt as they have it on the authority of one of their number, who is believed to be hand in glove with the authorities'. The Council, for their part, 'expressed themselves determined not to be dictated to as to which men shall be retained and which discharged'.[41] Inevitably, positions hardened and the men struck, though only for a few days. This was in April 1893; in June trouble flared up again after three men were in fact dismissed. The gas workers, now members of the London Gasworkers' Union, were led by the busy A. E. Schoon and strongly supported by Alfred Burrows of the Trades Council, who described the Council's gas stoking works as a 'little hell on earth'.[42] Again the trouble died down, but by this time the gas-workers were clearly alienated from the masters who ran the Council's Gas Committee. The advice which was given by R. L. Hattersley, the chairman of the Gas Committee at this time, that the men should remember 'the necessity, the absolute wisdom in your own interests of never quarrelling with your employers', adding that 'these agitators are egging men on to get their own salaries' and ending by emphasizing 'whatever else you do never have any disagreement with Mr Laycock [the Gas Works Manager]',[43] was very badly received by a workforce which had experienced the full power of the employer-dominated Council being used against them. Support for the men had come from committed working-class Labour activists, and the gas workers showed their understanding of this when in January 1894 they presented Alfred Burrows with a clock 'for services rendered during the recent dispute'.

The gas workers' conflict was between Council employees and elected members. At about the same time, in 1893, there was a major dispute at Haworth between the largely unorganized woollen workers and Merralls, one of the largest local manufacturers.[44] Again the workers discovered that their only support came from their own class, from socialists and trade unions. The immediate cause of the strike was the announcement of a reduction of wages by the firm. On hearing the news of the cutback, the workers voted to strike by 320 votes to 18. Merralls immediately locked out the workforce of 4,000 people. Few employees were in the union, but a strike committee was quickly organized and a meeting was attended by Ben Tillett, W. H. Drew and Alan Gee. Later speakers included John Lister and Margaret McMillan and leading local radicals such as John Moore, Alfred Burrows and Herbert Horner. The strikers were led by Alan Woodman, a weaver, who, 'it is alleged, was discharged from the employ of Messrs Merrall on account of the action he took on behalf of the Weavers Association'. He was also the chief ILPer in Haworth.

The strike emphasized the gap that was growing between the workers and the masters. The strikers felt that the time had come to act against grievances that had once been accepted, but were now felt to be intolerable. Workers alleged that Merralls 'regard their workpeople as mere tools in their hands to be utilised at the word of command'. Socialists emphasized the class differences between men and masters. John Moore, a founder member of the Keighley Labour Union, made a speech which affirmed that the conflict was rooted in class differences. The newspaper report said: 'perhaps the breeziest speech was made by Mr John Moore of Ingrow, who went "the whole hog" with regard to the Labour question. He made no attempt to conceal his belief that if the workers went up it would be at the expense of those at the top of the social scale.' At the same time, suspicion of the forces of the state increased. 'Some of the speakers gave vent to their indignation at the presence of the police in plain clothes, and suggested that the firm against whom they were fighting had much more control over the movements of the police than the average citizen and especially the workmen.'

Immediately after the strike, George Merrall, one of the leading members of the firm, demonstrated the way in which the industrial élite could use the law to impose their view of industrial relations on the workforce. He was one of three magistrates, all businessmen, who convicted three women who were brought to court for leaving their place of work without notice. Commenting, the *Keighley News* remarked:

> none can say the penalty inflicted was vindictive, or that a Bench otherwise constituted could have refused to convict under the law as it stands. But it is easy to understand how resentfully wage earners must regard the administration of laws so nearly concerning them by a tribunal composed exclusively of those whom they look upon rightly or wrongly as having interests antagonistic to their own.

W. H. Drew, on a recruiting drive in the aftermath of the lock-out, made great play with this insensitive decision: 'he held it to be extremely indecent for these three men [Magistrates Merrall, John Clough and John Sugden] to sit and try cases which so vitally affected their interests'. It was Keir Hardie who told the Keighley workers what they should do to control the power of the masters: join a trade union and support the ILP. The first action would make them strong in the workplace, and the second would enable them to capture the instruments of political power. Visiting the district at the time of the Merralls strike, he asked why there was 'such apathy and indifference on the part of the workers in the district':

> It was not because they lacked intelligence ... their countenances belied any such putting of the case; they were not degraded and demoralised by their condition; it could not be said that they were deficient in courage, for their late strike proved that when the occasion required their courage was not wanting. Why was it they were standing aloof from the great democratic movement that was sweeping over the country today, and which had for its object the uplifting of men and women, the giving of freedom and happiness to all, and the banishing of poverty with all its concomitant evils from this fair land.

The Merrall strike ended in a victory for the workers, thus proving the power of labour if properly organized. The reductions were withdrawn, but the workers came to see that they had won a battle, not the war. One speaker declared that 'almost twenty years ago a strike lasting something like seventeen weeks took place and Messrs Merrall were victorious. Another dispute five years ago resulted in the employees being defeated, but two years ago a proposed reduction of *6d.* a piece was resisted and finally withdrawn.' This time the workers had again been successful but W. H. Drew warned that Merralls would continue to press for changes to reduce labour costs: 'in plain words the introduction of the two-loom system. He took it they would have more backbone and grit than to allow this. If not it would hasten the time when the women would not only be wives and mothers, but breadwinners also, and he could not conceive a worse position for women.' In 1894 Merralls did indeed attempt to introduce the two-loom system.

The strike was also seen as part of a more general struggle between labour and capital. While the Haworth dispute was taking place, the Keighley plumbers and the Oakworth shuttlemakers were involved in their own fights, while the gas workers' quarrel had only just been resolved. At the same time, meetings in support of the Hull dockers were being organized by the Keighley Labour Union, where Alfred Burrows emphasized the class nature of industrial conflict: 'the fight at Hull was a struggle of capital versus workmen ... and its lesson was that all workers should band themselves together for defence against unscrupulous employers'. He also pointed out that the national Liberal government firmly supported the employers, 'a Government which prided itself upon its Liberalism lent its forces to help the capitalists to beat the aims of the workmen'.[45] Speeches at such meetings continually emphasized that neither the Liberal government nor the local Liberal magistrates and councillors could be trusted to look after the interests of the workers. Internationally, too, as Margaret McMillan pointed out, the local workforce was part of a wider class conflict. She said, during a meeting in support of the Merrall strikers, that 'they in Haworth, despite the friendly services of a few men and women, might feel rather lonely and helpless. But they ought not to be for there were thousands nay millions, of people in Germany, in France, in England and Scotland who were fighting the same battle of labour as theirs.'[46]

The strikes of the 1890s sharpened class antagonism; they showed how the masters used their control of the local state for their own purposes; they undermined the trust of the workers in local institutions and they brought home to the workers that they were part of a larger international struggle. Lastly, they showed that if the working class wanted to improve their condition, they must rely on themselves and not look for support from the masters. They thus played an important part in the political education of the Keighley workers.

The stoppages referred to above occurred when the Keighley Labour Union had only just been formed. However, similar conclusions were emphasized whenever a strike took place locally. Thus, during both the 1896 ironworkers' strike and the 1897 engineers' lock-out, the points that were made during the Merrall and the gas workers' strikes were repeated. On this occasion, however, an additional emphasis was given to the importance of political action in effecting permanent social change. In 1896 the *Keighley Labour Journal* asked: 'when will working men see how utterly futile strikes are to solve the wages problem? When will they realise the powerful influence of the vote?', adding that 'all improvement effected by strikes is purchased at too great a sacrifice ... and if you will only learn the lessons which the present is so plainly teaching, you will soon throw over the out of date weapon and take advantage of the political machine ready to your hand'.[47] When the 1897 lock-out started, there was a belief in the general goodwill of the local masters. Joseph Shackleton, a Keighley engineering workers' leader, believed that men and workers could come to a friendly agreement, declaring: 'if the employers that we now have to deal with are as good to treat with as they were last time, I think we shall get through this difficulty very smoothly and nicely. I have not a word to say against them. They have all treated us very civilly.'[48] It quickly became clear, however, that the masters' first loyalty was to their fellow employers and not to their workers. In a circular issued shortly after the start of the dispute, the masters acknowledged that 'the men's action is defensive'; but they argued that to allow the continued contributions to union funds 'would assist other workers in the country to fight the battle against the employers', and they concluded: 'that they were very sorry to have to resort to severe measures but recognizing a community of interest with all the employers in the country and feeling that the question is one of national importance they are bound to cut off supplies as far as they can.'[49] The local socialists recognized the logic behind the masters' position and, realizing the weakness of Keighley trade-unionism, surmised that the workers could best achieve their aims through political rather than industrial activity. They did not, however, neglect trade unions, for as an ILPer writing in the *Keighley Labour Journal* at the time said: 'I strongly hold that under any form of industry trade unions will be necessary, and I consider that any working man or woman who is not a member of a trade union has no reason but the densest ignorance to excuse him or her,' but he continued: 'the strike is a weapon of brute force, a relic of barbarism. With advancing civilisation reason must take the place of brute might. In a civilised community we have government and law to regulate all individual and social relationships.'[50]

To the ILP, the difficulty with the trade unions was that they accepted 'present economic conditions with the relationship of employer and employed', whereas the answer to industrial difficulties lay in changing the structure of society and this could only be done through the ballot box, for 'every question is a political question, the conditions attaching to all work, home life and religion, are governed by laws which may be changed by political means'.[51] The state itself was run by political parties which controlled the levers of power. Herbert Horner warned the striking engineers that 'the magistrates were often either employers or relatives or shareholders in similar concerns. The Bench, the Watch Committee of the Town and County Councils and Parliament itself were in the hands of capitalists who controlled the police and the naval and military forces.'[52] The leader of the Builders' Labourers' Union, Mr Mulligan, on a visit to Keighley at this time, gave the same message in more down-to-earth terms, warning the men 'to be careful in their picketings so as not to give the police a chance to interfere'.[53] In fact, seven strikers were found guilty of intimidation by local magistrates, causing the *Keighley Labour Journal* to note that 'a bench composed of employers, when judging workpeople, with the conflicting interests of one of their own class at stake, has no more notion of fair play, than has a cow of the beauty of the landscape on which it is grazing', adding: 'there is only one law, and that is the law made by the rich, made for the rich, and administered by the rich in their own interests'. The way to achieve equitable industrial relations, therefore, was through the ballot box:

> If trade unionism is to win greater victories in the future it has got to recognize the immediate and overwhelming importance of the legislative machine. Just as the trade-unionist alone would be powerless, just as the trade-unionist is often thwarted in his desires and attempts after better wages and conditions by the non unionist. Just so is the present suicidal division of working men into Liberals and Tories destroying their power to help one another by legislation ... it would cost far less, both in money and suffering to carry an eight hours day by legal enactment if working men would only unite in one solid party and convert Parliament to their opinion by sending those men only who represent those opinions and are prepared to carry them into effect.[54]

Seventeen years later, in 1914, a series of strikes took place which resulted in the bitterest industrial action in Keighley's history. Once again the engineering workers were involved, and the same point, that industrial strife was no substitute for political action, was made. The build-up to the strike was lengthy. In June 1911 the members of the Keighley ASE agreed to apply for an increase in wages of two shillings a week and a reduction in hours of work from fifty-four to fifty-two. By January 1912, the union's divisional organizer reported that 'the Keighley wage advance has required some attention and visits'; a month later he concluded that 'our difficulty is that there are so many small firms in the town (about 80 of them) and some of them appear to be living from hand to mouth and competing amongst themselves until there is no margin of profit left'. A year later, in 1913, two years after the original claim had been submitted, a conference was organized between the union and employers. Two employers turned up, and the patience of the engineers was exhausted. In April 1914, strike notices were posted and immediately fifteen small firms acceeded to the men's demands. The larger concerns, however, stood out against the claim.[55]

The dispute lasted four months and was uncompromising on both sides. As well as ASE members, the Toolmakers' Union was involved, and also large numbers of non-union men. At the same time, the Moulders' Union and Joiners' Union put in claims for extra wages. Workmen from all these jobs were soon on strike, and many more were sent home by the employers because there was no work for them to do.

The men were determined to 'at last make an attempt to lift the stigma of "black spot" from the district. We wish it to be remembered that we have determined that Keighley shall in the future stand for trade unionism, and never shall our district be the recognized stronghold of blacklegs and scabs.'[56] Pressure was put on those men who continued working. Joseph Wright, for instance, who worked for Haggert and Smith Machine Tool Makers, was accosted by a large crowd who jeered at him as a 'blackleg'. Emerging from the crowd, two men, Arthur O'Brien, a turner, and Herbert Binns, a fitter, took him by the arm and said:

O'Brien: Now then art tha bahn to join the club?
Wright: No I'm not.
Binns: Did you know one man got his neck broke last night? [They were referring to a cyclist brought down by a wire stretched across the road.]
O'Brien: It'll be tha turn next.[57]

In the week ending 11 July there was considerable rioting; non-union workers who were not on strike were bombarded with bricks, and groups gathered outside the house of Arthur Smith, of Dean, Smith and Grace, chanting songs and hurling abuse at him. Over seven workshops, including Prince Smiths, Dean Smith and Grace, and Hattersleys, had their windows smashed. For their part, the employers succeeded in having police reinforcements transferred to the town, and the *Bradford Observer* commented that 'there appears to be a quiet strengthening of the police force' which was 'due to the growing tendency of strikers to follow workers to their homes'.[58] Bad feeling grew between the strikers and the police, who were seen as supporting the employers. J. E. Davidson of the Moulders' Union, addressing a mass meeting, condemned police harassment of pickets and their protection of blacklegs.[59]

Although there were some who went back to work, the solidarity of the strikers generally, whether union or non-union, was remarkable and the local Labour politicians applauded what they saw as a new determination among the workers. William Bland, by this time prospective Labour candidate for the Division, commented that 'it shows that working men are beginning to be a great deal firmer in their attitude towards Trades Unionism than they were before'.[60]

What the ultimate result would have been is unknown. By July 1914, after four months, the great majority of the strikers remained out, while the major employers were adamant that they would not pay the increase in wages. There were various attempts at negotiation and on occasion agreement seemed close. On the masters' side, about twenty-five smaller employers had conceded the men's demands. Nevertheless, the situation was at an impasse. It was the outbreak of war which led to a hasty settlement, and the men's rise was granted.

The strike illustrated that industrial relations had improved very little since 1889. The masters were reluctant to meet trade-union representatives. Some firms, such as Hattersleys, would not negotiate with the unions but only with their workmen. The workers, on the other hand, felt that they were always under pressure from the local employers and from the local authorities, which were dominated by the manufacturers. William Bland declared that 'all the powers the authorities possessed was utilised against the workers when they tried to improve their economic lot'.[61] In particular, they thought that the press always gave the employers' view. 'A strike sympathiser' wrote to the *Keighley News* that when 'the worker seeks, by any means (no matter however creditable his toleration and endurance) to maintain his rights he is always put down as a rabble and treated as if he were a hooligan'.[62] They also thought that the laws were framed against them. Thus, after the mayor had threatened some strikers with creating a breach of the peace, a correspondent wrote to the newspaper saying: 'laws grind the poor and the rich make the laws. The laws governing the activities of trade unionism have been made by the class to which the Mayor of Keighley belongs.'[63] The laws on picketing were particularly resented, union supporters arguing that 'the right of peaceful picketing simply means that if a man chooses to work, he shall work and not be interfered with although a majority of his mates have decided in favour of joint action'.[64]

The strike also showed that the town was still poorly unionized. The largest group of those on strike were the non-union workers. It was said that in one of the largest engineering shops, employing a thousand people, only fifty were in the union, and although many joined after the start of the strike, with three hundred enrolling in the ASE in a week,[65] non-unionists always outnumbered organized labour.

In view of this resentment at the way in which the power of the authorities was used against them, and at the weakness of trade-unionism, it is perhaps not surprising that the solution offered to the workers was political action. Commenting on the refusal of the Council to implement school feeding, William Bland said: 'if the workers had sent a dozen labour men to the Keighley Town Council then the children [of the strikers] would have been fed in a proper manner'. Later he argued that although trade unions were the first line of defence for working men, yet their very existence depended on Parliament. It was necessary, he said, for workers to send MPs to the House of Commons who would represent their interests, for 'unless the working men elected Members of Parliament from their own class even the hard won privileges now enjoyed by them as trade-unionists might be filched away by professional politicians'.[66]

To the Keighley ILP, trade unions were important. They defended the workers' industrial gains and were a bulwark against exploitation by the masters. They helped to educate the worker by making him more conscious of his class loyalty. They made him look towards his fellow workers for help and support, rather than his employer. They provided the ILP with opportunities to recruit and educate members. They gave organizational and financial aid during election campaigns. Nevertheless, trade unions accepted the economic structure, seeking only to improve the workers' conditions within a capitalist framework. They were too weak to provide an adequate alternative to political action, which had to be the means of permanent social change. It was through Parliament that gains made by trade unions would be permanently secured. It was in the Council Chamber and the Board of Guardians that fair contracts clauses were to be implemented and the eight-hour day put into practice. Trade unions were important, but it was not through them that a socialist society was to be formed.

In any case, trade-unionism was only part of socialism. Equally important for many ILPers was the ethical and educational side of their work, and in order to understand the appeal of the ILP in Keighley, it is necessary to consider this side of their activities.

Notes

1. Thompson, *op.cit.*; Reynolds and Laybourn, 'Emergence of the Independent Labour Party in Bradford', *op.cit.*; Perks, *op.cit.*; Dawson, *op.cit.*; Hill, *op.cit.*; Bryher, *op.cit.*; Walton, *op.cit.*; P. Thompson, *Socialists, Liberals and Labour: the Struggle for London 1885–1914* (London, 1967); C. Wrigley, 'Liberals and the Desire for Working-Class Representation in Battersea, 1886–1922', in Brown, *op.cit.*
2. Clark, *op.cit.*
3. C. Parry, 'Gwynedd Politics 1900–1920: the Rise of Labour', *Welsh History Review*, 6 (1972), pp.313–28.
4. *Keighley News*, 19 November 1892.
5. *Ibid.*, 12 August 1893.
6. *Keighley Labour Journal*, 28 October 1894.
7. *Ibid.*, 16 May 1896.
8. Keighley ILP, Letter Book, 11 February 1907.
9. *Keighley News*, 25 February 1893.
10. *Ibid.*
11. *Ibid.*
12. Keighley ILP, Minutes, 27 February, 5 March 1896.

13. *Keighley Labour Journal*, 29 March 1896.
14. Keighley ILP, Minutes, 6 August 1896.
15. *Keighley Labour Journal*, 15 March 1896.
16. *Ibid.*
17. *Ibid.*, 24 October 1896.
18. *Keighley News*, 16 May 1896.
19. *Keighley Labour Journal*, 9 May 1896.
20. *Ibid.*, 29 May 1897.
21. *Ibid.*, printed in October of each year.
22. *Ibid.*, 20 October 1895.
23. *Ibid.*
24. *Ibid.*, 2 October 1897.
25. *Keighley Year Book*, 1909, p.198.
26. *Keighley Labour Journal*, 20 May 1905.
27. *Keighley News*, 9 December 1905.
28. *Ibid.*, 2 December 1905.
29. *Keighley Labour Journal*, 9, 16 and 2 May 1896.
30. *Keighley Year Book*, 1892–1910.
31. *Ibid.*, 1891–1906.
32. *Keighley Labour Journal*, 11 September 1897.
33. *Keighley News*, *passim*.
34. Information taken from *Keighley Year Book*.
35. *Ibid.*
36. B. Turner, *A Short History of the General Union of Textile Workers* (Heckmondwike, 1920), p.157.
37. *Keighley News*, 18 February 1893.
38. *Keighley Labour Journal*, 28 November 1896.
39. *Keighley News*, 17 February 1894.
40. National Woolsorters' Union Executive Committee, Minutes, 1900–1914, *passim*. Housed in West Yorkshire Archive Service, Bradford, Ref. No.21D82.
41. *Keighley News*, 1 April 1893.
42. *Ibid.*, 10 June 1893.
43. *Ibid.*
44. All information and quotations referring to the Merrall strike in the next few paragraphs are taken from *ibid.*, 1–29 July 1893, *passim*.
45. *Ibid.*, 24 June 1893.
46. *Ibid.*, 8 July 1893.
47. *Keighley Labour Journal*, 9 May 1896.
48. Quoted in Chambers and Holdsworth, *op.cit.*, p.15.
49. *Ibid.*
50. *Keighley Labour Journal*, 5 February 1898.
51. *Ibid.*, 21 August 1897, 5 February 1898.
52. *Ibid.*, 28 August 1897.
53. *Ibid.*
54. *Ibid.*, 17 July 1897.
55. Chambers and Holdsworth, *op.cit.*, pp.19–20.
56. ASE strike leaflet, 15 May 1914; quoted in Chambers and Holdsworth, *op.cit.*, p.22.

57. *Ibid.*
58. *Ibid.*, p.21.
59. *Bradford Observer*, 8 July 1914.
60. *Ibid.*
61. *Keighley News*, 15 July 1914.
62. *Ibid.*, 9 May 1914.
63. *Ibid.*, 16 May 1914.
64. *Ibid.*, 23 May 1914.
65. *Ibid.*, 2 May 1914.
66. *Ibid.*, 18, 23 July 1914.

CHAPTER SIX

Ethical Socialism, Socialist Culture and the Keighley Independent Labour Party

A number of historians have discussed the role of ethical socialism in the development of the British labour movement. Henry Pelling and K. S. Inglis have both examined the Labour Church and its importance in the growth of the ILP in particular and British socialism in general. Stanley Pierson has discussed the influence of ethical socialism on Labour leaders and party activists in the 1890s, and Stephen Yeo's article in *History Workshop* stimulated discussion on the 'Religion of Socialism'. Leonard Smith has recently examined the role of religion and the ILP and Tony Jowitt has argued the importance of religious belief in the development of the ILP in West Yorkshire.[1] Yet none of these works has examined the importance of ethical socialism in a specific locality, although Stephen Yeo, Keith Inglis, Len Smith and Tony Jowitt draw many of their examples from local groups. In his study of Colne Valley, David Clark emphasizes the part played by ethical socialism in the development of the local Labour party, regarding it as more important than trade-union support.[2] This chapter will examine why ethical socialism was important to the labour movement in Keighley, and how it became the accepted mode of expressing socialist ideas. It will maintain that the Labour Church made socialism accessible and acceptable to a section of the working class by putting it in a religious framework. In addition, it will be shown that the churches and chapels in the town were dominated by the manufacturing élite, who rejected the political aspirations of the working class. Further, this chapter attempts to demonstrate that the working class put forward their social and political demands in moral terms, concluding that this gave the ILP programme a moral bias and that concepts such as justice, freedom, brotherhood and equality became the basis of its socialism. At the same time, however, the Labour Church, the chief vehicle for their lectures, speeches and propaganda, at least in the early years, never developed into a Church in the formal sense. It remained chiefly the place where the Sunday meetings of the ILP were held. The trappings of a church service, such as hymns and recitals, tended to become secularized and sentimentalized, and were retained largely to give the audience a feeling of respectability and comradeship. Nevertheless, ethical socialism was of the first importance and remained the typical expression of the Keighley ILP beliefs.

Keighley was, of course, well provided with orthodox places of worship in the 1890s. There were seven Anglican and one Roman Catholic church, and twenty-eight Nonconformist churches and chapels, ranging from the Swedenborgians, with fifty participants, to the various Methodist denominations, each with several hundred members. Most of these bodies included the usual associated groups such as Sunday Schools and Mutual Improvement Societies.[3] In common with other institutions in the town, the churches and chapels were dominated by the manufacturers, who supported them both financially and with their social influence. Many of these churches were in need of financial assistance, as they were often in debt and, perhaps more importantly, thought of themselves as being in acute financial crisis. As S. J. D. Green says:

> Quite why they perceived the crisis of the early-nineties to be so acute is unclear. True many churches and chapels were very deeply in debt at that time, particularly as a result of a major surge in local church-building activity during the previous decade. Equally many societies were increasingly uncertain of their continuing income flows in a region of the country which was at the time enduring one of its worst economic downturns in living memory.[4]

In such circumstances, churches were often understandably reluctant to do anything which might antagonize their wealthier supporters. Nonconformist churches, in particular, were examples of the situation noted by Henry Pelling, where 'ministers were often hampered by dependence on the direct support of their congregations, and this frequently meant dependence on the most generous laymen'.[5] This point is made frequently by the *Keighley Labour Journal*. Herbert Horner, writing in 1898, says that:

> in too many cases a nonconformist minister must preach what suits a wealthy manufacturer or those golden pillars of the church will find means to get someone who will. They are used to subservient acquiescence in their employees in the shop and factory and they expect the same from their spiritual employees on Sunday.[6]

Such attacks were aimed largely at the Nonconformists, but the same pressures were present, though not so acutely, in the Church of England, which was supported by a number of Keighley's leading manufacturers. Nevertheless, because it was more difficult to remove Anglican incumbents, it was easier for some of Keighley's Church of England ministers to express radical views on social questions.

The extent of middle-class influence on the religious life of the town can be seen in the following examples: Joseph Summerscales, the washing-machine manufacturer, a JP and member of the School Board; Albert Rishworth, a leading local Tory; John Mitchell of Hattersleys, a JP and member of the Town Council – all were leading employers and influential in the parish church, as was C. H. Foulds, an early mayor. John Smith Naylor, a brass founder and Poor Law Guardian, Craven Laycock, a member of the School Board, and Jonathan Gill, a leading engineer and town councillor, were all important Congregationalists. James Groves and T. S. Clapham of the engineering firm were Baptists.[7] The Marriners' 'Christian Liberality was manifested on several occasions' towards the Methodist churches.[8] The Cloughs, too, were Methodists, the 'principal means of building the beautiful Methodist Chapel at Paper Mill Bridge and more recently in promoting the extension fund for building several additional Methodist Chapels in the Keighley Circuit'.[9] The Smiths of Laycock were 'very forward in promoting the interests of religious education'.[10] Obviously, such people and others like them did not use their power in the religious life of the town simply as a means of social control. They were sincere Christians doing what they thought was right. The point is that they had the power to ensure that their assumption of what was right was accepted by the churches. Allied organizations such as the temperance movement were equally dominated by the manufacturers. For example, the Keighley and District Band of Hope Union had William Clough as its president and J. J. Brigg, Swire Smith and J. W. Laycock amongst its vice-presidents. All four were major employers and members of the Keighley Liberal 300.[11]

Thus the churches and chapels were in no very strong position to resist endorsing the opinions of the middle-class élite or to make a favourable response to the awakening political and social demands of the working class in the 1890s. It is too simplistic to assume, however, that the situation was clear-cut and that opposition to working-class aspirations among the Keighley clergy was total. There were a number of ministers who were aware of the churches' failure to make contact with the workers, and who made efforts to make their religion relevant to the needs of that class. They included such people as the Revd E. Pringle, a Congregational minister who started the Pleasant Sunday Afternoon Movement in Keighley. There was the Canon F. D. Cremer, the rector of Keighley, whose 'Christian socialism ... permeated his sermons'.[12] A few ministers such as the Revd F. E. Chester and the Revd J. Stansfield, both Anglicans, called themselves socialists and co-operated closely with the ILP, particularly on the School Board and also in meetings to discuss social questions, although they never joined the party. Stansfield, however, married Mary Jane Dixon, the first ILP member of the School Board.[13] Even among these people, however, political questions were not their main concerns. They were chiefly interested in their churches and their congregations and the spiritual life of the community.

One openly socialist minister was the Revd S. J. C. Goldsack, a Nonconformist whose sympathies led him to form a Union of Socialists amongst members of his congregation. He was soon forced to resign his pastorate.[14] Other prominent churchmen occasionally came over to the socialist side. For example, W. E. Wallbank, an ex-town councillor and prominent Methodist Sunday School superintendent, declared himself a socialist because of the moral arguments, stating that 'he had come to the conclusion that socialism was the right thing, was a thing that all Christians should support and was bound to come in the future'.[15]

The concern of such people was by no means unique. In the Colne Valley, an area where ethical socialism was also strong, a number of Church of England ministers were among the earliest supporters of the ILP. In Bradford, Dr K. C. Anderson told his congregation that 'the socialist indictment against society is a true bill, we cannot answer the charge'.[16] However, the point about such men, both in Keighley and the rest of the country, is that though they formed an interesting minority, they were relatively scarce. Leonard Smith suggests that although there were national attempts to forge an unofficial alliance between the ILP leadership and influential religious leaders, relationships were never more than 'flimsy and fluctuating', and this is also true of Keighley.[17]

Nevertheless, the realization of the failure of religion to appeal to the workers did give rise to a number of attempts to bring them into the orbit of the organized Churches. The work of the Pleasant Sunday Afternoon (PSA) Movement has already been discussed, but it is worth mentioning that certain aspects of it had parallels with the Labour Church, which was started a little later. There was the same attempt to encourage people who did not attend a place of worship to join; there was an emphasis on fellowship and brotherhood; and both believed that the improvement of the character of the individual was necessary before social change could take place. It is possible, therefore, to see a considerable overlap between the ethical ideas put forward by the PSA and those of the Labour Church. The PSA showed that an ethical approach to social questions was one which could produce a response among the people of Keighley. What the ILP had to do was to put a socialist interpretation on such sentiments.

The attraction to the Keighley working class of a moral approach to solving society's ills is confirmed in other ways. In 1890 Alfred Burrows of the Trades Council and later the ILP gave trade-unionism a moral dimension when he called it a 'practical Christian Gospel',[18] and in the same year the *Annual Review* of the Keighley Trades Council pointed to the 'social and moral objectives'[19] of trade-unionism. During the 1893 strike at Merralls, W. H. Drew, discussed the propriety of holding a strike meeting on a Sunday:

> He held that if the founder of the Christian faith had been on earth now, he would have been with them, as his first care was the temporal needs

> of his people. He knew too well that unless people were contented in their daily walks there was no chance of raising their morals and making them better and nobler people. And so he held that the meetings were quite as religious as that conducted in any Church or Chapel … The Labour movement from end to end was filled with religious enthusiasm such as the Churches would do well to copy and he believed that if they intended to maintain that supremacy which they said ought to be theirs, but which they did little to obtain, their duty was to be with the toilers, and not with those opposed to them.[20]

Thus the successful establishment of a socialist movement in Keighley based on ethical concepts need cause no surprise. A few churchmen had taken a moral stand on social problems and in some cases advocated socialist solutions, and an influential part of the working class already phrased their demands for social change in moral terms. The official churches and chapels controlled by the middle-class manufacturers were unable and unwilling to accommodate this latent idealism, which was captured by the ILP and the Labour Church and later the Socialist Sunday Schools and converted into ethical socialism.

Ethical socialism was often called 'the religion of socialism'. The phrase was used as early as 1885 in the manifesto of the Socialist League, written by William Morris, and was used by many socialist pioneers during the 1880s and 1890s. Many early socialists experienced a process of conversion before they became committed to the cause, which often resulted in social ostracism and a breaking away from family and friends, and also in a sense of brotherhood and fellowship with other socialists. This phenomenon was much wider than those ILPers who were members of the Labour Church or the Socialist Sunday Schools. It was much wider than the ILP itself. Even meetings of the Social Democratic Federation could assume a religious character. George Lansbury recalled his membership of the Bow and Bromley SDF branch, where 'meetings were like revivalist gatherings. We opened with a song and closed with one, and often read together some extracts from economic and historical writings.' The 'religion of socialism' was particularly strong in areas like the West Riding, where Labour advanced among strong traditions of religious nonconformity.[21]

The appeal of ethical socialism in places like Keighley was especially strong among those sections of the working class which formed the membership of the local ILP. Once established, increasing numbers joined the ILP because they were attracted by the emphasis on ethical socialism. Unfortunately, it is difficult to find specific evidence of what made people join the Keighley branch, but there are indications that confirm that, for some, while the organized Churches had lost their attraction, the appeal of morality was strong. Speaking of G. J. Wardle, Edward Horner said that 'he [Wardle] had been led to socialism from its religious standpoint, while he [Edward Horner] had been led to it from its economic standpoint. Thus as all roads once led to Rome, so all roads now led to socialism.'[22] William Bramham seems to have found an inspiration in ethical socialism which he could not find in the established Church, declaring that 'for some time before almost the only attraction the chapel or the church had for him was the music, but being impelled to visit the Labour Union meetings he found there speakers with whom he could in the main agree and with whose objects he was in thorough sympathy'.[23] W. S. Wilkinson, choirmaster of the Keighley Clarion Vocal Union, also found the moral arguments for socialism compelling. He referred to 'the effect on his mind of reading the *Clarion*, Merrie England and Ruskin's Unto this Last and Sesame and Lilies ... [and] ... felt it his duty to choose sides ... and take his place under the banner of Labour'.[24]

Other ILPers retained their connections with religious organizations but also responded to the ethical appeal of socialism. Mary Jane Dixon was a well-known Primitive Methodist local preacher; Margaret Pickles, the ILP Board of Guardians candidate in 1898, was also prominently connected with the Primitive Methodists; Harrison Wallbank, an ILP candidate in Haworth, was 'qualified by experience in Sunday School ... to creditably discharge the duties of the position [on the Board of Guardians] in which his party are seeking to place him'.[25]

Ethical socialism was the most obvious way of spreading socialist ideas among the people of Keighley, and it was also the most effective way of gaining widespread backing. Because trade-unionism was weak in the town, it was difficult to translate the ILP alliance with the trade-unionists into mass support. It was necessary to find some other means of popularizing the ILP, and the ethical approach was the most hopeful alternative. By emphasizing the moral aspects of socialism as well as its value to organized labour, it became possible to attract support not just from the working class, but from other groups as well.

Before examining the Labour Church, the chief means of propagating ethical socialism in Keighley, and discussing its importance to the ILP, there are two questions which need to be considered. First, accepting that their concept of socialism was moral and visionary, how did the Keighley ILP reconcile the gap between their short-term political programme and their millenarian socialist ideal? Second, what did they mean by socialism? How far was their ethical socialism just rhetoric, camouflaging a reforming political programme, and how far was it a hope for a perfect society?

Stanley Pierson has remarked, when discussing Tom Maguire, that 'the tension ... between Socialism as a new religious faith and Socialism as a particular programme for advancing working-class interests, helped bring disillusion and an early death'.[26] Stephen Yeo has also pointed to the divergence between agency and goal, or what he calls 'here and nowhere', which he sees in the socialist movement in the late nineteenth century.[27] It is easy to identify a similar gap between aspiration and means in Keighley, and it is most clearly illustrated in the work of Philip Snowden.

Snowden was, without question, the ablest politician to participate in Keighley public life. He was prominent in local politics between 1895 and 1902, after which date he left the town and returned only as a visitor. His contribution to the local ILP was considerable. His talent as a speaker meant that he could express the ideas of the branch eloquently and coherently, in a way which had a wide appeal to members of the working class. His ability as a politician and administrator meant that the ILP could make intelligent and constructive contributions to the work of the Council and the School Board. He showed that socialism could offer practical policies as well as rhetoric.

Snowden had a superb speaking voice, which he used to great effect when making the case for socialism as an ethical system. Writing of his influence, Stanley Pierson says that 'no figure exhibited this appeal [of ethical socialism] more clearly than Philip Snowden who performed at this time a missionary work unsurpassed among his contemporaries ... in arousing the masses to self awareness'.[28] Locally, his talents fell on fertile ground and when he started to lecture in Keighley his ability was quickly recognized. Commenting on one of his early lectures, the *Keighley Labour Journal* remarked:

> Not only was the address remarkable for its impassioned eloquence, but it was full of that nameless power which seizes the hearts and consciences of men and carried the conviction along with it. We believe that the effect of such a speech cannot be merely transitory, but must result in a larger determination in the minds of those who heard it, not to tamely sit down with things as they are but to strive earnestly for the realisation of the brotherhood of man.[29]

And Snowden did not only appeal to committed socialists. On one occasion it was claimed that he addressed between eleven and twelve hundred people at the Mechanics Institute, 'crowded to excess, scores of people turned away'. Soon after his arrival in Keighley it was reported that:

> Last Sunday's meeting in point of numbers and enthusiasm was the most successful we have yet held. Hundreds of persons went away unable to get into the Hall, and it was a splendid tribute to the popularity of Mr Philip Snowden that so large and attentive an audience should come and hear him.[30]

His talents were, therefore, a unique asset to the Keighley ILP. In his lectures, 'argument and pathos, striking imagery and powerful appeal were beautifully blended', and to the local socialists he was 'the one and only Philip Snowden. Halifax may possess the towering Mont Blong but the mighty Snowden rears his stately crest in the vicinity of Keighley.'[31] Not only did he attract large audiences locally, inspiring the converted and converting the curious, but he rapidly became one of the most eloquent speakers in the socialist movement. His lectures were full of biblical phraseology and combined a vision of the future socialist society, and a sympathy for the present situation of the workers, with razor-sharp attacks on the capitalist class. In a lecture in 1895 he declared that:

> socialism aimed at something beyond mere restricted demand for higher wages; its object was to realise those aspiring mutterings which had been faintly heard for ages, and to establish for the workers a true life – the development of the whole of man's capacities, the expanding of affections and the co-operating with Divine Order of the universe. Socialism did not claim to establish any new principle of morality or religion, but it did claim to understand the moral law more clearly and perfectly than current philosophy or religion … It was a religion that believed with Ruskin that whether there was one God, whether there were three gods, or 10,000 gods little children should have their bellies filled and their bodies kept warm. It was a religion which judged men not by creeds, but by deeds.[32]

One of his most famous lectures was called *The Christ that is to be*, and the final passage illustrates the religiosity of his style. He said:

> But the only way to regain the earthly paradise is by the old hard road to Calvary – through persecution, through poverty, through temptation, by agony and bloody sweat, by the crown of thorns, by the agonising death. And then the resurrection to the New Humanity – purified by suffering, triumphant through sacrifice.[33]

However, Snowden's talents as a speaker were not confined to spreading the utopian message of ethical socialism. His intellectual abilities, wide range of interests and eloquence enabled him to debate the social, political and economic problems of the day with authority and skill. These talents gave the Keighley ILP a greater local political standing than it otherwise would have had, for with Snowden in the party it was unconvincing to brand its members a mere rabble-rousing group of irresponsible agitators. He was also able to convince even some of the more sceptical people that the ideas of socialism were worth serious consideration. For example, a typical lecture at nearby Steeton in 1897 on 'Labour and Politics' drew 'a capital audience including many well-known Liberals', who:

> listened with great interest and keen attention to the admirable and lucid statement of the Socialist position and programme and it was quite evident that the people of Steeton fully appreciate the point of the

> lecture ... Mr William Clough said that before he came to the meeting he had been told that if he asked any questions he would get nothing but impudence, but he wanted to say that just the opposite was the case, and he desired to express his thanks to the Chairman and the speaker, for the courtesy shown to him. There is no doubt that Mr Snowden has by his earnestness, ability and sincerity made an impression on Steeton and will at another future visit, be sure of a welcome here.[34]

Snowden's speaking ability, supported by carefully thought out political positions, gave him considerable standing in the local community and stamped an authority even on his most unpopular views. For example, at the time of the Boer War he was able to take an anti-government line and yet 'Sunday evening's meeting was a triumph. Mr Snowden spoke on "Imperialism" and although his language was not measured, and his statements were against the popular opinion, yet there was not a whisper of dissent, not a single question.'[35]

Snowden's speeches were, therefore, broadly of two kinds. The first type aimed to spread the ethical socialism of which he was a prime exponent in the north. The second type aimed to analyse and comment on the current political situation. However, for him, as for most ethical socialists, there was, as Colin Cross noted, a difficulty in that 'between the two principal styles – the emotional and the factual – there was a gap. He could describe the distant dream of Socialism and he could analyse current affairs. What he could not do was to describe how the transition to the perfect Socialist State was to be achieved.'[36] It was a failing that was seized on by the local Liberals. In 1895 the *Keighley News* examined this very point after Snowden had made a particularly abusive attack upon the Liberal manufacturers:

> We will take for granted for the sake of argument, that the evils of society are as terrible as they are represented to be by Mr Snowden and that he and his followers are absolutely infallible in the indications that they give of an effectual cure for them; that of the pooling of all the property and resources of society in one common fund to be dispersed for the common good. Mr Snowden has been good enough to admit that this is a 'large order' and that it will take some years, perhaps some generations to execute. Now it would be of some service if Mr Snowden would be kind enough to indicate what the owners of land and wealth are to do in the meantime.[37]

The Keighley ILP was aware of the difference between aspiration and means. On the one hand there was the hard slog of political campaigning, with its petty gains and inevitable compromises; and on the other hand the belief in 'socialism as the Kingdom of God'. How was the first to lead to the second? The Keighley socialists proposed two solutions. First, they suggested that it should be accepted that socialism was going to be a long time arriving – 'let us not ignore facts', they wrote, 'mountains are not removed in a day. We have a long and stubborn fight before us. But we have right on our side and can afford to wait, working all the time as strenuously and as earnestly as if victory were close at hand.'[38] Their successes in local government were seen as the first small steps in a long-drawn-out historical process. Second, their ethical socialism put considerable emphasis on local reforms. They argued that socialism could be achieved only if the mass of the people underwent individual conversion, for 'our business is to make socialists. We can never hope to realise our ideals until we convert people to them.'[39]

The necessary prerequisite for such conversions were improvements in living and working conditions. By improving the environment, the circumstances would be created whereby the individual would be given the leisure and facilities to arrive at socialism. This belief, suggesting that it was environment which largely influenced people's development, probably derived from the writings of Robert Blatchford, although its origins are, of course, much older. G. J. Wardle outlined the arguments in 1895:

> One of the strong points in the Socialist movement is its insistence on the importance of Environment in its relation to character and life … 'We are moulded by our Environment' and to expect 'Saints' to grow up in slums, in overcrowded insanitary workshops … is clearly to expect the impossible … The Socialist therefore affirms and the Labour Church reiterates the affirmation that to seek to alter the condition at the same time as you seek, to develop the personal character, is the only way to bring about 'The Kingdom of Heaven on Earth' for which all … so ardently long.[40]

Philip Snowden made the same point in his article 'The Two Salvations', which was published in the *Labour Prophet*:

> We are entirely at one with those who see the necessity for individual regeneration … To change these conditions which are preventing the individual regeneration of the masses is the social salvation which it is necessary to preach and put into practice as the complement to the preaching of individual salvation. And by improving the conditions under which people live we make the work of individual regeneration easier and possible.[41]

It was in this way that the Keighley socialists attempted to reconcile the differences between long-term aspirations and short-term commitment. If it was necessary to improve the environment before people could become socialists, then municipal socialism was an essential preliminary to the creation of 'the kingdom of heaven on earth'.

What, however, was this socialism that the Keighley ILPers so ardently desired? In the economic sense, the question is easy to answer. When the

Keighley Labour Union was formed in 1892, it had three objectives, which were radical rather than socialist: to secure the direct representation of labour on all municipal bodies; to restore the land to the people by the taxation of land values; to municipalize monopolies and extend municipal powers. When it was affiliated to the ILP in 1893, these were replaced by 'the collective ownership and control of the means of production, distribution and exchange'.[42] However, socialism was clearly seen as more than mere economic collectivism: to many, it contained elements akin to religion or a religious substitute. As has been seen, G. J. Wardle regarded it as nothing less than 'the realisation of the Kingdom of Heaven on Earth'.[43]

As this phrase indicates, ethical socialism was a matter of feeling and emotion rather than precisely defined beliefs. It is, nevertheless, possible to identify some of its more salient features, an important one of which was that it cut across class lines. An article in 1895 declared that it was 'a great mistake to suppose that the line of division between the socialist and the anti-socialist is the same as between the upper and lower classes. Many of the most earnest, able and certainly most self sacrificing champions today belong to the wealthy and cultured class.'[44] Attacks on the working class were not infrequent; 'the majority of the lower classes are intellectually incapable of understanding socialism', commented the *Keighley Labour Journal* in 1895, and in the same edition the 'respectable working man' is told that 'socialism is not for him. Such a man is as incapable of understanding or appreciating the intellectual life which it is the object of socialism to make universal as a toad is of soaring with the lark into the cloudless summer sky.'[45]

This attitude is perhaps explicable when the importance that the ILPers placed on the environment as a moulder of character is remembered. Also, many of the ILPers held middle- or lower-middle-class jobs, and this may have made them unsympathetic to the priorities of the labouring classes. For example, the Horners were teachers, Snowden was a journalist who had been a civil servant and Mary Jane Dixon was a manageress. Inevitably, also, there was a feeling of disappointment that the majority of the working class persisted in electing Liberals and Tories to the Council, the School Board and the Boards of Guardians, instead of ILPers. This disappointment could at times lead to an attitude of élitism, as the above quotation indicates.

This rejection of the class war, as well as a belief that socialism had as much to do with ethics as with economics, is well illustrated in a report on a talk given by J. R. Widdop to the Keighley Labour Church. Widdop was a member of the SDF and seems to have outlined a Marxist interpretation of historical change. The *Keighley Labour Journal* commented that:

> While agreeing with the speaker to some extent, we are bound to confess we cannot go with him altogether, as the changes which have taken place ... have been brought about by a multitude of causes, not the least of

> these being the power of ideality working towards some perfect system and the influence of morality and true religion in persisting in the application of those ideals even when it has been against the interest of the dominant class.[46]

As an alternative to the class analysis of Widdop, the Keighley ILPers emphasized moral concepts such as brotherhood, justice and equality. The following two passages give the flavour of their appeal, both in terms of the vocabulary used and in the stress on emotion rather than logic. The first bases socialism on an appeal for justice:

> You cannot take up a newspaper … but you will find … amid the records of gambling, drunkenness, gluttony divorce and luxury … tales of how helpless women are starved to death and brave men driven to desperation … I doubt sometimes if there be a man amongst us who has one atom of humanity in his body. If there were I think his indignation would be fiery enough to burn up the cant and callousness which can tolerate such ghastly inhumanity to one another. What need we of theories and programmes? Is it past the wit of man to save one from dying of starvation while another is satiated with abundance? Is it God's will that the idle and vicious shall roll in wealth and the industrious and virtuous pine to death.[47]

The second is an argument in favour of equality:

> One of the most common objections to socialism is based on the argument that Socialism would destroy all incentive to effort, that it would do away with what is called the struggle for existence and thus produce uniformity … we preach a socialism which is based on such principles as 'All for one and each for all' … Socialism would compel every man to work, not as it is now, in many cases against his fellow, but for him … It proposes to transfer the struggle to a conflict with nature; to an attempt to wring from her all the glorious possibilities that lie in her for the benefit of mankind, to turn her vast treasury into a store house from which the wants and needs of every man can be satisfied.[48]

A further moral concept important to the Keighley socialists was the idea of individuality. Socialism should not lead to uniformity. Philip Snowden was the best-known interpreter of the view that, under socialism, there would be created 'a condition of things favourable to the development of a higher type of individuality'. This view was expressed in a number of articles and speeches, including his influential pamphlet *The Individual Under Socialism*, where he attacked the capitalist system as chaining workers:

> for eleven hours a day to monotonous toil with the eye of the overseer and the fear of dismissal spurring them on to an exertion which leaves them at the end of their day's work physical wrecks, with no more ambition but to restore their wasted energies at the nearest public house.
>
> The system effectively prevented the working man or woman from displaying any originality or individuality in his work or leisure. Under socialism work would be, 'good, useful and honourable' having an elevated effect on men's character and there would be abundant time for the satisfaction of individual desires.[49]

Finally, the Keighley ILPers expected the road to socialism to be peaceful and evolutionary. With its emphasis on class collaboration and individual conversion, this is not surprising. For all their rhetoric, they believed that:

> The only possible way to change the system is from within ... The socialist ... knows that Society is one organic whole, and it is impossible to split it into sections without destroying the life of the body. The Socialist leaven working in our body will gradually leaven the whole Society. There is no wrong, no outraging our principles in doing what necessity compels us to do. It is enough if we are ready to change the system, and if we are doing all we can to bring about this change as gradually, but as rapidly as we can.[50]

This gradualist form of ethical socialism, depending on individual conversion and brought about by arguments based on moral precepts, was clearly not original. The writings of William Morris, Robert Blatchford and the Fabians all influenced the Keighley ILPers. Yet it is important to note that their ideas were disseminated in articles and speeches whose vocabulary contained a strong vein of religious imagery. Socialism, it was argued, was a form of Christianity which would eventually replace the organized religion of the older Churches. In this way, the 'transfer of religious energy from religion to politics'[51] was brought about.

The Keighley socialists believed in their ethical socialism deeply and sincerely, although its lack of intellectual content may have lead, as Pierson suggests it did in some places, to 'their moral and religious rhetoric ... [simply] ... serving class or sectional interests'.[52] The branch's reaction to the death of Caroline Martyn is one example of the depth of their commitment to their kind of socialism. Like the rest of the labour movement, they were stunned, moving in their monthly meeting 'that a letter of condolence be sent to the relatives of the late C. E. D. Martyn expressing our deepest sympathy with them in their bereavement and also the great loss the socialist movement has sustained by her death'. The minutes then added: 'this was carried everyone rising to their feet'. It was the only time such a letter was sent or such an act of respect paid, the point being that it was paid to one of the leading ethical socialists of the day. A month later it was resolved 'that a full length portrait ... of the late Carrie Martyn be recommended to be purchased and framed by the Club Committee'.[53]

It is perhaps not surprising that the activities of the Labour Church became a focal point of the branch's activities. As early as January 1893, 144 Labour Hymn Books at 1*d.* (0.5p) each and 36 at 2*d.* (1p) each were purchased by the union.[54] Later in the year a permanent home was found for the Labour Church, the minutes recording significantly that it was the Primitive Old Chapel that was to be 'engaged from the Co-Op Soc. at 8*s.* [40p] per Sunday evening 6.15–8.15 subject to no smoking being allowed'. From time to time other buildings were considered for these Sunday meetings. In March 1895 a deputation was ordered 'to attend and view the Spiritual Temple with a view to opening it as a Lab. Ch. and Club if suitable', and in 1899 an attempt was made to raise funds to establish a Socialist Hall. None of these proposals appears to have proceeded any further, largely because of financial difficulties. However, in December 1899 a Socialist Sunday School was established.[55]

Perhaps surprisingly, the Keighley Labour Church did not affiliate with the Labour Church Union for two years, and the reason would seem to have been financial. In January 1895 the Executive agreed that 'we call our Sunday Evening Meetings the Labour Church any alterations to be left with the Lecture Committee as to details of the service, but no additional financial burdens in the shape of affiliation fees to be acted upon'. Three months later, however, it was agreed to join the Labour Church Union. The chief supporter seems to have been G. J. Wardle, who in 1896 was a member of the Labour Church Union Conference.[56]

Irrespective of the details of organization, however, the meetings of the Labour Church were very popular. The party recognized that they were its best means of propaganda, and in December 1894 it commented that 'our most successful work has ... been the Sunday services and the crowded audiences who have listened to the new gospel and drunk with avidity the teaching put forth by the various speakers will no doubt furnish many recruits and staunch adherents'. By the end of 1896 it was claimed that four to five hundred people attended their meetings, 'the great majority of whom are strong believers in our principles'.[57] Nevertheless, there seem to have been some indications that this popularity was confined only to a section of the working class. H. C. Rowe, writing in the *Labour Prophet* about a visit he made to the town, said: 'in the Co-operative Hall, between three and four hundred people found comfortable seating room on the Sunday evening, strong, sober, plain people'.[58] The impression is that the ILP was attracting the more respectable members of the working class, a pattern that was found nationally, as well as in Keighley.

One other important aspect of the Keighley Labour Church should be considered: to what extent was the weekly service regarded as a religious occasion, or how far was it merely a convenient name for a Sunday political meeting, where, 'with a prayer and a couple of hymns … you got a Socialist lecture to thousands who otherwise you'd never see'.[59] K. S. Inglis, in his article on the Labour Church movement, points out that this was a national problem. He argues that the visiting speakers were not a source of strength to the Labour Church as a movement. One of the reasons was the eclectic nature of the subject-matter of the addresses and the wide variety of speakers' views. A leader of the Nottingham Labour Church summed up this confusion: 'on one Sunday they would have an orthodox speaker, and perhaps the next an aggressive secularist. People went away wondering what the Labour Church stood for.'[60] For many of the speakers, the Labour Church was simply a useful platform, while for other attenders it was an opportunity to see the leaders of the labour movement in a comfortable and congenial atmosphere, where the religious fervour of the meeting helped to reinforce a sense of respectability and familiarity.

The Keighley Labour Church seems to have experienced this difficulty, and it is understandable that they should do so, even though socialism in Keighley was strongly ethical and the meetings were held in a former church. The fact is that the Labour Church was established by the ILP as part of its propaganda machine. It was never, as was the case in Leeds, for example, a separate organization. There were, of course, similarities between the Keighley Labour Church services and ordinary religious services; for example, hymns were sung, but these seem to have been more a matter of preference than of religious conviction. Religious formats were retained only for as long as people wanted them. Thus, many of the recitals given at the end of each service were distinctly secular. Poems and songs such as 'Christmas Day in the Workhouse', 'Home Sweet Home', or 'Hope Told a Flattering Tale' were recited and sung, and amateur musicians played such tunes as the 'Wedding March' on the concertina.[61] The tendency was for such offerings to be sentimental rather than religious. At the same time, the speakers were drawn from a wide range of backgrounds and expressed a variety of opinions. Many of the addresses were concerned with an ethical approach to socialism, and such titles as 'Did Christ Teach Socialism', 'Religion and Social Duty', and, of course, Philip Snowden's 'Religion of Socialism' were popular, but other speakers concentrated on the political and economic aspects of the ILP programme. In November 1894, for example, the speakers were Fred Jowett on 'Municipal Experiences', J. R. Clynes on 'Political Parties and Reform', and Joseph Guy on 'The Utility of Trade Unions'. Similarly, in November 1897 there were talks on 'The Extermination of Fever Under Socialism', 'Employers and Employed', and 'Slum Landlordism'. Table 6.1 (p.175) lists the titles and speakers in the Labour Church between 1893 and 1899, after which information becomes unavailable, and it can be seen that the discussions of economic and social questions were prominent, although talks on ethical socialism were always highly regarded. But the important point is that the desire to have a wide variety of speakers and subjects militated against the Labour Church becoming anything more than a place where talks were held. The appeal of the meetings lay in the audiences being able to hear different speakers, usually from outside the locality, each week. Many of these speakers were leaders of the labour movement and it was this fact that was the criterion for inviting them to speak. The religious aspects of the service that were retained were a matter of form rather than belief. Perhaps the most significant comment on the Labour Church can be found in a minute of 13 July 1899, which said 'that we have all first class lecturers and go outside the Socialist movement if necessary'.[62] It was the lecturer that was important; and although the form of the service was popular, there was little commitment to the Labour Church as a spiritual movement.

But it remained the fact that ethical socialism was the characteristic means of expressing socialism in Keighley. The failure of the established Churches to harness the moral feelings of the respectable working class led to them transferring their religious energy to the labour movement. At the same time, however, the spirituality of religion as expressed in the Labour Church was debased and sentimentalized, and became a matter of form. Notwithstanding this, the moral approach to social questions determined the kind of socialism which developed in the town. It was classless, evolutionary and gradual, and based on a belief in such concepts as justice, equality and freedom.

The Labour Church, however, was only one aspect of a wider counter-culture developed by the Keighley socialists. They attempted to create a socialist culture in which more was involved than simply agreeing with the ILP's political programme and voting for them at the elections: it was to encompass a whole way of life, much of it based on the concept of fellowship.

The activities making up this culture were diverse but, before examining them, mention must be made of the ILP Club which was the organizational centre of the branch. Almost the first act of the Labour Union was to establish its club.[63] It was obviously used as a social centre, and in this it probably resembled not only the other Working Men's Clubs that were in existence, but also the various Liberal and Conservative Clubs. Games were provided, including a darts board, a portable bagatelle and a full-sized billiard table, bought after much discussion from the Ingrow Liberal Club. For many years, the Club could not afford a piano, although the importance of acquiring one was regularly minuted. This purely recreational side, however, was subordinated to the political and ethical work of the party. On Sundays, no billiards or darts were allowed, and the Club Room was closed while the Labour Church services were held.

The question of whether or not the Club should sell drink throws an interesting light on some of the social and cultural influences which were important in the party. The power of temperance, with its implications of self-control and self-reliance, was strong. There was an active group in favour of selling liquor, but it was in a minority. In February 1894 it moved 'that we consider the selling of drink in the Club'. This proposal was quickly squashed, the majority resolving 'that no intoxicating drink be sold in the Club as a source of revenue'. The drink lobby returned to the attack the following month, moving 'that drink be sold in the Club as a source of revenue'. Exasperated, the majority moved 'that the drink question be not discussed again for twelve months'.[64] Nevertheless, the question of selling drink was revived at regular intervals. The temperance group included such leading party members as the Horners, Philip Snowden, Mary Jane Dixon and G. J. Wardle. Both Wardle and Mary Jane Dixon preached in Nonconformist churches, as did another temperance advocate, Mrs Roe. The Nonconformism and temperance which have been seen as important influences on the ILP are evident here, and were more important than the financial advantages of selling alcohol.

In less contentious areas, the Club was regarded as a legitimate means of raising money for the party and for bolstering the alternative culture of the ILP. For example, in December 1893, 'the club committee be authorised to organize a social and dance', for which tickets were sold and a profit made and which became a regular fund-raising event. In addition, the Club sold various domestic items: 'The Club Secretary drew the attention of members to the advisability of members making their purchases of tobacco, tea and ILP matches from the Club in order to assist in reducing expenses.' It was also used as an educational centre, where arithmetic and shorthand classes and discussion groups were held and a library of 'works on labour questions' was housed. Ultimately, however, its chief importance must have been the simple fact that it was the headquarters of the branch, where its political campaigns were organized, its committees met, its meetings held and its paperwork done. It was, in short, the administrative headquarters of the party.[65]

As membership grew, clubs were established in other parts of the Division. These resembled the Keighley Club, but membership was smaller. Unlike Bradford, where there were over twenty clubs differing in size but maintaining their independence, the Keighley Club dominated the District. This does not mean that the others always accepted the leadership of Keighley. In 1903, Tom Mackley wrote sharply to the Haworth secretary that 'I have yet to learn that this Committee are under any obligation to write Haworth to inform them what they are doing in Keighley.'[66]

Although the Club provided the physical headquarters of the branch, it was the various Clarion organizations which best expressed the concept of fellowship which was so important to Keighley socialism. The most successful was the Clarion Vocal Union, led by W. S. Wilkinson. A music teacher, he joined the ILP in 1892, attracted by its moral appeal. At a meeting in January 1894 it was recorded that:

> When first approached he had declined to preside over the meeting and had begged to be allowed to sing or do something else in a humble way to show his sympathy with the movement. When he thought of the objects of the Labour Union and of their attempts to bind men together to help their less favoured brother workers he thought he must obey the call of duty so 'he had arrived'.[67]

Clearly, for him, joining the party was a moral as much as a political decision. While a member, he stood unsuccessfully for the Borough Council, but his main interest lay with the Clarion Vocal Union. His work was much appreciated and was regarded as valid a contribution to the party as the political work of the Horners and the Snowdens.

The Vocal Union made various contributions to the success of the branch. It helped to recruit new members; it made political meetings more attractive; and it often accompanied distinguished speakers. For example, it toured with Keir Hardie when he visited the area in 1897, rendering 'valuable assistance at all meetings'. More important, however, it helped to create the fellowship which motivated many members to join the ILP. An account of a trip to Ilkley organized by the Vocal Union gives some of the flavour of such activities:

> At half past two we wended our way to the fountain in the centre of the pleasure seekers, and there the Clarion Vocal Union rendered some splendid music to the astonishment of the crowd of people, who quickly gathered round, with many enquiries as to who these singers could be. No one seemed to know until one of the party began to give out 'Merrie England', when one old gent who evidently had seen better days, cried out 'Why they are socialists', and echo answered, 'Right old friend'.[68]

Such outings were more than just propaganda, they were a way of showing that socialism was about enjoying a fuller life, 'one of the pleasantest days out it has ever been my lot to join', as it was said of the above trip. The effort put into the Vocal Union showed that the ILP was not only concerned with the eight-hour day or fair contracts, but also about a more positive approach to life than was possible under capitalism. As the *Keighley Labour Journal* said, echoing William Morris: 'under the pressure of our industrial system, maypoles and many of the joys of May have disappeared, men have become like machines. They have not time to enjoy themselves.'[69] It was the attempt to show that men did not have to become machines that made the cultural side of ILP life so important. It was seen by them as an integral part of socialism, providing a foretaste of what life would be like. An account of a joint meeting of several vocal unions in the *Keighley Labour Journal* brings this out: 'several thousands of Socialists were present, and all seemed to enjoy themselves in good humoured and true socialist fashion. Is it possible that in the quiet and orderly gathering which graced the glades and woods of Bolton lies the real significance of the future.'[70]

The Vocal Union was probably the most important, but it was not the only Clarion organization which was incorporated into the activities of the Keighley ILP. The Clarion Scouts were formed in 1894, and in 1897 a Clarion Cycling Club was established.[71] Again, the justification for forming these groups was the idea that brotherhood and socialism were moral commitments as well as political ones, as the *Keighley Labour Journal* said about the cyclists:

> Apart, however, from the social advantages to be acquired by membership, there is work to be done which only cyclists can do, and the way to do it effectively is by some organised, systematic method, this method can most easily be developed by a well disciplined Clarion Cycling Club, composed of men who are willing to do something however humble, to spread the truths of socialism.[72]

Later, a Clarion Fellowship was set up, 'to develop social intercourse among socialists'.[73]

As well as these groups, the social life of the branch was carried on by regular dances, teas – particularly ham teas – and 'free and easys'. This range of activities gave the branch a social and cultural life of considerable richness and variety, as can be shown in a report by the *Keighley Labour Journal* for April 1901, discussing the work of the branch in the previous three months:

> We have had discussions in our rooms on Sunday evenings on various subjects by men of various shades of opinion. These discussions have been a source of pleasure, and I believe education to those who have attended ... a committee have arranged several successful evening socials at which members of the Clarion Prize Vocal Union have given their services. We have also carried through our annual tea, concert and dance which was ... very successful financially ... We intend to renew our former active open-air propaganda. A Committee is appointed to arrange a series of picnics including, if possible, a boat trip to Farnhill Crags on the canal.[74]

Enterprise on this scale can have left the local ILP enthusiasts little time for anything else but the work of the party. Apart from organizing events and attending various ILP functions, they were in constant demand as speakers or at public meetings. Philip Snowden was, of course, exceptionally popular, but his claim in 1901 that he had addressed a public meeting every single weekend for five years was probably not much greater than some of the others, such as Herbert Horner.

The moral approach towards socialism created a counter-culture in Keighley, as elsewhere, which put forward a value-system that was an alternative to capitalism. This ILP culture was based on a belief in brotherhood and was intended as an example of what life would be like when socialism was achieved. This hopefulness about the future is summed up in the phrase frequently used in the branch: 'we shall arrive'. It had a political connotation, but also a moral one. When all men were brothers, then socialism will have arrived. It was the adoption of this ethos of fellowship which separated the Keighley ILP from the other two parties and made it into a crusade rather than just a political machine.

Notes

1. Pelling, *op.cit.*, ch.vii; K. S. Inglis, 'The Labour Church Movement', *International Review of Social History* (1958), pp.445–60; S. Yeo, 'A New Life: The Religion of Socialism in Britain', *History Workshop*, 4 (1977), pp.5–56; L. Smith, 'Religion and the ILP', in James, Jowitt and Laybourn (eds), *The Centennial History of the ILP* (Halifax, 1992); L. Smith, *Religion and the Rise of Labour*, *op.cit.*; A. J. Jowitt, 'Religion and the Independent Labour Party', in Laybourn and James (eds), *The Rising Sun of Socialism*, *op.cit.*: this work contains a list of relevant writings.
2. Clark, *op.cit.*, pp.50–2, 145–50, 186–8.
3. *Keighley Year Book*, 1895.
4. S. J. D. Green, 'The Death of Pew-Rents, the Rise of Bazaars, and the End of the Traditional Political Economy of Voluntary Religious Organisations: the Case of the West Riding of Yorkshire, *c.*1870–1914', *Northern History*, XXVII (1991), pp.219–20.
5. Pelling, *op.cit.*, p.129.
6. *Keighley Labour Journal*, 14 May 1898.
7. Information on Summerscales and Mitchell in *Keighley Year Book*; obituary of Albert Rishworth in *Keighley News*, 28 August 1937; obituary of C. H. Foulds in obituaries file in Keighley Reference Library; obituary of John Smith Naylor in *Keighley News*, 1 May 1915; obituary of Craven Laycock, *ibid.*, 27 December 1927; obituary of Jonathan Gill, *ibid.*, 19 January 1930; obituary of James Groves, *ibid.*, 10 June 1916; obituary of T. S. Clapham, *ibid.*, 20 February 1915.
8. Hodgson, *op.cit.*, p.55.
9. *Ibid.*, p.67.
10. *Ibid.*, p.99.
11. *Keighley News*, 12, 19 October 1889.
12. *Keighley Labour Journal*, 14 May 1898.
13. Information on the activities of Pringle, Chester, and Stansfield is to be found in the *Keighley News* and *Keighley Labour Journal*, *passim.*
14. *Keighley Labour Journal*, 19 September 1895.
15. *Ibid.*, 29 December 1895.
16. Brockway, *op.cit.*, p.31.
17. Smith, *op.cit.*, p.259.
18. *Yorkshire Factory Times*, 15 August 1890.

19. *Ibid.*, 7 January 1891.
20. *Keighley News*, 8 July 1893.
21. Quoted in Smith, *op.cit.*, p.262.
22. *Keighley Labour Journal*, 1 April 1898.
23. *Ibid.*, 13 February 1895.
24. *Ibid.*, 14 January 1894.
25. *Ibid.*, 15 March 1896, 1 April 1898, 18 March 1899.
26. S. Pierson, *Marxism and the Origins of British Socialism: the Struggle for a New Consciousness* (Ithaca, 1973), p.148.
27. S. Yeo, *Religion and Voluntary Organisations in Crisis* (London, 1976), pp. 253–89.
28. Pierson, *British Socialists*, *op.cit.*, p.48.
29. *Keighley Labour Journal*, 10 November 1895.
30. *Ibid.*, 6 November 1897, 1 December 1895.
31. *Ibid.*, 30 October 1898; *Labour Leader*, 27 February 1897.
32. *Keighley News*, 9 February 1895.
33. P. Snowden, *The Christ that is to be* (London, 1903). For a discussion of *The Christ that is to be*, see Smith, in James, Jowitt and Laybourn (eds), *Centennial History of the ILP*, *op.cit.*, pp.268–70.
34. *Keighley Labour Journal*, 31 July 1897.
35. *Ibid.*, 4 November 1899.
36. Cross, *op.cit.*, p.38.
37. *Keighley News*, 4 May 1895.
38. *Keighley Labour Journal*, 7 October 1894.
39. *Ibid.*, 30 December 1894.
40. *Ibid.*, 3 February 1895.
41. *Labour Prophet*, April 1898.
42. *Keighley Year Book*, 1893; Keighley ILP, Minutes, 12 October 1892; *Keighley Year Book*, 1895.
43. *Keighley Labour Journal*, 17 January 1895.
44. *Ibid.*, 22 May 1896.
45. *Ibid.*, 2 May 1896.
46. *Ibid.*, 1 March 1896.
47. *Ibid.*, 5 January 1896.
48. *Ibid.*, 15 December 1895.
49. Philip Snowden, *The Individual Under Socialism*, Keighley ILP pamphlet, 1903, available in the Snowden collection, Keighley Reference Library.
50. *Keighley Labour Journal*, 5 December 1896.
51. Pelling, *op.cit.*, p.132.
52. Pierson, *Marxism*, *op.cit.*, p.40.
53. Keighley ILP, Minutes, 6 August, 2 September 1896.
54. *Ibid.*, 9 May 1893.
55. *Ibid.*, 7 September 1893, 7 December, 10 January 1899.
56. *Ibid.*, 3 January 1895; *Labour Prophet*, February 1896.
57. *Keighley Labour Journal*, 30 December 1894, 19 December 1896.
58. *Labour Prophet*, November 1895.
59. Poirier, *op.cit.*, p.55.
60. Inglis, 'Labour Church Movement', *op.cit.*, p.456.

61. *Keighley Labour Journal*, February–March 1984.
62. Keighley ILP, Minutes, 13 July 1899.
63. *Ibid.*, 2 November 1892, establishes a Club Committee, *Keighley Year Book*, 1893, gives the Club address as Upper School Green.
64. Keighley ILP, Minutes, 1, 22 February, 1 March 1894.
65. *Ibid.*, 7 December 1893, 9 August 1894, 4 October 1893.
66. Keighley ILP, Letter Book, 19 November 1903.
67. *Keighley Labour Journal*, 14 January 1894.
68. *Ibid.*, 24 April 1897.
69. *Ibid.*, 24 March 1894.
70. *Ibid.*, 2 June 1897.
71. Keighley ILP, Minutes, November 1894; *Keighley Labour Journal*, 27 November 1897.
72. *Ibid.*, 26 February 1898.
73. *Ibid.*, April 1901.
74. *Ibid.*

Table 6.1 Meetings at Keighley Labour Church, December 1893–March 1899

Date	*Speaker*	*Subject*	*Chairman*
24 Dec. 1893	Margaret McMillan	Peace on Earth (ethics)	Mrs T. Roe
31 Dec. 1893	J. B. McKenzie	The Land for the People (land question)	Thomas Dewhirst
7 Jan. 1894	Leonard Hall	Trade Unionism and Politics (new unionism)	Daniel Ogden (Printer)
14 Jan. 1894	J. Fotheringham	Social Ideals (ethics)	G. J. Wardle
21 Jan. 1894	Fred Jowett	The Municipal Question	J. Bateman (Pres. TC)
28 Jan. 1894	Ernest Johnson	Political Economy and the Workers	Ellis Foster (Overlooker and ILP)
4 Feb. 1894	W. K. Hall	The Solution of the Labour Problem	William Robinson (ILP & TC)
11 Feb. 1894	F. Brocklehurst	Socialism and Character (ethics)	Edward Horner
18 Feb. 1894	Robert Morley	The Problem of Poverty (attack on temperance, ethics)	Ernest Butterfield
25 Feb. 1894	Revd R. Roberts	Social Salvation (ethics)	John Moore
(Meeting held in Queens Theatre; collection for Cottage Hospital and Cinderella Fund)			
4 Mar. 1894	Dan Irving	Socialism and Freedom (ethics)	George Gill (TC not ILPer)
11 Mar. 1894	Hanson Hey	Our Dangerous Classes (ethics)	Arthur Green
18 Mar. 1894	A. T. Markes	The Political Outlook (government as employer of labour)	Walter Clayton
(Summer Break)			
7 Oct. 1894	Ernest Johnson	Political Power: A Retrospect	William Robinson
14 Oct. 1894	Robert Morley	Did Christ Teach Socialism? (ethics)	W. Butler
21 Oct. 1894	E. R. Hartley	The Coming Revolution (ethics)	N. W. Scholefield

28 Oct. 1894	James Fotheringham	Religion and Social Duty (ethics)	Herbert Horner
4 Nov. 1894	Fred Jowett	Municipal Experiences (ILP should capture control of municipal government)	W. F. Hardy (Trade-unionist, ILP and later borough councillor)
11 Nov. 1894	J. R. Clynes	Political Parties and Reform (current political problems)	J. Bateman
18 Nov. 1894	Joseph Guy	Utility of Trade Unions	Alfred Burrows
25 Nov. 1894	Fred Brocklehurst	A Living Wage (ethics)	E. Horner
2 Dec. 1894	H. Horner	The Gothenburg System	R. Mackley (Co-ops, ILPer, trade-unionist)
9 Dec. 1894	Enid Stacy	Modern Shams (ethics)	Mrs T. Roe
16 Dec. 1894	Caroline Martyn	The Brotherhood of Man (ethics)	Mrs N. W. Scholefield
23 Dec. 1894	Margaret McMillan	Goodwill to Men (ethics)	Mary Jane Dixon
30 Dec. 1894	Hanson G. Hey	Review of the Year (politics)	None given
6 Jan. 1895	Leonard Hall	From Socialism to Slavery (ethics)	John Moore
13 Jan. 1895	James Parker	An Ideal Municipality (gas and water socialism)	Thomas Cawthron
20 Jan. 1895	Ben Riley (Sec. Warwickshire Labourers' Union)	Agricultural Labourers and Parish Councils	Thomas Mackley (unsuccessful ILP candidate for Council)
27 Jan. 1895	M. Condon	Socialism and the Gospel of Christ (ethics; slides shown)	William Bramham
3 Feb. 1895	F. Gazeley	Folks Who Try to Walk On Their Heads	George Gill
10 Feb. 1895	Short addresses by local speakers, including Alfred Burrows and Mrs T. Roe		
17 Feb. 1895	Philip Snowden	The Religion of Socialism (ethics)	H. Horner
24 Feb. 1895	James Parker	The Unemployed, its Causes, Changes and Remedy	Thomas Dewhirst

3 Mar. 1895	Arthur Spencer	How to live a Hundred Years even in Keighley (public health)	B. Atkinson
10 Mar. 1895	Thomas Atkinson	A Plea for Humanity (ethics)	E. Butterfield
17 Mar. 1895	Philip Snowden	The Cry of the Children (ethics)	G. J. Wardle
(The Cinderella Club; meeting held in Theatre)			
24 Mar. 1895	R. Morley	Christ and Commercialism (ethics)	T. Moorhouse
6 Oct. 1895	S. D. Shallard	Christ or Barabbas: Which?	P. Snowden
13 Oct. 1895	James Sexton	The Art of Happiness	Tom Mackley
20 Oct. 1895	Robert Morley	Contrasts	E. Butterfield
27 Oct. 1895	H. C. Rowe	The Sovereign People	James Teale
3 Nov. 1895	Revd H. Bodell Smith	The Socialist Gospel	H. Horner
10 Nov. 1895	I. L. Tudor	Evolution or Revolution	Bruce Atkinson
17 Nov. 1895	Herbert Burrows	The Unemployed; the Danger; the Cause; the Remedy	W. S. Wilkinson
24 Nov. 1895	F. W. Potter	An Ideal City	Ellis Foster
1 Dec. 1895	P. Snowden	The Social Problem	G. J. Wardle
8 Dec. 1895	Tom Anderson	Critics of Socialism	R. Thistlethwaite
15 Dec. 1895	A. W. Hildreth	Civilisation	W. Parker
22 Dec. 1895	T. Shaw	Trade Unionism Past and Present	W. Robinson (Pres. TC)
29 Dec. 1895	James Fotheringham	Shakespeare and Human Life	E. Foster
5 Jan. 1896	J. Grady	Is Our Movement of God?	T. Roe
12 Jan. 1896	Mr Dyson	The Industrial Revolution	Heaton Hollings
19 Jan. 1896	W. W. Greaves	Poverty and Luxury: their Cause and Remedy	None given
26 Jan. 1896	F. D. Cremer (Canon of Keighley church; not Socialist)	Grandmotherly Legislation	G. J. Wardle

2 Feb. 1896	Fred Brocklehurst	Socialism and Evolution	Mr Whitaker
9 Feb. 1896	J. Johnston	The Socialist Ironworks at Guise	D. Smith
16 Feb. 1896	Tom Shaw	War Unchristian and Barbarous	W. F. Hardy
23 Feb. 1896	Ralph Harvey (Vice-pres. Bradford TC)	The Resurrection of a Great Ideal	None given
1 Mar. 1896	J. R. Widdup (SDF)	Social Development Historically Considered	J. Teale
8 Mar. 1896	J. R. Clynes	A Christian Life	T. Mackley
15 Mar. 1896	P. Snowden	Is Socialism Practicable?	Ellis Foster
22 Mar. 1896	F. E. Chester (Keighley socialist, clergyman)	Piers Plowman	P. Snowden
29 Mar. 1896	Enid Stacy	The Causes of Poverty	Mary Jane Dixon
(Summer Break)			
3 Oct. 1897	E. J. Hart	Patriotism	E. Horner
10 Oct. 1897	M. MacMillan	Education and Socialism	Mary Jane Dixon
17 Oct. 1897	T. B. Duncan	David and Goliath Up to Date	Joseph Hargreaves
24 Oct. 1897	Fred Brocklehurst	Social Progress	G. J. Wardle
31 Oct. 1897	P. Snowden	A Municipal Programme	H. Horner
7 Nov. 1897	Dr A. W. Martin	The Extermination of Fever under Socialism	J. Whittaker (Bradford)
14 Nov. 1897	Revd E. J. Sale	Employers and Employed	D. Townson
21 Nov. 1897	Ada Nield	The Duty of Women as Citizens	Miss Pickles
28 Nov. 1897	F. W. Potter	The Land Question	None given
5 Dec. 1897	H. R. Aldridge	Slum Landlordism	W. Robinson
12 Dec. 1897	Joe Burgess	The Latest Unauthorised Liberal Programme	R. Mackley
19 Dec. 1897	Styan Cooper	Modern Slavery	None given

26 Dec. 1897	Robert Morley	Christ: His Message	J. Ridgion
2 Jan. 1898	E. R. Hartley	Elocution Recital	E. Horner
9 Jan. 1898	Paul Bland	The Work Before Us	T. Mackley
16 Jan. 1898	Ramsey MacDonald	Socialism and Politics	H. Horner
23 Jan. 1898	C. A. Pease	Child Labour	None given
30 Jan. 1898	R. Morley	An Evening with Burns	H. Hollings
6 Feb. 1898	Canon Cremer	Justice	E. Horner
13 Feb. 1898	Enid Stacy	Poor Law Administration	None given
20 Feb. 1898	Musical Service by the Clarion Vocal Union		
27 Feb. 1898	Tom Taylor	Trade Union Leaders and Their Actions Towards Socialism	James Teale
6 Mar. 1898	Revd E. J. Sale	None given	None given
13 Mar. 1898	Joe Burgess	None given	None given
20 Mar. 1898	Keir Hardie	Is Democracy a Failure?	G. J. Wardle
(Summer Break)			
16 Oct. 1898	Leonard Hall	The ABC of it	William Prosser
23 Oct. 1898	Fred Brocklehurst	Socialism at Work	J. Hargreaves
30 Oct. 1898	P. Snowden	The Individual Under Socialism	H. Horner
6 Nov. 1898	J. B. Glasier	England as it might be under Socialism	Allan Woodman (Haworth)
13 Nov. 1898	A. Priestman	Trade Organisation	None given
20 Nov. 1898	F. E. Chester	The Social Message of John Ruskin	E. Horner
28 Nov. 1898	J. R. MacDonald	Lessons from Recent Labour Struggles	Tom Mackley
4 Dec. 1898	Joe Burgess	Socialism at the Trade Union Congress	C. Whitehead (KTC)
(Winter Break)			

29 Jan. 1899	T. B. Duncan	Successful Failures: Co-operation, Trade Unions, Temperance	W. Prosser
5 Feb. 1899	Katherine Conway	Life in a Village: A Socialist Survey	Mrs Roe
12 Feb. 1899	Mona Wilson and Ben Turner	The Organisation of Women	James Smith
19 Feb. 1899	Robert Morley	Modern Socialism	None given
26 Feb. 1899	D. B. Foster	None given	None given
5 Mar. 1899	G. A. H. Samuels ('Marxian')	Capitalism	Tom Mackley
12 Mar. 1899	Musical Service by the Clarion Vocal Union		

CHAPTER SEVEN

Women and the Keighley Independent Labour Party

From its foundation, the ILP claimed to be the most sympathetic of all the political parties towards the aspirations of women. Joseph Clayton, secretary of the Leeds branch in the 1890s and a historian of the socialist movement, noted that 'in the early ILP women were a great deal more than mere helpers to men, they were quite literally the co-leaders', and gave it a tendency to look upon women's suffrage as a reform of vital need.[1] Isabella Ford of Leeds, a member of the NAC between 1903 and 1907, claimed that she had joined the ILP because it was the only party that 'stood for equality and opportunity for the whole human race ... women had never had such equality before'.[2] Keir Hardie said that:

> ours is the one political organisation wherein women stand on terms of perfect equality with men. Women are eligible for election to the National Council of the party, and to the various offices on the same terms as men. From its earliest inception the ILP has taken a decided stand on the side of women's claim for political equality. In the sphere of industry the same claim is put forth: equal pay for equal work.[3]

In Keighley, too, the ILP regarded the support of women as important. In 1894 Elizabeth Roe, one of the most important of the Keighley women ILPers, said, when introducing Margaret McMillan, that 'she wished to make a special appeal to the women who were present in large numbers to help on the good work and further the cause of socialism'. Five years later 'Mrs Roe spoke of the claims the movement had on the women and urged them to join in the work, so as to get better conditions for themselves, their husbands and their children.'[4] Mary Jane Dixon, a successful ILP candidate in the 1896 School Board election, said that the 'cause of Social reform was that which lay closest to her heart, and that if they could only get the women thoroughly in earnest about the matter, the cause would be sure to triumph'.[5] In October 1894 the *Keighley Labour Journal* wrote:

> working men and women whether you have been Liberals or Tories or of no particular party, cease fighting one another, unite on the common

> ground of your common interests in Labour and help to form a strong and united workers party ... You all want healthy dwellings, fresh air, pure streams, shorter hours of labour, and better conditions of work. Therefore we appeal to the working men and women of all parties to vote straight for the Independent Labour Party candidates.[6]

The Labour Church meetings, too, were seen as appealing to women as well as men. 'We hope', wrote the *Keighley Labour Journal*, 'that as a result of these meetings the working men and women of Keighley will realise that the Labour cause is their cause, that it is the cause of humanity, and that it demands their allegiance and support.'[7]

Some of the most important historians of the ILP have shown little interest in the contribution of women to the party or in the impact of feminist questions on ILP politics. Henry Pelling draws attention to the 'new women' such as Katharine St John Conway, Enid Stacy, Caroline Martyn, but, in singling out these speakers, gives the impression that they were unusual rather than the most prominent representatives of a widespread movement.[8] David Howell is also dismissive of the role of women in the party. He suggests that the influence of the group of peripatetic women lecturers was short-lived: 'Carrie Martyn died in 1896; Katharine Conway and Enid Stacy tended to be less active after their marriages.' Of other well-known ILP women, he argues that Margaret McMillan's activities were largely limited to Bradford municipal politics, and that the Pankhursts and Theresa Billington came to concentrate predominantly on women's issues and to drift away from the ILP.[9] Nevertheless, he agrees that women could play a significant part in some branches, citing the Lancashire towns, where the patterns of employment and widespread unionization in the cotton trade gave women both economic independence and organizational confidence. However, he suggests that even in these places women were given traditional roles such as making the tea after ILP demonstrations, and he argues that the lack of women delegates at party conferences indicates how unimportant they were in the overall running of the party.[10]

Local studies, too, have tended to ignore the role of women in the development of local branches. Laybourn and Reynolds make few references to women members in their study of the party in West Yorkshire, and a recent analysis of the ILP in the Yorkshire textile district also ignores the contribution of female members, apart from passing references to travelling lecturers such as Enid Stacy and Katharine Conway.[11] Only in David Clark's Colne Valley are the activities of women members referred to in detail. He suggests that 'women played an important part in the development of the CVLU [Colne Valley Labour Union] and its associated Labour clubs'.[12]

A number of historians have argued, however, that women's contribution to the party was substantial. Olive Banks suggests that it was 'feminist from its inception',[13] and Jill Liddington and Jill Norris say that 'the ILP, more than any other party was sympathetic to the aspirations of feminism',[14] and show how industrial experience and trade-union organization laid the basis for working women's involvement in socialist and suffrage politics after 1900. These 'radical suffragists' demanded the vote as part of a broader campaign to achieve equality at work and in the home, and they pursued these objectives within the labour movement. The Liddington and Norris research was based largely on Lancashire, where the women cotton workers were 'by far the highest paid and best organised of all working women'. They may not, therefore, be typical of working women in the country as a whole. June Hannam has written two important articles on women and the ILP, including one which concentrates on the West Riding. In this she argues that although a weak trade-union membership made it difficult for women workers to exert an influence on the ILP as an organized group, individual women were politically active and made an impression in the branches.[15]

It is certainly true that visiting lecturers such as Caroline Martyn, Enid Stacy and Katharine St John Conway were enormously popular. An advertisement placed by the Weavers' and Textile Workers' Association announced to the people of Haworth in 1896: 'look out your old friend Katharine St John Conway is coming'.[16] Enid Stacy first visited Keighley in 1894, when she lectured on 'Women and Socialism',[17] and returned in 1896, when her speech was described by the *Keighley Labour Journal* as 'exceedingly able and brilliant'.[18] Caroline Martyn visited the area in 1895 and was 'a decided success'. When she died, the *Keighley Labour Journal* reported that she was 'one of the most energetic and unselfish of women, and her early death was doubtless caused by the whole-hearted and unsparing service she has tried to render to the cause'.[19]

It is also true that such middle-class independent socialist women were part of a wider phenomenon. Examples included Ethel Annakin, who had connections with Keighley, as well as Margaret McMillan of Bradford and Isabella Ford. Of Ethel Annakin, Tom Mackley, secretary of the Keighley ILP, wrote that she 'bids fair to fill the very wide gap caused by the lamentable death of Miss E. Stacy'.[20] In Keighley a local example was Mary Jane Dixon. She was young, a Methodist lay preacher, a manageress – which, if not quite middle-class, was socially grander than a mill worker – and she later married an Anglican minister who shared many of her opinions and had no objection to her continuing her political career. She was elected to the School Board and remained active in the ILP until at least 1910.

It is important to ask how far women such as Mary Jane Dixon and Elizabeth Roe were exceptions, to what extent they were involved in the activities of the Keighley ILP, what their contribution was, and whether the 'woman question' was considered important in the debates of the party.

There were women members in the Keighley ILP from the beginning, some of whom played an active role in the life of the branch. By December

1893, Mrs Elizabeth Roe, one of the most prominent female Keighley ILPers, was elected a member of the Executive Committee, and in 1894 there were three women on the Committee out of a total of sixteen. Throughout the 1890s there were usually at least three female members on the Executive, and they were often among its most regular attenders. Mrs Roe, for example, attended all eleven meetings in 1897. By 1898, there were six women on the Executive, with Mrs Emmott attending all twelve meetings, Mrs Roe ten, Mary Jane Stansfield (formerly Mary Jane Dixon) five, Mrs Stell eight, and Mrs Barnes of Silsden none. Mrs Barnes may have had difficulties, as Silsden is some distance from Keighley. The attendance record of the women was thus generally good, certainly as good as the men of the same year.[21]

Unfortunately, the minutes for 1900–3 are missing, but in that period Mrs Roe was elected a vice-chairman, though there were no other women on the Executive. However, women always stood for the Committee even if they were not elected.[22] It was in 1906 that the women again achieved success, with Mrs Roe, Mrs Glover, Mrs Waterworth (probably the wife of J. W. Waterworth a prominent local ILPer), and Miss Minnie Glyde being elected, and they retained this number in the following year, with Mrs Stansfield replacing Mrs Glover, while the others held onto their seats. By 1908, women's representation dropped to two – Mrs Roe and Miss Wilson – and in 1909 Mrs Roe was again the sole female representative, thanks to her re-election as vice-president, though later that year she and Mrs Warrington were both elected. Thus, although their numbers sometimes dropped, it was usual for at least some women to be on the chief administrative body of the branch. On occasion, as many as a quarter of the Executive could be female, and there seems to have been no prejudice against women being at the highest level of branch life, although the men invariably outnumbered the women.

Some women became involved at the same time as their husbands; for example, Mr and Mrs Ellison both joined at the same meeting in April 1910. Even the formidable Mrs Roe's husband was an ILPer. Sometimes married members left the district together, as when in 1896 'this meeting of the Labour Union learns with regret of the departure of Comrades N. W. Schofield and Mrs Schofield of the Womans Labour Union'. Such departures could be a damaging blow to the branch. Mr and Mrs Roe also left for a short time in 1895 to work in Nelson, and the branch recorded its 'heartiest thanks' for 'their great and valuable services to the Keighley Labour Union'.[23] Fortunately, they were back in Keighley within six months. Among the unmarried female members, the most prominent were Mary Jane Dixon and the Glyde sisters.

It is difficult to find evidence of how many women were ordinary members of the branch and how their numbers compared with those of the men. Between 1903 and 1911, 93 women were referred to in the minutes, either as being admitted as members or as contributing to the work of the party. Of course, some of these dropped out during that period and some were never very active, but 62 of them made some contribution other than being just a member. They may have been on one of the party's many committees – for instance, the Social, the Lecture, or the Refreshment Committee, the Concert Party or the Festival Committee, the Visiting Committee or even the committee responsible for buying wallpaper for the Labour Institute. They might have been an officer of the branch, such as assistant to the literature secretary, or a representative for one of the wards, or a subscription collector. There were also mentions for doing something as humble as baking a cake for an ILPer who was ill.

Most of the branch meetings, it would seem, were attended by at least a few women, although the minutes rarely give their names. However, at the General Meeting of 5 October 1905, where names were recorded, five of the eighteen members present were women; and at the meeting of 5 December 1910 fifteen people attended, six of whom were women. These two meetings may be quite untypical, but, if they are representative, it would indicate that women were a significant minority among the branch activists. Some were very active indeed. Between the years 1903 and 1910 Mrs Roe made at least 220 interventions at ILP Executive and General Meetings. Mary Jane Stansfield, Margaret Pickles and the three Glyde sisters were also prominent members, often quite as busy as any male in the life of the branch.

Like a number of branches, the Keighley ILP established a separate women's group. In December 1893 a Women's Labour Union was formed and a room was 'set apart once a fortnight for the use of the lady members'; social evenings were held in the Co-operative Restaurant, where 'the gathering was bright and happy, and everybody enjoyed themselves'.[24] By 1896, however, they were accepted as fully-fledged members of the Keighley ILP and the separate women's group may have died out by the late 1890s. The object of these groups had been to encourage women to join the ILP and give them an opportunity to use their special talents. These were seen chiefly as organizing socials, teas and other events. In 1894, for example, 'delegates from the [Keighley] ILP join with the Ladies Council delegates in having a Ball at the Drill Hall', and in 1896 the Keighley Woman's Labour Union organized a Grand Ball for the branch.[25]

Even after the disappearance of the Women's Labour Union, the work of women members tended towards the social side of branch life. For example, they were always responsible for organizing the annual tea, dance and social. The *Keighley Labour Journal* remarked of the 1896 event: 'the provisions etc., are being given by members and friends. The ladies are working hard to make it a thorough success.'[26] These teas were major events in the Keighley ILP year, with five hundred people attending in 1897 and eight hundred in 1898. Clearly, organizing such affairs required considerable planning and preparation, but they seem to have been greatly enjoyed by those who attended. In 1899:

> The second part of the concert programme was sustained by the Clarion Lady Minstrels, who made their first appearance. They are seventeen in number and the only gentleman of the troupe was Mr Walter Wilkinson, who arrayed in a tie of unusual dimensions, acted as interlocutor and general conductor. The general get up of the minstrels left nothing to be desired.[27]

Other committees also had a majority of women. In 1903 eight of the eleven members of the Festival Committee were women, as were three out of four members of the committee set up to buy the new wallpaper for the Labour Institute.[28] They also formed a majority on the Social Committee, with ten of the seventeen members in 1903 being women.

Those committees more directly involved in the political side of branch life tended to be male-dominated, though there was usually a female presence. Mrs Roe, Mrs Slater and Mrs Spencer, for instance, were all members of the Lecture Committee. By 1898 the Committee consisted of four women and fourteen men, and in 1903 and 1904 there were three women. Anything to do with politics or elections or the selection of candidates was seen as men's responsibility, though again women were represented. In 1894, Mrs Roe was voted on to the Joint Election Committee for municipal elections, as well as the committee to select the candidate for the ILP District Council. By 1899, she, Mary Jane Dixon (now Mrs Stansfield) and Mrs Barnes were among the delegates to the District Council, but the remaining eleven representatives were men. In 1897, Mrs Roe and Mary Jane Dixon were elected as delegates to the meeting to discuss the Keighley Divisional ILP Council, but they were the only two women out of twenty-one representatives.

On most of the branch committees there was female representation, often numbering between a quarter and a half of the total members. This, of course, may have been the proportion of male to female members in the branch as a whole. Nevertheless, it seems clear that there was a demarcation between those activities seen as belonging to men and those regarded as women's responsibility. Those which fell into what was thought to be the women's sphere might, at first, be seen as largely social. However, many ILPers considered the non-political side of their work as important as electing members to the Council, the School Board or the Board of Guardians. There was a fervent belief in creating a socialist society within the framework of the existing system. Living the life of a socialist was important, and the activities organized by women helped to create that socialist society. As David Clark points out when discussing the women ILPers of the Colne Valley:

> But the value of teas and socials was not only that they provided a source of revenue and attracted adherents to the Labour cause, but also that they stimulated the involvement of women in the working of the Labour clubs and the Labour Union. This involvement was important because it meant that the Labour movement became a family institution and this helped the development of a series of social activities which became a 'counter culture' in later years.[29]

A similar situation applied in Keighley. Providing the framework for being a socialist was as important as electing representatives, particularly in the early years of the branch. Much of the work done by Keighley women ILPers helped to develop a socialist culture.

At the same time, much of their work raised money. The annual tea, dance and social helped to provide funds for more political work. In 1894 the *Keighley Labour Journal* commented: 'we are glad that the Dance at the Drill Hall proved such a success, and that a substantial balance has been realised towards defraying the expenses incurred during the Municipal Elections', and in 1896 it remarked of the same event: 'the financial success was very agreeable and will help to materially lessen the Labour Union debt'.[30]

Thus, although much of women's activities tended to be confined to the social and fund-raising side of ILP work, it was seen as important. In addition, they did have an active political role in Keighley. Not only were they voted on to the Executive, but they were also nominated for elective office. In 1895, before Philip Snowden was selected as parliamentary candidate, the branch considered nominating a lady. The minutes recorded that 'the question of a lady candidate was referred to the parl. com'.[31] This suggestion never came to anything, but the parliamentary committee who selected Snowden did have two women members, Mary Jane Dixon and Mrs Spencer, and does suggest that the position of women in politics and in society generally was receiving some attention.

However, women were more usually proposed for places on the School Boards and Boards of Guardians. In 1896 Mary Jane Dixon was successfully nominated for the School Board and she was re-elected three years later. There was nothing particularly unusual in this. The 1870 Education Act entitled women not only to vote, but to be elected. By 1889 there were nearly one hundred women on the Boards, a number which had doubled by 1900. Indeed, most Boards probably had one or two women amongst their members, and several had served as chairman. Initially, women activists were strongest in and around London and in those cities, such as Bradford, which had a strong women's movement often based on the Liberal party. The 1890s, and the rise of organized labour, saw women seeking public office in many of the industrial towns of the north. In doing so, they made women's political role more acceptable to the electorate, and showed up the reluctance of the existing political parties in many towns to give women a proper part in political life.

The system for electing School Board members could work in favour of women candidates. No qualifications were needed to stand, and each voter had as many votes as there were seats and was able to plump them all for one candidate. In addition, education was seen as appropriate work for women because many teachers were female and because infants and girls were thought to need a woman's understanding. A woman candidate, therefore, often had a good chance of being elected because she could usually count on many female voters plumping all their votes for her and she could also expect support from friendly groups, such as clergy, doctors and charity workers, and from some sections of the working men. She might also reasonably expect a fairly friendly press.

These factors seem to have helped Mary Jane Stansfield when she stood as Keighley's first woman School Board candidate in 1896. She argued that education work was a proper area of women's interest: 'it will surely be helpful to have a woman on the Board, seeing that there are scholars and teachers of both sexes, whose interests are bound up with the proper administration of the Board', and claimed that '[o]ur schools are filled by scholars and teachers of both sexes, and it is only fitting that there should be a lady on the Board to specially care for the interests of the female teachers and scholars'. She also appealed to women to vote for her, as she was the only woman candidate standing: 'working women support the only unsectarian lady candidate before you, by giving the whole of your 11 votes to Miss Dixon'. In addition, she was seen as a good Labour candidate:

> We have in Miss Dixon an exceptionally good candidate. Her sympathies are certainly in the right direction, and she has acquired by her experiences as a lay preacher, the coolness and courage necessary to do public work. She is thoroughly in touch with the educational aspirations of the age.[32]

By the 1899 School Board election, Mary Jane Dixon had married the Revd Robert Stansfield, himself a member of the Board. They were attacked by the Conservative *Keighley News* but defended by the *Keighley Labour Journal*, which argued that the ILP was the party which truly accepted women's equality and women's rights:

> Has a woman to have no thoughts of her own, no individuality, no independence. We ask every woman who has a vote in this election to show fair mindedness and acknowledgement of what is due to her sex by voting straight for Mrs Stansfield. The Labour Party believes in equal rights for women. We are fighting against the idea that when a woman marries she has to sacrifice her own opinions to her husband. We want to free women from such slavish submission. A woman who has the courage to express her own opinions is looked upon by Liberals as a moral monster.[33]

Mary Jane Dixon, therefore, could claim to be campaigning not only as a socialist, but as a woman demanding equal political rights for all members of her sex. Thus she could hope for a considerable number of votes from women as well as from Labour supporters. How successful she was once she had been elected is difficult to judge.

Much of her time was spent fighting for the rights of the workers rather than of women. She tried to get a fair contracts clause inserted into the Board's contracts, but failed. She opposed salary increases for the Board clerk and headmasters, on the grounds that ordinary clerks and teachers should have the raise, and she did achieve an increase in pay for the Keighley teachers in 1898: 'We have to thank Miss Dixon, the Rev. R. Stansfield, Mr Chester and Mr Rudd for their efforts to induce the Keighley Board to accept a more reasonable course.'[34]

Her election manifesto, however, was a mixture of expected ILP demands and attention to the needs of children. Thus she wanted the nationalization of education from the elementary school to the university; equal opportunities for all; no sectarian teaching; a fair contracts clause; and a reduction in the School Board rate. She also demanded a better moral training for children; more attention paid to their physical development; the appointment of a medical officer of health to the Board; school feeding; visits to the baths at a cheap rate; smaller classes and more individual attention given to pupils; and, lastly, that the children should be made happy.[35] She was thus a mixture of those interests which were seen as especially the concern of women and those concerning the more general working population. When she was the only ILPer on the School Board, she was a lone, if plucky, voice; when she was joined by Philip Snowden, the ILP presence was more important than their numbers would suggest.

It was possible for a woman to get on to the School Board by a combination of the votes of women and of sympathetic groups of men, and, in the case of Mary Jane Dixon, the party vote. It was much more difficult for women to get elected to Boards of Guardians. Poor Law Guardians had to have a property qualification, which, in the case of female candidates, usually meant their home, so they had to be relatively affluent. Political parties tended to be less interested in Poor Law elections, for the boundaries were not the same as parliamentary constituencies, the people who used the Poor Law rarely had the vote, and issues were not generally political, at least until the rise of socialism. Nevertheless, a number of women were elected to the Boards, and by 1889 some eighty women were Guardians. When the property qualifications were removed in 1894, their numbers rose, and by 1900 there were nearly a thousand female Guardians.

By the end of the nineteenth century, many of the inhabitants of the workhouse were women and children, the old and the sick. Female Guardians were often seen as the people who could best offer support and compassion because their special sphere of interest allowed them to understand the needs of such people. This was certainly the appeal made by the ILP when they nominated Mrs Roe and Mrs Pickles as Guardians in the elections of 1898 and 1901. The ILP argued that there was a need for women representatives on the Board:

> The *Herald* thinks that we have made a mistake in bringing out two lady candidates. Well there has only been one lady representative for the Borough on the retiring Board ... So that all things considered, it is not too much to affirm that the women representatives, especially on Boards of Guardians, may be safely and wisely increased.[36]

It also maintained that Mrs Pickles and Mrs Roe would make excellent candidates: 'Mrs Pickles is a motherly body, one to whom the unfortunate class referred to will instinctively turn to for sympathy and help, and one to whom they will not turn in vain.' She had 'considerable experience as a workhouse visitor' who, if elected, 'would do the work as a labour of love'. Furthermore, '[Mrs Roe] is well known to all connected with political and social reform work in Keighley. She has a wide knowledge of the Poor Law and Labour questions and is a fluent and pointed speaker.' In 1901 Mrs Pickles was elected to the Board, where she was appointed to the Infirmary, Cottage Homes and Workhouse Visiting Committees, all of which might be expected to make use of her 'kind and sympathetic nature'.[37]

Both on the School Board and as Guardians, the female ILP representatives seem to have played an active part, and their presence was appreciated by the male members of both bodies. Writing in 1901, the *Keighley Labour Journal* said:

> We may add that the respect which has been shown to the Socialist member of the Guardians is not exceptional to the general treatment which socialist members on the public bodies in Keighley have received. Neither on the School Board ... have the socialists any cause to complain of being unfairly debarred from their share of administrative work. So far as we are aware no obstacle has ever been thrown in their way to prevent them from obtaining access to any information they required.[38]

Soon after the turn of the century, the opportunities for women in elected office started to disappear. In 1902, Town and County Councils took over responsibility for education services and School Boards were abolished. Mary Jane Dixon had already expressed concern about such a change: 'should any of that machinery [education] be captured by the County Council, she was afraid it would pass beyond the reach and control of the workers, for none, save men and women of means and leisure could undertake the duties of the County Council'.[39] Certainly, the disbandment of the School Boards forced her out of public life. The *Keighley Labour Journal* commented: 'By the retirement of Mrs Stansfield the Keighley

School Board loses one of its most active and able members. She has been unremitting in her activities and her ability enabled her to obtain a knowledge of the work seldom equalled by a public representative.'[40]

It also seemed possible that Poor Law responsibilities might be passed to Town Councils. This did not happen, but it was not until 1907 that women could be elected to either Town or County Councils. In Keighley, after the death of Margaret Pickles in 1906, no other female ILPer was elected to any body until after the First World War.

There is considerable strength in the argument that, on those bodies to which they were elected, it was the ILP women who provided the humanity, while the men made the hard-headed decisions. This interpretation is, of course, over-simplified. Men as well as women were put forward by the ILP to stand for the School Board and the Board of Guardians and the party's manifesto applied to all candidates. At the same time, other representatives were aware of the needs of children in schools, and the old, the sick and the infirm in the workhouse. The point is that women ILPers largely accepted their role and rarely questioned it.

The 1890s were years of great activity for the women's movement, and the question of the most effective way for them to improve their lot was widely discussed by women ILPers. A variety of positions was taken on this question: Enid Stacy, for example, dismissed women's rights as a 'middle-class fad'; Isabella Ford of Leeds, on the other hand, wanted co-operation between the ILP and the women's movement. She linked economic and political questions, arguing that, whatever its imperfections, the vote was at least a recognition of equality and that most industrial evils arose from the fact that women were treated as inferiors. Ethel Annakin, later Mrs Philip Snowden, was committed to the campaign of women's suffrage. She toured the country on behalf of the National Union of Women's Suffrage Societies, and wrote two books and a pamphlet on the plight of women. By 1907 she had decided to commit herself full time to the question of the vote, and in 1909 she resigned from the ILP.

The Keighley ILP seems to have been divided in its support for women's suffrage. Tom Mackley, the branch secretary, writing about the question in 1902, struck a somewhat gloomy note: 'I submitted enclosed Petition to my Executive Meeting tonight and they unanimously decided that the President and myself should sign it. Wishing you every success in what I consider a very doubtful question.'[41] In the event, 33,184 people throughout the country signed the petition. Similar doubts were to appear in later minutes, as the following extracts show: on 2 July 1906 the following resolution was passed: 'That we put up an appeal for fund for the Women's Social and Political Union movement'; later at the same meeting a counter-resolution, that 'we do not as a Party identify ourselves with the Woman's Suffrage movement', was put and lost. On 6 August 1906 the resolution 'that we endorse resolution re Women's Suffrage agitation and forward same to proper authorities' was proposed, only to be queried because of the 'charges made against the Social and Political Union in the bye election at Cockermouth'. Eventually, the resolution was passed, but only on the chairman's casting vote.

The branch believed that women's best interests were served through working with the ILP. Tom Mackley wrote to Ethel Annakin in 1903: 'Now I have always believed the ILP was the only political party that did take up these questions [woman's suffrage] in a serious way, and ... was advocating them in season and out.'[42] There is little evidence that the main ILP women activists in Keighley took a particular interest in the women's movement outside the context of the party. They wanted the vote, but the needs of the party came first. Mrs Roe, Mary Jane Dixon, and the three Glyde sisters never raised the subject with any persistence, although Mrs Roe did propose that the branch 'put up an appeal for the Women's Social and Political Union'.[43]

The position of the Keighley ILP was not unusual in Yorkshire. From its inception, the party had to grapple with the conflicts between the specific interests of women as a sex and its overall emphasis on the need for unity between men and women of the working class. It failed to challenge women's unequal position in the workplace or in the home. The predominance of male trade-unionists in the Yorkshire ILP, the weakness of female workers and the deeply rooted commitment to family life, in which women were seen as central, makes this understandable. However, the ILP was prepared to concede that women should have political equality with men. Keighley is a good example of a branch that allowed its female members to play a full part, albeit with an emphasis on social and ethical socialist activities. It elected women on to its Executive Committee and supported them fully when they stood for public office. Despite some limitations, the Keighley ILP did support the rights of women, and the women members seemed to feel that this was enough to secure their support.

Notes

1. J. Clayton, *The Rise and Decline of Socialism in Great Britain* (London, 1926), p.84.
2. I. O. Ford, 'Why Women Should be Socialists', *Labour Leader*, 1 May 1913.
3. K. Hardie, *After Twenty Years: All About the ILP* (1913), p.13.
4. *Keighley Labour Journal*, 7 January 1894, 28 January 1899.
5. *Ibid.*, 30 December 1894.
6. *Ibid.*, 28 October 1894.
7. *Ibid.*, 8 October 1898.
8. H. Pelling, *Origins of the Labour Party*, 2nd edn (Oxford, 1965), p.155.
9. D. Howell, *British Workers and the Independent Labour Party, 1885–1906* (Manchester, 1983), p.334.

10. *Ibid.*, p.335.
11. Laybourn and Reynolds, *Liberalism and the Rise of Labour 1890–1918*, *op.cit.*; Laybourn and James, *'The Rising Sun of Socialism'*, *op.cit.*
12. Clark, *op.cit.*, p.48.
13. O. Banks, *Faces of Feminism* (Oxford, 1981), p.123.
14. J. Liddington and J. Norris, *One Hand Tied Behind Us; the Rise of the Women's Suffrage Movement* (London, 1978), p.125.
15. June Hannam, 'Women and the ILP, 1890–1914', in James, Jowitt and Laybourn (eds), *Centennial History*, *op.cit.*, pp.205–29; June Hannam, 'In the Comradeship of the Sexes lies the Hope of Progress and Social Regeneration: Women and the West Riding ILP *c.*1890–1914', in Jane Rendell (ed.), *Equal or Different: Women's Politics 1800–1914* (Oxford, 1987).
16. *Keighley Labour Journal*, 28 November 1896.
17. *Ibid.*, 16 December 1894. In the afternoon Enid Stacy lectured on 'Women and Socialism' and in the evening on 'Modern Shams'.
18. *Ibid.*, 3 October 1896.
19. *Ibid.*, 24 November 1895, 1 August 1896.
20. Keighley ILP, Letter Book, 28 September 1903.
21. The attendances for men were, W. F. Hardy 7, J. Teal 1, C. Whitehead 11, E. Horner 8, T. Mackley 12, H. Horner 11, W. Pickles 10, W. R. Hall 12, R. Mackley 1, P. Snowden 7, J. Scruton 7, W. Prosser 0, B. Roff 12, R. Bradley 10, S. P. Holmes 4, W. Richardson 7.
22. For example, in 1904 Miss Moorhouse, Mary Glyde and Miss Pattinson all stood for the Executive, although they were not elected, and in 1905 Mary Glyde and Mrs Barron stood unsuccessfully.
23. *Ibid.*, 6 February 1896, 3 January 1895.
24. *Ibid.*, 7 December 1893; *Keighley Labour Journal*, 25 March 1894.
25. Keighley ILP, Minutes, 8 November 1894; *Keighley Labour Journal*, 21 November 1896.
26. *Ibid.*, 16 February 1896.
27. *Ibid.*, 1 April 1899.
28. Keighley ILP, Minutes, 13 June 1903.
29. Clark, *op.cit.*, p.48.
30. *Keighley Labour Journal*, 16 December 1894, 15 March 1896.
31. Keighley ILP, Minutes, 1 November 1895.
32. *Keighley Labour Journal*, 8, 15, 22 March 1896.
33. *Ibid.*, 21 March 1899.
34. *Ibid.*, 9 October 1897, 13 March 1897, 29 January 1898.
35. *Ibid.*, 21 March 1899.
36. *Ibid.*, 1 April 1898.
37. *Ibid.*, 12 March 1898, 19 March 1901.
38. *Ibid.*, 27 April 1901.
39. *Ibid.*, 16 July 1898.
40. *Ibid.*, 25 April 1902.
41. Keighley ILP, Letter Book, 27 August 1902.
42. *Ibid.*, 1 October 1903.
43. Keighley ILP, Minutes, 2 July 1906.

CHAPTER EIGHT

Conclusion

Keighley was at the heart of the labour movement in the years before 1914. It was where Philip Snowden first became prominent, and by 1900 its ILP membership was one of the largest in the country. However, it was unable to build on these achievements and suffered a decline after 1902. The reasons for its early success were various, and included the antagonism of the local Liberals towards the demands of labour, both in the workplace and politically, which resulted in working-class political activists realizing that the only way to have a voice in government, whether local or national, was by forming their own party. There was also the growth of organized labour in the 1890s, largely through the work of socialists, who helped to establish the Trades Council and participated in a series of industrial disputes. And the appeal of ethical socialism, as personified by Philip Snowden, turned the ILP into a moral crusade as well as a movement to secure practical improvements in people's lives. Connected with this was the creation of a socialist culture which emphasized brotherhood and fellowship.

Keighley, therefore, is an appropriate community from which to study the decline of Liberalism and the rise of the labour movement. It is possible to examine the reasons for the failure of the Liberals to come to an accommodation with Labour; the tensions between those who wanted an alliance of socialists and those who favoured an agreement with the trade unions; and the attraction of the religion of socialism. Nationally, there are two debates: one concerns the reasons for the failure of Liberalism and the other the causes of the rise of organized labour. In both of these, events in Keighley can illuminate the discussion.

The Decline of Liberalism

After the decline of Chartism, the Liberals secured the political support of the working class, which they retained until the end of the 1880s. As a result, before a Labour party could be created, the appeal of Liberalism had to be undermined. How and when this took place, both nationally and in West Yorkshire, is a matter of debate.

In George Dangerfield's 1935 classic, *The Strange Death of Liberal England*,[1] it is argued that the Liberals succumbed to the development of class politics as the working class attached itself to the political ambitions of the Labour party. As more material became available and more research was undertaken, this analysis was revised. In 1954, Henry Pelling wrote his influential *The Origins of the Labour Party 1880–1900*, whose key argument was that the success of the ILP and the Labour party lay in their alliance with trade unions.[2] More recently, Ross McKibbin accepted this approach, arguing that 'the Labour Party was based upon a highly developed class-consciousness and intense class loyalties'.[3] According to these historians, this transfer of political loyalties to Labour by the working class was clear before the First World War and was the chief reason for the decline of the Liberal party. Keith Laybourn and Jack Reynolds, in their study of West Yorkshire politics, also argue that this shift in loyalties was taking place and that the trade-union alliance was essential for the creation of a Labour party.[4]

This approach has not gone unchallenged. Some historians have explained the deterioration of the Liberal party by reference to the changes brought about by the First World War and the conflict within the party which resulted from the replacement of Asquith by Lloyd George in 1916. It was the war that was responsible for Liberal decline, for the party was politically healthy in 1914 and Labour was struggling to secure support.

Much of this debate has centred on the success of so-called 'New Liberalism'. This was an attempt in the years after 1890 to secure working-class support for the Liberals by offering them a series of social reforms and compromises. It offered industrial conciliation to solve industrial disputes; public ownership where appropriate; and opposed sectional interests with communal responsibility. It tried to create a framework whereby harmony would replace class conflict, and attempted to reconcile the growing demands of Labour with the need to maintain the political unity of the Liberal party. However, in many areas, such as the north of England, the party relied upon the support of wealthy industrialists, many of whom were opposed to the aspirations of the working class, and this meant that the accommodation of New Liberal ideas was never going to be easy. At the same time, a growing number of workers were becoming mistrustful of the sincerity of their employers when they claimed to be representatives of the interests of all sections of society. Events such as the Manningham Mills and Keighley engineers' strikes showed how correct this analysis was and how untouched the West Yorkshire Liberals, at least, were by New Liberal ideas.

Nevertheless, historians such as P. F. Clarke argue that New Liberalism, with its greater emphasis on social reform, was the key to a Liberal revival before the First World War.[5] Clarke suggests that the changing fortunes of the Liberals in Lancashire were the result of New Liberal ideas put forward by the *Manchester Guardian*, Winston Churchill and Lloyd George. He argues that what applied to Lancashire was also true of other regions. This opinion has been challenged and it is suggested that, even where the Liberals were successful, the reason may have had little to do with New Liberalism. In Wales, K. O. Morgan concludes that Liberalism was successful because of its traditional commitments to free trade, peace, retrenchment, reform, Nonconformity and Welsh nationalism.[6]

In the West Riding textile region, New Liberalism made little impact. Its most prominent exponent was William Pollard Byles, who owned the *Bradford Observer* and the *Keighley News*. He tried to mediate in the Manningham Mills strike, and in 1892 was the successful Liberal candidate for Shipley. However, he was defeated in the 1895 election when several prominent local Liberals sided with his Unionist opponent. In 1901 he stood as a Labour candidate in Leeds East, but returned to the Liberal party soon after that, though eventually he was forced to leave the district for Lancashire, whose politics he found more congenial.

Generally, traditional Liberalism dominated the local parties in West Yorkshire. There were some initiatives by New Liberals, but on the whole they came to nothing. In Bradford, J. W. Jarratt helped to formulate a progressive municipal programme for the Liberal Association, and in 1900 he stood down as Liberal candidate in Bradford West to give F. W. Jowett a clear run against the Tories in the general election. None of these initiatives came to anything, however, and 'Old Liberalism' retained its dominance. C. P. Trevelyan was returned for Elland in a parliamentary by-election in 1899. Although his collectivist views eventually led him to join the Labour party in 1918, there is little evidence that he was inclined to New Liberalism before 1906. Walter Runciman stood for election in Dewsbury in 1902. He was open to the new ideas, being attracted to notions of 'national efficiency', supporting the miners' eight-hour day, and ready to use the power of the state to intervene in economic affairs. He won the seat when he defeated Harry Quelch of the SDF, but his support came from traditional Liberals. In Halifax, the policies of the Liberal party continued to be shaped by an old-fashioned leadership which opposed intervention by the state in industrial and social matters and supported 'individualistic' methods for the relief of poverty. It was the same in Huddersfield, where the Liberals were generally successful, although New Liberalism was almost unknown.

Keighley resembled other Yorkshire textile towns, in that the ideas of New Liberalism went unheeded. Despite the fact that the *Keighley News* was owned by William Pollard Byles, there is no evidence that the local party was affected by the ideas of Liberal reformers. The alliance of Nonconformist millowners, deeply imbued with the ideas of *laissez faire*, self-help and individualism, combined with a widely held belief in the importance of temperance, in improving the condition of the working class and a commitment to solve the question of Ireland before any other reforms could be undertaken, was sufficient to keep the Liberal party in power for most of the period before 1906. Local campaigns such as that to ensure adequate space for Nonconformists in the local burial ground, or the passive resistance to the 1902 Education Act, showed how potent the appeal to Nonconformist interests could still be. No concessions were made by the Liberals to such working-class demands as the eight-hour day or fair contracts, both of which were seen as a threat to the profitability of trade. Neither is there evidence that career politicians were preferred to local men when candidates were chosen. Indeed, much of the success of Keighley MPs such as Isaac Holden or John Brigg in parliamentary elections was due to their being local men. The Keighley Conservatives, for their part, realized that having to have outside candidates weakened their parliamentary campaigns, and they regularly regretted their inability to persuade one of their local supporters to stand for Parliament. Thus the ideas of New Liberalism were antipathetic to the deepest-held beliefs of the Keighley Liberal party.

Throughout the Yorkshire wool region, therefore, New Liberalism was not of major importance. Nor, in the 1880s, is there convincing evidence that the West Yorkshire working class as a whole was dissatisfied with the traditional Liberal party as the representative of their political ambitions. Indeed, it was in that party that a number of future Labour leaders had their first taste of political activity: in Keighley, both Herbert and Edward Horner were active Liberals, with Herbert applying for the post of Liberal agent; and Philip Snowden was a committed Liberal for a number of years before converting to socialism.

One of the reasons for the Liberals' success in retaining the political trust of the workers was that many of the party leaders were also major employers in their localities. Many workers paid deference to the millowner and had a loyalty to their place of work and community which transcended obligations to class. This phenomenon of paternalism has attracted the attention of historians. Patrick Joyce, for instance, although chiefly concerned with Lancashire, does refer to the West Riding textile belt and describes and analyses the way in which paternalism worked;[7] other historians have also studied the phenomenon, with particular respect to West Yorkshire.[8] In such works, we can find several references to Keighley, where the community was small and close-knit and where paternalism was especially effective in retaining the commitment of the employees to a place of work and to the boss. The manufacturers seem to have had an almost instinctive ability to retain the respect and loyalty of their workers, whether with regard to temperance, Nonconformity or politics, while at the same time never allowing any familiarity, and this created considerable difficulties for the Keighley ILP when it was formed. It was not until these personal loyalties to the mill or the master had been demolished, and it became clear that employers were unwilling to help the working class, that popular support for independent political action became possible.

The Rise of the Labour Movement

Historians are agreed that, in the Yorkshire textile belt, the success of the ILP, and later the Labour party, was due to the creation of an alliance between socialists and the trade unions. Nevertheless, there is some debate as to whether or not this alliance was the only means by which a successful working-class political party could be formed. David Howell has pointed out that, nationally, 'there is little evidence to suggest in the 1890s the ILP was revealing itself as clearly more suited than the [Social Democratic] Federation to British conditions',[9] and Martin Crick, in various studies, has questioned whether or not the trade-union alliance was necessary for Labour's success in West Yorkshire.[10] He suggests that the socialist movement in the 1890s was notable for its eclectic nature and regional diversity, with socialists moving easily between the SDF and the ILP, and that the formation of a branch was often dependent on individuals. In particular he argues that the politics of the 'heavy woollen' district between 1893 and 1912 demonstrate that the ILP was not the inevitable standard-bearer of British socialism and that the Labour alliance was not the only viable strategy for British socialists. He stresses that trade-unionists and socialists were split over the best way to achieve their aims, or even over what those aims should be. However, after the failure of Harry Quelch in the 1902 election, independent labour representation in the heavy woollen district was pursued in alliance with trade unions and the strategy of spreading socialism was subordinated to the business of electioneering. It was the ILP preoccupation with electoral effectiveness that gradually undermined the socialist vision. Thus, while arguing that the ILP/trade-union alliance was not necessarily inevitable, Crick does accept that it became the key to Labour's political success.

This tension between those who saw the trade-union alliance as essential to electoral success and those who resented its primacy can be found in other branches, including Keighley. In particular, after the disappointments of the 1895 general election, there was considerable discussion about the best way to revive the socialist movement. Stephen Yeo argues that it was at this time that the pursuit of electoral success began to undermine the original ideals of winning people over to socialism. Opposition to this view came from trade-unionists and from ILPers, both of whom resented any connection with each other. The most prominent of the latter group was E. R. Hartley, president of the Bradford Labour Church. He was antipathetic to trade unions, viewing them as a reactionary force holding back the working-class movement. Keith Laybourn and Jack Reynolds argue, however, that the activities of the Clarion movement, the Labour Church and later the Socialist Sunday Schools, which provided the framework for the socialist way of life, 'were not so much countervailing as complementary in West Yorkshire' to the trade-union alliance.[11]

Their conclusion seems to apply to the Keighley branch, where the leading ILPers were often both trade-unionists and enthusiastic ethical socialists. People like the Horners and G. J. Wardle were as equally at home in the Labour Church as at a trade-union meeting. Edward Horner recalled that Wardle had been brought to socialism by its moral arguments, even though he was a prominent member of the local branch of the ASRS. W. S. Wilkinson, the conductor of the Clarion Vocal Union, was a music teacher by profession and never belonged to a trade union, and he was attracted to the ILP by its ethical appeal. Despite his not being a trade-unionist, he was an admired and respected member of the local branch. Philip Snowden was, of course, best known for his ethical socialism, but he always urged his audiences to become members of trade unions. Nevertheless, the Keighley socialists, although arguing that workers should be active in trade unions, had two reservations. Firstly, they argued that permanent reforms could only be achieved through politics and that political action should have primacy over trade-union activity. Secondly, they usually agreed that it was not necessary to be a trade-unionist if one was to be a socialist. Given the serious weakness of local trade-unionism, both these opinions are understandable. Being a socialist in Keighley meant having a range of choices and activities within which to express your commitment. These could range from the Clarion Vocal Union, to the Labour Church, to trade-union work, or to standing for elected bodies. All were seen as equally valid expressions of the socialist ideal, and it was this variety of interests which led to the creation of a culture and value-system which could be put forward as an alternative to capitalism. This ILP culture was intended to be an example of what life would be like when socialism was achieved. It was the adoption of this moral dimension which helped to separate the Keighley ILP from the other two parties and made it into a crusade rather than merely a political machine.

Why ethical socialism and the ideas of the Clarion movement should have been so popular in West Yorkshire is still a matter of debate. A recent article suggests that there was a close relationship between religious impulses and the development of the ILP in the West Riding which was crucial to the party's development and which continued to exert an influence for many years.[12] Much of the ILP membership, it is argued, came from skilled workers, artisans and small businessmen; the kind of people who would have attended regular Sunday services and been reared in the culture of the Chapel. They were therefore receptive to the ethical appeal of speakers such as Caroline Martyn, Katharine St John Conway and Philip Snowden. For some, the ethical appeal was the core of socialism and it had a greater attraction than the practical issues of municipal socialism. Stephen Yeo[13] suggests that the greatest success of ethical socialism was in the 1890s. It is certainly true that in parts of West Yorkshire a cross-fertilization of religion and socialism took place in these years, and Keighley is one place where Yeo's analysis convinces. The local Labour Church was established soon after the Labour Union, but it was the massive popularity of Philip Snowden, who arrived in the town in 1895, that made ethical socialism the chief characteristic of the local labour movement. For a few years, ethical socialism combined with the work of the Clarion groups, and club life dominated the work of the local ILP, arguably at the expense of creating a political organization and building up the trade-union movement. The popularity of these meetings was never in doubt. Even before Snowden emerged as a leading ILPer, the party could remark that the most successful part of its activities was 'the Sunday services and the crowded audiences who have listened to the new gospel',[14] and by 1896 they were claiming audiences of between four and five hundred for their meetings. Nevertheless, there is evidence that the kind of people who were attracted to the Keighley Labour Church were those identified in A. J. Jowitt's article as being steeped in the culture of the Chapel, namely the respectable working class; the kind of people who might under other circumstances be found in the local Methodist church.

K. S. Inglis[15] has identified a further characteristic of ethical socialism which was experienced in Keighley. This was the tendency of the Labour Church services to become secularized, although the religious forms were preserved. As already suggested, the most significant reference to the Keighley Labour Church is recorded in the minute of 13 July 1899, 'that we have all first class lecturers and go outside the socialist movement if necessary',[16] which sums up the ultimate failure of the Labour Church movement in Keighley. It was the speaker rather than his point of view which was of overriding importance. Nevertheless, in the absence of strong trade unions, ethical socialism, particularly while Snowden lived in the town, was an effective means of mobilizing the Keighley working class to the cause of Labour.

However, despite the appeal of ethical socialism and the tensions between socialists and trade-unionists, it was the connection between the two that gave the labour movement in West Yorkshire its influence and was the basis of its political success. In Keighley, the trade-union connection was crucial to the existence of the party, although, as has been said, the appeal of ethical socialism was used to supplement the weakness of trade-unionism. The party continually emphasized the benefits of trade-union membership, for 'wherever trade union membership is strong wages are from 15 to 25 per cent higher than those paid for similar work where unionism is weak or non existent'.[17] The Keighley ILP leadership, with the exception of Philip Snowden, consisted almost entirely of active trade-unionists, and the branch was seen from the start as the political ally of the unions. Similarly, the local Trades Council was controlled by ILPers. ILP candidates in elections were usually trade-unionists and were often jointly nominated with the Trades Council. Solidarity was always expressed with trade unions in the election manifestos, and much of the ILP programme aimed directly at improving the conditions of the workers through such demands as that for the eight-hour day and fair contracts clauses. After 1905, with the gradual withering away of the appeal of ethical socialism, the connection became more important in the town, and the creation of a local LRC completed the alliance. The ILP was well represented on the LRC, with six members coming from the party itself and eight as trade-union representatives, and it is illustrative of the importance of the unions to the party that the candidate in the 1906 election was a trade-unionist rather than an ethical socialist. This belief in the trade-union alliance was tempered, however, by a commitment to political, rather than industrial, action as the most effective way of improving the conditions of the workers, for 'strikes ... brought in their train starving husbands, starving wives and starving children', and it was better to 'send men of their own class to the House of Commons'.[18] Given the weakness of unions in the town, this belief in politics was logical.

Obviously, trade unions hoped that an independent political party would be electorally successful. Yet if the results of parliamentary elections are examined, the ILP/LRC/Labour party performance nationally was weak before 1914. In West Yorkshire, Labour won no seats before 1906 and held only three or four parliamentary seats at any one time between that year and 1914. The Liberal party normally gained the other nineteen, and in the Keighley constituency Liberal success was never in doubt. Isaac Holden retained the seat until 1895, and John Brigg until 1911, even in years such as 1900 when nationally the Liberals were in difficulties. Even when a candidate was not a local man, as in 1911 when Sir Stanley O. Buckmaster stood, the result was not in doubt.

However, historians have argued that parliamentary elections are not the clearest guide to assessing the state of the political parties in West Yorkshire.[19] Local election results, it is argued, may give a fairer picture of the state of the parties in the years before 1914, when, for instance, Labour was making significant gains in local elections in several parts of West Yorkshire. In 1891 there were 6 ILP representatives on elected bodies in West Yorkshire; by 1900 this had risen to 53, by 1906 to 89 and by 1914 to 202. Obviously, this pattern varies from place to place, but overall the labour movement was increasing its support from 1900, and after 1906 'Liberalism was no longer garnering the working-class support which it once commanded and the real drift of that support to Labour appears in the enormous surge of Labour's municipal and local victories, especially after 1910.'[20]

Keighley does not fall into this pattern. Its success in local elections came early and then declined. By 1900 it had four representatives on the Borough Council, three on the School Board and in 1901 it elected its first member to the Board of Guardians. An ILPer had also been voted borough auditor. After 1902 the School Boards were abolished and by 1904 the Labour borough councillors were reduced to one, who was not returned at the next contest. The only other success was in 1907, when Herbert Horner was returned to the County Council, and in 1912, when he was re-elected to the Borough Council. The reasons for this failure were local rather than national. A number of labour activists left the town, or dropped out of politics, and were not replaced. One of the reasons for the lack of new blood can be found in the splits which bedevilled the branch in the early years of the twentieth century, leading to the threat by Herbert Horner in 1913 that he would start a new party. There was also an organizational failure which neither the ILP nor the LRC seemed able to overcome, and enthusiasm was no substitute for a party machine. Nevertheless, although their appeal in local contests remained weak, their vote at parliamentary elections was creditable, at over a quarter of the votes cast, and the groundwork was laid for better success after 1919.

David Howell has noted[21] that the course of early labour history was indirect and that each community differed in its approach to the emergence of the ILP. The varied industrial structure, the role of individuals, the success of the paternalism of the industrial masters, all helped to ensure that the movement developed in separate ways in every town. This pattern is particularly evident in the Yorkshire wool textile belt, where the diversity of products led to widely uneven economic and social experiences. For example, Bradford, dominated by worsteds, with its large female and juvenile workforce, was different from Halifax, whose worsteds were balanced by a large engineering sector. Large towns such as Bradford, Halifax and Huddersfield were very different from the more rural communities of the Colne Valley; and middling towns such as Dewsbury, Batley and Keighley all had their own traditions and cultures.

The labour movement thus developed unequally in these communities. By 1914 the most successful towns were probably Bradford and Halifax. In other places, accomplishments were more volatile. The triumph of Victor Grayson in Colne Valley was followed by his defeat in 1910. In Huddersfield, the Liberals retained much of their support; in Dewsbury the attempt to form a union of socialists failed and was followed by the creation of a trade-union alliance. In Keighley, early success was followed by years of failure, relieved by the unexpectedly good result in 1906 but then followed by internal wrangling.

However, a number of common factors throughout the district can be discerned. There were the economic imperatives of the great depression, which resulted in employers putting increasing pressure on their workforce to raise output and cut costs. Accompanying this was the indifference of the local Liberal parties, often dominated by local manufacturers, to the demands of labour. This indifference often turned to antagonism as labour formed independent political parties. There was the connection between ethics and socialism, which gave the movement the quality of a moral crusade and appealed to the culture of the chapels which many early labour activists had imbibed. There was the tension between socialism and labour which caused difficulties in some constituencies. However, probably most important was the involvement of trade-unionism in labour politics.

By allying itself with trade-unionism and by abandoning socialism for the present, the ILP and Labour party in West Yorkshire secured increasing political success. From the 1890s to 1906 they made many local gains. In 1906 they won three parliamentary seats, to which they added Colne Valley in 1907. From 1910 onwards, Labour was eroding the Liberal power base in many parts of the region and by 1914 the Liberal party was having real difficulty arresting the growth of Labour.

Keighley was not one of the ILP successes in West Yorkshire. Its early promise was not fulfilled, and by the outbreak of the Great War the socialists were still riven by internal disputes and lacked significant representation on elected bodies. In a number of ways, however, it conforms to the West Yorkshire pattern of development. There is no doubt that the local ILP was founded as a result of the Liberal manufacturers' indifference to their workers. Economically, this was demonstrated in the 1889 engineers' strike and in other disputes in the early 1890s. Politically, it was demonstrated by their unwillingness to allow working-class activists any say in the local Liberal party. There was a trade-union/ILP alliance from the very first and the agreement between the two groups was never lost. The town was also a centre of ethical socialism and the alternative culture of the early labour movement. There were branches of the several Clarion organizations, and there was a Labour Church. In Philip Snowden, the Keighley ILP had one of the most popular ethical socialists in the country, as well as an able local politician. For its size, it had one of the largest and most successful ILP branches, and even during its decline it had its successes. It performed well in the 1906 election and maintained its percentage of the vote in later parliamentary contests. Its alliance with the trade unions gave it a viability which meant that, when it had settled its internal problems, it was able to mount a realistic threat to both Liberals and Tories and elect Keighley's first Labour MP in 1922.

Notes

1. George Dangerfield, *The Strange Death of Liberal England* (London, 1935 and 1970).
2. Pelling, *op.cit.*
3. R. I. McKibbin, *The Evolution of the Labour Party 1910–1924* (London, 1974).
4. Laybourn and Reynolds, *Liberalism and the Rise of Labour*, *op.cit.*
5. Clarke, *op.cit.*
6. Morgan, *op.cit.*

7. Joyce, *op.cit.*
8. Jowitt (ed.), *op.cit.*
9. D. Howell, 'Was the Labour Party Inevitable?', *Bulletin of the North West Labour History Society* (1984), p.15.
10. Crick, 'Labour Alliance or Socialist unity?' *op.cit.*; Crick, *History of the Social-Democratic Federation*, *op.cit.*
11. Laybourn and Reynolds, *Liberalism and the Rise of Labour*, *op.cit.*, p.95.
12. Jowitt, 'Religion and the Independent Labour Party', *op.cit.*
13. Yeo, 'A New Life', *op.cit.*
14. *Keighley Labour Journal*, 30 December 1894.
15. K. S. Inglis, *Churches and the Working Classes in Victorian England*, *op.cit.*, ch.6.
16. Keighley ILP, Minutes, 13 July 1899.
17. *Keighley Labour Journal*, 9 May 1896.
18. *Keighley News*, 12 August 1893.
19. Laybourn, *The Rise of Labour*, *op.cit.*, p.15.
20. Laybourn and Reynolds, *Liberalism and the Rise of Labour*, *op.cit.* p.142.
21. Howell, *op.cit.*, pp.277–82.

Bibliography

PRIMARY SOURCES

1. Manuscript

Minutes of the Keighley ILP 1892–1903, 1905–14. Housed in Keighley Library.

Letter Book of the Keighley ILP, 1901–8. Housed in Keighley Library.

Minutes of the Keighley Divisional Liberal Association, 1885–1914. Housed in Keighley Library.

Minutes of Keighley Borough Liberal Association, 1885–1914. Housed in Keighley Library.

Minutes of Central Conservative Association for the Keighley Division, 1885–92. Housed in West Yorkshire Archive Service, Bradford.

Minutes of Keighley Divisional Conservative Association, 1892–1914, includes minutes of Conservative and Liberal Unionist meetings. Housed in West Yorkshire Archive Service, Bradford.

Minutes of Keighley Borough Conservative Association, 1903–14. Housed in West Yorkshire Archive Service, Bradford.

Executive Committee Minutes of the National Woolsorters' Union, 1900–14. Housed in West Yorkshire Archive Service, Bradford.

J. Lister, 'Early History of the ILP Movement in Halifax'. MS copy in West Yorkshire Archive Service, Calderdale.

2. Printed

Keighley Year Book: a manual of local information and reference, published annually by the Keighley News, 1877–1917.

P. Snowden, *The Christ that is to be* (London, 1903).

P. Snowden, *The Individual Under Socialism* (Keighley, 1903).

3. Newspapers

Bradford Observer
Clarion
ILP News
Keighley Echo
Keighley Herald
Keighley Labour Journal
Keighley News
Labour Leader
Labour Prophet
Yorkshire Factory Times

SECONDARY SOURCES

1. Books

A. Almond, *Biography of James Ickringill Esq*. (Keighley, 1919).

O. Banks, *Faces of Feminism* (Oxford, 1981).

L. Barrow, *Independent Spirits: Spiritualism and English Plebians, 1850–1910* (London, 1986).

M. L. Baumber, *A Pennine Community on the Eve of the Industrial Revolution: Keighley and Haworth between 1660 and 1740* (Keighley, n.d.).

M. L. Baumber, *From Revival to Regency: a History of Keighley and Haworth 1740–1820* (Keighley, 1983).

F. Brockway, *Socialism Over Sixty years: the Life of Jowett of Bradford 1864–1944* (London, 1946).

S. Bryher, *An Account of the Labour and Socialist Movement in Bristol* (Bristol, 1929).

Sir F. W. L. Butterfield, *My West Riding Experiences* (London, 1927).

L. Caffyn, *Workers' Housing in West Yorkshire 1750–1920* (London, 1982).

D. Clark, *Colne Valley: Radicalism to Socialism. The portrait of a northern constituency in the formative years of the Labour Party 1890–1910* (London, 1981).

P. F. Clarke, *Lancashire and the New Liberalism* (London, 1971).

J. Clayton, *The Rise and Decline of Socialism in Great Britain* (London, 1926).

M. Crick, *The History of the Social-Democratic Federation* (Keele, 1994).

C. Cross, *Philip Snowden* (London, 1966).

W. Cudworth, *Condition of the Industrial Classes of Bradford and District* (Bradford, 1887, reprinted Queensbury, 1974).

G. Dangerfield, *The Strange Death of Liberal England* (London, 1935 and 1970).

I. Dewhirst, *A History of Keighley* (Keighley, 1974).

Eboracorum Lodge Independent Order of Foresters, *Good Fellowship in Keighley, 1823–1923* (Keighley, 1925).

G. Firth, *Bradford and the Industrial Revolution: an economic history 1760–1840* (Halifax, 1990).

H. Forbes, *The Rise, Progress and Present State of the Worsted, Alpaca and Mohair Manufactures* (Bradford, 1852).

K. Hardie, *After Twenty Years: All About the ILP* (1913).

J. Hodgson, *Textile Manufacture and Other Industries in Keighley* (Keighley, 1879).

D. Howell, *British Workers and the Independent Labour Party 1888–1906* (Manchester, 1983).

P. Hudson, *The Genesis of Industrial Capital: a study of the West Riding wool textile industry c. 1750–1850* (London, 1986).

K. S. Inglis, *Churches and the Working Classes in Victorian England* (London, 1963).

D. James, *Bradford* (Halifax, 1990).

D. James, J. A. Jowitt and K. Laybourn (eds), *The Centennial History of the ILP* (Halifax, 1992).

P. Jennings, *Inns and Pubs of Old Bradford* (Bradford, 1985).

J. A. Jowitt (ed.), *Model Industrial Communities in Mid-Nineteenth Century Yorkshire* (Bradford, 1986).

P. Joyce, *Work, Society and Politics: the Culture of the Factory in Late Victorian England* (Brighton, 1980).

W. Keighley, *Keighley Past and Present* (Keighley, 1879).

T. Koditschek, *Class Formation and Urban Industrial Society: Bradford 1750–1850* (London, 1990).

K. Laybourn, *Philip Snowden: a biography 1864–1937* (Aldershot, 1988).

K. Laybourn, *The Rise of Labour: the British Labour Party 1880–1979* (London, 1988).

K. Laybourn and D. James (eds), *Philip Snowden: the First Labour Chancellor of the Exchequer* (Bradford, 1987).

K. Laybourn and D. James (eds), *The Rising Sun Socialism: the Independent Labour Party in the Textile District of the West Riding of Yorkshire between 1890–1914* (Wakefield, 1991).

K. Laybourn and J. Reynolds, *Liberalism and the Rise of Labour* (London, 1984).

J. Liddington and J. Norris, *One Hand Tied Behind Us; The Rise of the Women's Suffrage Movement* (Virago, 1978).

A. M. McBriar, *Fabian Socialism and English Politics 1880–1914* (London, 1966).

R. I. McKibbin, *The Evolution of the Labour Party, 1910–1924* (London, 1974).

Men of the Period: Portraits and Pen Pictures of Leading Men (Biographical Publishing Company, 1897).

A. E. Musson, *British Trade Unions* (London, 1972).

C. Pearse, *The Manningham Mills Strike in Bradford, December 1890 – April 1891*, Occasional Papers in Economic and Social History, No.7 (Hull, 1975).

F. Peel, *The Risings of the Luddites, Chartists and Plug Drawers* (Heckmondwike, 1881, reprinted 1968).

H. Pelling, *Origins of the Labour Party 1880–1900*, 2nd edn (Oxford, 1965).

S. Pierson, *British Socialists: the Journey from Fantasy to Politics* (Harvard, 1979).

S. Pierson, *Marxism and the Origins of British Socialism: the Struggle for a New Consciousness* (Ithaca, 1973).

P. Poirier, *The Advent of the Labour Party* (London, 1958).

R. Price, *Masters, Unions and Men* (London, 1980).

Jane Rendell (ed.), *Equal or Different: Women's Politics 1800–1914* (Oxford, 1987).

J. Reynolds, *The Great Paternalist: Titus Salt and the Growth of Nineteenth-Century Bradford* (London, 1983).

J. Rhodes, *Half a Century of Co-operation in Keighley, 1860–1910* (Manchester, 1911).

G. Sheeran, *Brass Castles: West Yorkshire New Rich and Their Houses 1800–1914* (Halifax, 1993).

E. M. Sigsworth, *Black Dyke Mills* (Liverpool, 1958).

L. Smith, *Religion and the rise of labour* (Keele, 1994).

K. Snowden, *The Master Spinner: a Life of Sir Swire Smith LL D, MP* (London, 1921).

P. Snowden, *An Autobiography* (London, 1934).

Spectator (C. W. Craven), *Keighley School Board and its History* (Keighley, 1890).

R. Spence Hardy, *Memorials of Jonas Sugden* (London, 1858).

P. Thompson, *Socialists, Liberals and Labour: the Struggle for London 1885–1914* (London, 1967).

B. Turner, *A Short History of the General Union of Textile Workers* (Heckmondwike, 1920).

S. and B. Webb, *The History of British Trade Unionism* (London, 1894, reprinted 1920).

D. G. Wright, *The Chartist Risings in Bradford* (Bradford, 1987).

D. G. Wright and J. A. Jowitt (eds), *Victorian Bradford* (Bradford, 1982).

S. Yeo, *Religion and Voluntary Organisations in Crisis* (London, 1976).

2. Articles

A. Briggs, 'Industry and Politics in Early Nineteenth-Century Keighley', *Bradford Antiquary*, New Series, XXXV (1950).

A. Briggs, 'David Urquhart and the West Riding Foreign Affairs Committee', *Bradford Antiquary*, New Series, IX (1958).

A. Briggs, 'Keighley 1848–1948', in M. Bancroft, A. Briggs and E. Treacy (eds), *One Hundred Years: the Parish of Keighley 1848–1948* (Keighley, 1948).

M. Crick, 'Labour Alliance or Socialist Unity? The Independent Labour Party in the Heavy Woollen area of West Yorkshire', in K. Laybourn and D. James (eds), *The Rising Sun of Socialism* (Wakefield, 1991).

M. Crick, 'A Collection of Oddities: the Bradford Branch of the Social Democratic Federation', *Bradford Antiquary*, Third Series, No.5 (1991).

P. A. Dawson, 'The Halifax Independent Labour Movement: Labour and Liberalism 1890–1914', in K. Laybourn and D. James (eds), *The Rising Sun of Socialism* (Wakefield, 1991).

G. Firth, 'The Bradford Trade in the Nineteenth Century', in D. G. Wright and J. A. Jowitt (eds), *Victorian Bradford* (Bradford, 1982).

I. O. Ford, 'Why Women Should be Socialists', *Labour Leader*, 1 May 1913.

S. J. D. Green, 'The Death of Pew-Rents, the Rise of Bazaars, and the End of the Traditional Political Economy of Voluntary Religious Organisations: the Case of the West Riding of Yorkshire, *c.*1870–1914', *Northern History*, XXVII (1991).

June Hannam, 'Women and the ILP, 1890–1914', in D. James, J. A. Jowitt and K. Laybourn (eds), *The Centennial History of the ILP* (Halifax, 1992).

June Hannam, 'In the Comradeship of the Sexes lies the Hope of Progress and Social Regeneration: Women and the West Riding ILP *c.*1890–1914', in Jane Rendell (ed.), *Equal or Different: Women's Politics 1800–1914* (Oxford, 1987).

J. Hill, 'Manchester and Salford Politics and the Early Development of the Independent Labour Party', *International Review of Social History*, 26 (1981).

E. Hobsbawm, 'The Labour Aristocracy in Nineteenth Century Britain', in *Labouring Men* (London, 1964).

D. Howell, 'Was the Labour Party Inevitable?', *Bulletin of the North West Labour History Society* (1984).

K. S. Inglis, 'The Labour Church Movement', *International Review of Social History* (1958).

D. James, 'Philip Snowden and the Keighley Independent Labour Party', in K. Laybourn and D. James (eds), *Philip Snowden: the first Labour Chancellor of the Exchequer* (Bradford, 1987).

D. James, 'Paternalism in Keighley', in J. A. Jowitt (ed.), *Model Industrial Communities in Mid-Nineteenth Century Yorkshire* (Bradford, 1986).

J. A. Jowitt, 'The Pattern of Religion in Victorian Bradford', in D. G. Wright and J. A. Jowitt (eds), *Victorian Bradford* (Bradford, 1982).

J. A. Jowitt, 'Copley, Akroyden and West Hill Park: Moral Reform and Social Improvement in Halifax', in J. A. Jowitt (ed.), *Model Industrial Communities in Mid-Nineteenth Century Yorkshire* (Bradford, 1986).

J. A. Jowitt, 'Religion and the Independent Labour Party', in K. Laybourn and D. James (eds), *The Rising Sun of Socialism* (Wakefield, 1991).

J. A. Jowitt, 'Textiles and Society in Bradford and Lawrence, USA, 1880–1920', *Bradford Antiquary* (1991).

K. Laybourn, 'Trade Unions and the ILP: the Manningham Experience', in J. A. Jowitt and R. K. S. Taylor (eds), *Bradford 1890–1914: the Cradle of the Independent Labour Party*, Bradford Centre Occasional Papers No.2 (Bradford, 1980).

A. E. Musson, 'Class Struggle and the labour aristocracy', *Social History*, vol.1, 3 (1976).

H. F. Moorhouse, 'The Marxist Theory of the Labour Aristocracy', *Social History*, vol.3, 1 (1978).

H. F. Moorhouse, 'The Significance of the Labour Aristocracy', *Social History*, vol.6, 2 (1981).

K. O. Morgan, 'The New Liberalism and the Challenge of Labour: the Welsh Experience', in K. D. Brown (ed.), *Essays in Anti-Labour History* (London, 1974).

C. Parry, 'Gwynedd Politics 1900–1920: the Rise of Labour', *Welsh History Review*, 6 (1972).

C. Pearse, 'The Manningham Mills Strike in Bradford, December 1890–April 1891', Occassional Papers in Economic and Social History, No.7 (Hull, 1975).

H. Pelling, 'The Concept of the Labour Aristocracy', in *Popular Politics and Society in Late Victorian Britain* (London, 1968).

R. B. Perks, 'The Rising Sun of Socialism; Trade Unions and the Independent Labour Party in Huddersfield', in K. Laybourn and D. James (eds), *The Rising Sun of Socialism* (Wakefield, 1991).

M. Pugh, 'Yorkshire and the New Liberalism', *Journal of Modern History*, vol.50, 3 (1978).

J. Reynolds and K. Laybourn, 'The Emergence of the Independent Labour Party in Bradford', *International Review of Social History* (1975).

C. Richardson, 'Irish Settlement in mid-nineteenth century Bradford', *Yorkshire Bulletin of Economic and Social Research*, 20 (1968).

D. Russell, 'The Pursuit of Leisure', in D. G. Wright and J. A. Jowitt (eds), *Victorian Bradford* (Bradford, 1982).

E. M. Sigsworth, 'William Greenwood and Robert Heaton', *Bradford Textile Society Journal* (1951–2).

J. Smith, 'The Strike of 1825', in D. G. Wright and J. A. Jowitt (eds), *Victorian Bradford* (Bradford, 1982).

L. Smith, 'Religion and the ILP', in D. James, J. A. Jowitt and K. Laybourn (eds), *The Centennial History of the ILP* (Halifax, 1992).

R. Storch, 'The Plague of Blue Locusts: Police, Reform and Popular Resistance in Northern England, 1840–1855', *International Review of Social History*, XX, 1 (1975).

E. P. Thompson, 'Homage to Tom Maguire', in A. Briggs and J. Saville (eds), *Essays in Labour History* (London, 1960).

J. T. Ward, 'Some Industrial Reformers', *Bradford Textile Society Journal* (1962–3).

M. Warwick, 'W. E. Forster's Work in Burley-in-Wharfedale, 1850–1886', *Yorkshire Archaeological Journal*, vol.43 (1971).

T. Woodhouse, 'The Working Class', in D. Fraser (ed), *A History of Modern Leeds* (Manchester, 1980).

D. G. Wright, 'The West Riding Textile Districts in the Mid-Nineteenth Century', in J. A. Jowitt (ed.) *Model Industrial Communities in Mid-Nineteenth-Century Yorkshire* (Bradford, 1986).

C. Wrigley, 'Liberals and the desire for Working-Class Representation in Battersea, 1886–1922', in K. D. Brown (ed.), *Essays in Anti-Labour History* (London, 1974).

S. Yeo, 'A New Life: the Religion of Socialism in Britain', *History Workshop*, 4 (1977).

3. Unpublished theses

J. M. Chambers and T. Holdsworth, 'The Worm Turns: the Amalgamated Society of Engineers in Keighley 1889–1914' (unpublished essay deposited in Keighley Library, n.d.).

M. Crick, 'A Call to Arms: The Struggle for Socialist Unity 1884–1914', unpublished MA thesis (Huddersfield Polytechnic 1980).

M. Crick, 'To Make Twelve O'Clock at Eleven: the history of the Social-Democratic Federation', unpublished Ph.D. thesis (Huddersfield Polytechnic 1988).

P. Dawson, 'Halifax Politics, 1890–1914', unpublished Ph.D. thesis (Huddersfield Polytechnic, 1987).

H. J. O. Drake, 'John Lister of Shibden Hall: 1847–1933', unpublished Ph.D. thesis (University of Bradford, 1973).

K. M. Feather, 'Nineteenth-Century Entrepreneurs in Keighley', unpublished BA dissertation (University of Liverpool, 1983).

G. Firth, 'The Genesis of the Industrial Revolution in Bradford 1760–1830', unpublished Ph.D. thesis (University of Bradford, 1974).

C. W. Garnett, 'Irish immigration and the Roman Catholic Church in Bradford, 1835–1870', unpublished MA thesis (University of Sheffield, 1983).

G. Ingle, 'The Marriner Textile Firm', unpublished MA thesis (University of Leeds, 1974).

K. Ittmann, 'The Manufactory of Men: Society and Family Life in Bradford, West Yorkshire 1851–1881', unpublished Ph.D. thesis (University of Princeton, 1989).

E. Jennings, 'Sir Isaac Holden 1807–1897: the First Comber in Europe', unpublished Ph.D. thesis (University of Bradford, 1982).

C. Johnstone, 'The Standard of Living of Worsted Workers in Keighley during the Nineteenth Century', unpublished D.Phil. thesis (University of York, 1976).

R. B. Perks, 'Liberalism and the Challenge of Labour in West Yorkshire, 1885–1914, with special reference to Huddersfield', unpublished Ph.D. thesis (Huddersfield Polytechnic, 1985).

W. D. Ross, 'Bradford Politics 1880–1906', unpublished Ph.D. thesis (University of Bradford, 1977).

D. Russell, 'The Popular Music Societies of the West Yorkshire Textile District 1850–1914', unpublished D.Phil. thesis (University of York, 1980).

M. Smith, 'Robert Clough Ltd., Grove Mill, Keighley. A Study in Technological Redundancy 1835–1865', unpublished MA thesis (University of Leeds, 1982).

R. L. Walton, 'The Labour Movement in Blackburn 1880–1914', unpublished MA thesis (Huddersfield Polytechnic, 1981).

Index

FOR A COMPLETE LIST OF KEELE UNIVERSITY PRESS BOOKS
PLEASE WRITE TO
KEELE UNIVERSITY PRESS
KEELE UNIVERSITY, STAFFORDSHIRE ST5 5BG, ENGLAND